OUR BOYS IN INDIA

OUR BOYS IN INDIA

BY

HARRY W. FRENCH

GYAN

Published by

GYAN

Gyan Publishing House
5, Ansari Road
Daryaganj, New Delhi-110002
Phone: 011-47034999, 9811692060
E-mail: books@gyanbooks.com

Distribution Network
gyanbooks.com
India, USA, Canada, UK, Australia, France

ISBN: 978-81-212-7202-5 (PB)
First Published, 1883

2nd Impression 2023

Printed at: Gyan Press, Delhi.

OUR BOYS IN INDIA
Author: HARRY W. FRENCH

THE ELEPHANT FIGHT.

OUR BOYS IN INDIA

THE WANDERINGS OF

TWO YOUNG AMERICANS

IN HINDUSTAN

WITH THEIR ADVENTURES ON THE SACRED RIVERS
AND WILD MOUNTAINS, ETC.

BY

HARRY W. FRENCH

AUTHOR OF "CASTLE FOAM," "EGO," "NUNA, THE BRAMIN GIRL,"
"GEMS OF GENIUS," ETC.

With One Hundred and Forty-Five Illustrations

BOSTON
LEE AND SHEPARD, PUBLISHERS
NEW YORK
CHARLES T. DILLINGHAM
1883

TO MY FRIEND,

REV. CHARLES W. PARK,

American Missionary of Bombay,

AS A FEEBLE EXPONENT OF A TROPICAL ESTEEM,

This Book is Dedicated.

CONTENTS.

LIST OF ILLUSTRATIONS.

OUR BOYS IN INDIA.

OUR BOYS IN INDIA.

CHAPTER I.

A FLASH OF LIGHTNING.

MANY who were boys in Massachusetts only a few years ago will well remember a startling notice that was printed in the newspapers, and was posted in conspicuous positions throughout the State, declaring in great letters, —

A CHILD MISSING! — TWENTY THOUSAND DOLLARS REWARD.

Paul Clayton, the youngest son of Benjamin Clayton, president of the Merchants' and Shippers' Bank of Boston, has been missing from home since Aug. 10.

It is supposed that the boy was stolen, between the hours of eight and nine on the night of the 10th of August, from the summer residence of Mr. Clayton, at Beverly Farms. He was six years old, had long, brown curling hair, a full face, light complexion, blue eyes, and rosy cheeks. He was a particularly happy-tempered and affectionate child, large for his age, and unusually mature and intelligent.

Any one giving information that shall result in his recovery will receive the sum of twenty thousand dollars.

(Signed) PHINEAS SHARP,

Chief of the Boston Detective Bureau, Boston, Mass.

There may be some who even followed one clew or another, partly out of sympathy for little Paul Clayton, and partly attracted by the large reward. But the first five days went by without the desired information.

The farmers had almost finished their haying, and they were glad of it; for upon that 15th there was a terrible thunder-storm, that tore up and threw down every thing in the fields

HAYING.

that would yield to it. At six o'clock the sun came out again; but in an hour it set in dense clouds, and a lingering storm set in, that lasted several days.

Richard Raymond had returned from India only two days before. He went directly to his sister's house in Beverly. She was his only living relative; and that was the old homestead that he had left, as a boy, now nearly twenty years before. Anxious to see the old landmarks again, and supposing that the storm had broken up, he took advantage of the cool air and the momentary sunshine to go out for a stroll.

In fifteen minutes he was buried in the pine forests, that every one who has ever been there will remember, extending between Beverly and Beverly Farms. The dry, sandy soil had rapidly absorbed the water that had poured down upon it; and Richard Raymond wore a pair of boots so thick, that he did not even notice the drops yet clinging to the ferns and blueberry-bushes. He was thirty-five years old; but he felt like the boy of fifteen again, as he once more pushed his way through the low branches, stopping now and then to pick a leaf of winter-green, hard and tasteless, though it was in the middle of August.

His heart was full of sunshine. He did not even notice that the real sunlight was again enveloped in dense clouds, and rapidly fading out of the east, till drops began to patter on the leaves, and the wind to sigh in a moist and rainy way through the branches of occasional oaks that grew among the pines; but it sounded so natural, — so much like what he had often heard when a boy, — that he only laughed, and felt so much the more at home.

Still he kept on his walk, till suddenly he realized that it was becoming very dark; and he stopped for a moment to wonder where he was, and what direction he should take to go back again. Every thing was changed, to the very forests. He did not remember the old paths so well as he thought, even those that were the same as they had been twenty years before. In fact, he very soon came to the conclusion that he was lost. And, as if the clouds were laughing at him, they began to pour down the rain almost as fast as they had in the afternoon. Then the lightning flashed: but this was fortunate, for in the light he discovered that he was very near a road; and, reaching it as soon as possible, he drew himself close to the trunk of a tree, to wait there till some team should pass or the rain should cease.

Neither of these things happened at once; but, before he had been there very long, he heard some one muttering. It was a woman's voice: she was talking to herself. In a moment more a flash of lightning disclosed the figure of a woman, with torn clothes and a very pale face, creeping along the road, dripping with water, wringing her hands, and wailing in words that he could not understand.

RODERICK DENNETT'S WIFE.

Richard Raymond spoke to her. She gave a faint cry of fear at first; but then she caught his hand, and burst into tears. He could just see her as she stood close beside him.

"O sir! save me, save me!" she cried. "Find my husband for me, and I will give you — I will give you — any thing, any thing!"

The woman was evidently insane; and, as she clasped Richard's hand, something that she was holding fell to the ground, but she did not notice it.

"Is your husband lost, my good woman?" asked Richard gently. "What was his name?"

The poor woman dropped his hand, and, covering her face, began to cry again, sobbing, "Oh, his name was Roderick,

Roderick Dennett! and we were married only a month ago; and now he has left me forever. He has been gone five days. Oh, he has gone forever! Yes, gone forever, I know."

Richard Raymond started when the woman pronounced that name; and in the darkness and the pouring rain, and a strange conflict of thoughts that had been produced by the sound of the word that was very familiar to him, he did not notice that the woman had suddenly left him. But she was gone. He could not tell in which direction. He called, but she did not answer. He remembered that she had dropped something, and stooped and picked it up. It was evidently a little watch and chain. He walked rapidly down the road, but could not find her.

RICHARD RAYMOND.

A few minutes later Mr. Raymond had discovered lights in windows close at hand, and soon found himself sheltered in a little station a few miles from Beverly, on a branch road. He was still repeating that name "Roderick Dennett;" for he and Roderick Dennett ran away to sea together twenty years before, and together wandered as far as India. There Richard had dropped the sowing of wild oats, and by diligent application had become a wealthy man; but Roderick had lived by deceiving every one with whom he had any thing to do. At the end of ten years he left India, and Richard knew no more of him, till now he suddenly heard the name again; and, as ever, it was connected with crime.

Richard looked at the little watch that he still held in his hand. It was a silver hunting-case. He opened it. It had run down. On the inside of the cover the name "Paul" was engraved in the silver. He shut it up again, and went on thinking, while he waited for a train.

As he sat there, his eyes wandered over the room, and finally rested on a notice calculated to attract attention. It was under the large head-line, —

"A CHILD MISSING!"

and three times he read the notice through, then suddenly opened the little watch again, and read the name engraved on the cover, "Paul."

He began putting the facts together that had so curiously come under his notice all in a single hour.

"He left her five days ago," he said to himself. "Five days ago was Aug. 10. I wonder if there can be any connection between the Paul Clayton on the notice there, and the Paul whose name is in this watch, and Roderick Dennett, whose wife was carrying it an hour ago!"

A train whistled, and drew up at the station. Richard seated himself in it, and safely reached his home. The next day he went to Boston, and soon learned that the name of Roderick Dennett was upon many lips as connected with a crime more bold than he had ever committed in India, and that the man had disappeared. Officers were eagerly searching for him, but with no clew; and no one connected him with the abduction of the missing child. Richard said nothing of his suspicions: but, at the earliest possible opportunity, he went to New York; and, after a week of work that would have surprised even the Boston Detective Bureau, he came to the conclusion that a Benjamin Shipman and daughter, who sailed from there upon a Mediterranean steamer, of the Anchor Line, at noon on the 11th of

August, were none other than Roderick Dennett and the missing Paul Clayton.

He had no real authority for this, and the police-officers would have laughed at him had he told them upon what frail ground he based his belief. Yet he felt so sure of it, that, had he had the power, he would have had this Benjamin Shipman arrested, and brought back to America: but the steamer had been gone for thirteen days before he became positive, and by that time she would have passed the Straits of Gibraltar; and he fancied that Roderick Dennett would have taken passage upon the first connecting steamer for India.

Richard Raymond had now become thoroughly interested in the matter; and, though he saw the folly of laying his suspicions before the officers, he was resolved to see the father of the missing child, and, placing the facts before him, offer his services.

While he is on his way back to Beverly, intent upon going over at once to the Farms, let us, too, turn to the home of the little Paul Clayton as it was upon the evening of the 10th of the month.

BY THE SEA, AND THE PINES AND THE OAKS.

CHAPTER II.

THE WISHBONE NIGHT.

BENJAMIN CLAYTON'S cottage at Beverly Farms was one of the prettiest in that beautiful forest skirting the coast. It was built in the old Gothic style, with long windows; and when the lights shone through them at night, they seemed like some of the old castle windows of Europe. The sea dashed against the rocks upon one side of the road, and the pine forest surrounded the house on the other. Beverly Farms is so near to Boston, that Mr. Clayton could go to the bank in the city every day almost as conveniently as though he remained at his city home; so that all summer and every summer his four happy children, Scott, Bess, Paul, and Kittie, romped in the forest, or played upon the seashore.

Kittie was the baby-girl. Paul was the youngest boy. On the tenth day of August he was six years old. Bess was nine, and Scott was fourteen. They were all the world to each other, and their happy home was almost a heaven to them.

The Gothic cottage was filled with children on this 10th of August. Paul was enjoying a birthday party with his friends. It was the lucky "six," and hence was made a wishbone party; and every little couple was given a wishbone to secure for themselves the best thing that heart could think of on this auspicious occasion. There was something superstitiously sacred in the wishing; and there was something so sacred to the brothers and sisters in each other, that they stole away by themselves, after the wishbones had been distributed, to break them where no one else could see or hear.

"What do you wish for, little Paul?" cried Bess with a merry laugh.

Paul was thoughtful. His brow contracted in a studious way; his blue eyes wandered up and down the brittle bone.

"What do you wish for, Bess?" he asked doubtfully.

"I?" said Bess. "Oh! I wish you many happy returns of the day, of course; but you must wish for something for yourself, you know."

"Well," said Paul at last, "I wish that I might visit that wonderful land of India, that aunt Jane was telling us about this afternoon. I wish I might go all over India."

"I withe tho too," lisped little Kittie.

"And I," said Scott, looking over Bess's shoulder, "I wish for an opportunity to be a hero."

"What a funny wish!" cried Bess; "but pull, brothers, pull! Now: one, two, three!" and the wishbones snapped.

Paul ran away to find his father, and tell him of the result.

In the library sat Mr. Clayton and another gentleman. It required but a glance at the two to tell at once that both were in desperate earnestness over something.

For two days Benjamin Clayton had worn a very serious face in his private office at the bank, for something had been going wrong. No one had noticed this at home; for, while Mr. Clayton thought of nothing but his business in the city, he never brought any of it home with him, in his face at least, where the children could see it. He was the president of the largest bank in Boston; and two days before, he had discovered something in the cashier's accounts that the great bank examiner

THE WISHBONE NIGHT.

had overlooked; and the deeper he studied those accounts, the greater the fraud appeared, till, to his horror, he found that the cashier was a defaulter and a robber to the amount of nearly a half-million dollars. It seemed incredible that every one had been so blinded; yet there were the figures, when Mr. Clayton gave them his attention, and the securities that had been left with the bank were gone.

Mr. Clayton had said nothing to his cashier; but with the quick suspicion of a guilty mind, that Shakspeare talks about, the cashier had discovered that he knew all about it, and to-night, in spite of the party, he had come out to the Farms, and was in earnest conversation with the president.

Mr. Clayton listened without a word, while the cashier laid the whole matter before him, and ended in this way: —

"Now, Mr. Clayton, the deed is done, and you have found it out. You were too smart for me by about a week. What I propose to do is this: I shall be at the bank late at night, on the last of the month, settling the accounts. I shall be attacked by men that I shall hire. They will break into the safe, and the next day there will have been a terrible robbery. As you have found me out, I shall have to divide with you. I shall take charge of disposing of the securities, and will give you, in good money, one quarter of a million dollars."

Mr. Clayton was a man who had learned by long trial to control himself, and act carefully; but this was something that was beyond his utmost will. He sprang to his feet. His face was flushed with anger.

"Roderick Dennett!" he exclaimed, "had you come to me with any show of penitence, I could have forgiven you, and done all in my power to make others forgive you too. But not for all the money in the world would I help you to cover up a crime."

"Then you will expose me?" said Roderick sullenly.

"Most assuredly!" replied Mr. Clayton, sitting down again.

"You will be exposing yourself," said Roderick. "No one will believe that a half-million dollars could have been taken from the bank by the cashier without the knowledge of the

THE INTERVIEW.

president; and it would be much better for you and the bank, as well as for me, if it went as a robbery."

"I do not care if every one suspects me! I do not care if I am imprisoned for life!" exclaimed Mr. Clayton. "I would not aid you to steal a pin for all the money in Boston, or any other consideration. You are a miserable scoundrel! a black-leg! a villanous dog! I will denounce you!"

"Stop!" cried Roderick Dennett angrily. "Be careful! I'll make you suffer for what you are saying!"

Just as Mr. Clayton was about to reply, Paul came running into the room with the broken wishbone in his hand.

"Papa, papa!" he cried, "come down and wish with us. Oh, we are having such fun! I've just wished that I might go to India, and I've got my wish. I know I'm going; for it's the lucky night, you know."

Here little Paul hesitated; and with the broken bone in one hand, and his curly little head hanging to one side, he looked from his father to the stranger, and back again, for he saw that something was the matter.

"Run away now, Paul," said his father: "you must not disturb me. I will come down by and by." He said it very kindly: but, after all, it was so different from the way in which he had always spoken, that Paul felt a great lump gather in his throat; and, instead of going back to the merry party of children, he crept out on the veranda all alone, and began to cry.

Some terrible words passed between the two men as soon as Paul had gone out, but no one ever knew what they were. The stranger went away very soon, but Mr. Clayton did not come out of the library. No one saw him till over an hour later, when his wife and Scott and Bess, in great anxiety, came hurrying into the room. For a moment they forgot their errand; for there sat Mr. Clayton, just where Paul had left him, ghastly pale and terribly agitated. He did not notice them till his wife bent over him, and anxiously asked, —

"What is it, Benjamin? What is it? Has any thing happened to Paul?"

"To Paul?" Mr. Clayton started to his feet; for little Paul was his petted boy, and at that moment, at least, seemed the dearest thing on earth to him.

"We cannot find him. We have hunted everywhere," cried Bess, who could no longer restrain herself.

With his eyes fixed in a terrible stare, Mr. Clayton turned toward his wife. In her face he read the truth. With one groan he staggered backward, and fell upon the floor. It was a severe stroke of paralysis, and the night was sad enough in that happy family.

The terrible danger in which the father stood distracted the attention partly from little Paul; and at best they could not have known which way to turn, for no one knew of Roderick Dennett and the conversation that had passed in the library. No one knew of the terrible threats he had made, and of how little Paul had come into the library just when he was trying to determine what he could do to make Mr. Clayton suffer most.

Mr. Clayton could have turned the search in the right direction, and doubtless have arrested the fugitive and villain before he could have escaped, which Roderick Dennett was very fearful would come to pass. But the father's lips were sealed with paralysis; and for weeks after the shock he did not speak a word, or hardly know what was transpiring about him.

The sudden disappearance of the cashier, and the illness of the president, annoyed the officers of the bank: and, though the defalcation was not at once discovered, matters looked strangely suspicious; and in two days the whole was known, and officers were sent to search for the fugitive. But it was two days too late. Roderick Dennett escaped without suspicion; and, had it not been for one contingency, he might have lived for years, and perhaps died, without having any search properly directed. That contingency was the very last that he had looked for,— the presence of Richard Raymond on the scene.

CHAPTER III.

BEING HEROES.

IT was on the thirtieth day of August that Richard Raymond introduced himself in the disconsolate home. He was ushered into the library; and as Mrs. Clayton was engaged in assisting the doctor with her husband, it was some time before she appeared. Scott sat by the centre-table, with an open book before him; but his eyes were swollen with crying, and his cheeks were wet with tears. He was not reading. The stranger came in so suddenly, that Scott had no opportunity to leave the room; but he was ashamed to be found crying, and hid his face.

Richard Raymond, with the true sympathy of an honest heart, realized the position: and, to try and make friends with the poor boy, he threw himself carelessly into an easy-chair beside him; and, taking a book from the shelves at hand, he pretended for a time to be engaged in reading. Scott turned his head away, and rested his cheek in his hand, struggling to stifle the sobs that kept forcing themselves from his sad heart. This gave Mr. Raymond an opportunity to study him carefully for a moment, before he attempted to draw him into conversation; and, as he was a kind-hearted and shrewd man, he was at last able to succeed.

"I used to roam about here when I was a boy like you," said Richard; "but there were no houses here then. And beyond the woods we used sometimes even to see wolves and foxes. Once, when I was ten years old, I went in the winter to a field about half a mile from here with a boy who was older than I. We were pretending that we were pioneers, and had gathered some sticks to build a fire, and had brought some apples and potatoes from home to bake. While we were at work, I looked up, and saw a large animal just springing upon me. I could not tell whether it was a fox, or a wolf, or only a savage dog; but, as I turned to run, he leaped, and threw me down. I fell upon my back, and he stood over me, with his great red tongue hanging out of

RICHARD RAYMOND AND SCOTT CLAYTON.

his mouth, as I held him for life by the long hair on his throat. The boy who was with me had turned to run: but, when he saw me in trouble, he stopped; and, coming back with the axe that we brought to cut the wood for the fire, he struck the creature a terrible blow behind the shoulders that almost cut him in two."

"He was a very brave boy," said Scott. "Did he live to grow up a hero?"

"It takes more than bravery to make a hero," replied Mr. Raymond.

"I wish I were a hero," said Scott with a deep sigh. "I have great need to be one now." And he turned his head away again; and Richard, seeing that he was once more struggling with the tears, endeavored to change the subject by saying, —

"Yes, the boy did live; and he has grown up to be a sort of a hero in one way, but I fancy it is not the kind of a hero that you would like to be."

"Tell me about him, sir," said Scott. "What is his name?"

"It is Roderick Dennett," said Richard.

"Roderick Dennett!" exclaimed Scott, looking up. "Why, that is the name of the cashier of papa's bank."

"It is the very same man," replied Richard.

"But they say that he has run away with some of the bank money," said Scott in surprise.

"That is being one kind of a hero, is it not?" asked Richard.

"A very bad hero," said Scott.

"That is precisely what I meant, that it takes more than bravery to be a true hero. It took bravery to rob the bank, but he would have been much stronger had he resisted the temptation."

"Are there any wolves about here now, or foxes?" asked Scott with a shudder.

"Not many, I think," replied Mr. Raymond. "But why do you ask?"

IT TAKES MORE THAN BRAVERY TO MAKE A HERO.

"I was wondering if it could have been one of them that carried off brother Paul," said Scott, bursting into tears.

"That is what I have come to see you and your mother about," Mr. Raymond replied at last; "for I think that I know something about your brother Paul." Scott started to his feet; but Mr. Raymond continued, "I believe it is the man who saved my life that has taken Paul away."

"Mr. Roderick Dennett!" exclaimed Scott.

"Yes, Mr. Roderick Dennett. Do you know if he was about here on the night of the party?" asked Richard.

"Yes, sir, he was," replied Scott; "for Bess and I saw him go through the hall, and go out, just a little while before we missed our brother. He hurried past us. Bess said, 'Good-evening, Mr. Dennett;' but he never noticed us. We thought it very strange, for he was always so kind when he came up to see papa. But I had forgotten all about it since then."

"Do you know whose watch this is?" asked Mr. Raymond, showing Scott the little silver watch that the poor woman had dropped on the ground.

Scott seized it eagerly, exclaiming, with tears in his eyes, —

"O sir, it is Paul's! It was his birthday present from papa. He wore it in the evening."

Richard Raymond was satisfied that he was right, though all that he had built upon would have been thought a very frail foundation to a legal detective. Just then Mrs. Clayton came in with the good news that her husband was much better, and seemed thoroughly conscious again, though still unable to speak. Mr. Raymond told her briefly his suspicions, and the ground for them. His name was not entirely unknown to her; and she put such confidence in what he said, that it was decided that he should see Mr. Clayton, even in his weak condition.

Scott went with them to the sick-room, where, very simply and calmly, Richard Raymond reported all that he knew.

"You must not think me an adventurer," said he, "urged on by any thought of the reward that is offered. I have an independent fortune; and until I know that I am right, at least, I wish to pay my own expenses. You can move your left hand, I see; and if, when you assent to what I say, you will lift it from the pillow, it will be all that is necessary. I can say in a few words all that I know, and I trust you will not let it excite you. I have thought that your cashier, Roderick Dennett, might know something about Paul."

An eager flush for an instant tinged the pale cheeks, and the hand was instantly lifted. It was evident to all that there was no doubt in Mr. Clayton's mind that it was Roderick Dennett. Mr. Raymond continued, —

"I knew the man in America when he was a boy. I knew him for ten years in India. I think that he left New York with the child, on the Anchor Line, for India, on the 11th of August. If you will permit me, I will start at once for India; and I am sure, that, sooner or later, I shall know all about your son."

Again the trembling hand was lifted from the pillow.

"Two things are absolutely necessary: my suspicions must be kept a secret with you here, or he might easily hear and baffle every endeavor; and I must have some one with me who could instantly recognize the little boy through any disguise that might be put upon him, — some one who has known him very well at home."

A shadow passed over the sick man's face. There was a momentary silence in the room. Richard Raymond did not look at Scott; but he knew the thoughts he was thinking, and he felt sure that the boy who wanted to be a hero would come to his aid.

A moment later Scott knelt by his father's side, and earnestly whispered, —

" Father, let me go with him, and bring back brother Paul."

BESS AND HER PET

It was a terrible struggle. Mrs. Clayton, with one arm about her son, knelt weeping by the bed. For a moment it seemed too much, and Richard thought that Mr. Clayton was again wandering in his mind; but the left hand trembled on the pillow, and then slowly rose. Scott seized it, but gently and reverently, and pressed it to his lips.

Bess was left to love little Kittie, and be the ministering angel in the sick-room. In the long, weary days that followed, when the house seemed so still and deserted that had been so bright before, her one great duty was a thing that seemed impossible to perform, — to keep a happy face to cheer her father;

and sometimes thoughts would come that were too much even for the bravest little heart; and with her pet canary on her shoulder chirping, and trying to kiss her, and seeming to do his very best to express his sympathy, she would go to the window to hide from her father the tears that would well up from the full fountain. And there she would think over again all the little incidents of that last half-hour when they were all together, when they stole away from the rest of the children to break their wishbones on that sacred birthday night.

"Perhaps little Paul is having his wish," she would sob; "and surely Scott will have his. Oh, if I were only a man, I would be a hero too, and help find little Paul!"

Brave little Bess! She never thought that she was the greatest hero of them all, and performing the very hardest duty and the noblest work. But so it is; and those who are real heroes are oftener those who do not know it than those who do.

CHAPTER IV.

OUT ON THE OCEAN.

THERE have been so many stories told of the Atlantic, that Scott had a good idea of what was before him for the first nine days of the voyage; and he was so sad, that he found it hard to yield to the partial novelty, and to Mr. Raymond's untiring efforts to make him forget himself. But he was going in search of Paul. That alone made him happy, and gradually overcame the terrible homesickness that seemed to lie like a heavy weight upon him all the time. The days dragged on with almost unendurable slowness at first: it seemed a year since he had left the cottage home among the pines, though they had only been six days upon the sea, when an event occurred that opened Scott's eyes to his real position, and showed him that, after all, he had much to be thankful for, and that, while there were hosts of people in the world who were worse off than he, it was not only foolishness, but cowardice, to give himself up to mourning for the past.

Scott was sitting under the awning, aft; for it was perfectly calm and excessively hot, even on the ocean. Richard laughed, however, and told him that he would think it a delightfully cool afternoon by the time he had experienced a few days upon the Red Sea. There were many emigrants on the steamer, who had either failed to make the fortunes they had hoped for in America, or had earned enough to visit the old country again, and were going home. Suddenly Scott realized that a very

WHERE SCOTT FORGOT HIMSELF.

solemn company was gathering upon the deck, far forward. He asked Mr. Raymond what it was. Richard had not spoken of a death that had occurred on board, dreading to make the boy more melancholy; but now he was obliged to tell him that it was a funeral. Scott shuddered; and in spite of Richard's suggestion that it was among the emigrants, and that they had better remain where they were, he slowly rose, and walked forward, with his eyes fixed on the gathering throng, as though it had some subtle charm that was enticing him.

With a sad face, Richard followed him. The body of a man, made heavy with lead weights, so that it would sink, and bound up in coarse canvas, lay stretched upon the deck. Beside it, in great distress, knelt a woman, evidently the widow. Clinging to her neck, and crying bitterly, was a little boy; while on the other side knelt the minister, solemnly repeating the last prayer. Then four seamen came forward, with bare heads; and, putting the body upon a sort of litter of plain pine, they carried it to the edge of the steamer, and let it fall into the sea. As the splash sounded, the poor woman shrieked, and fell fainting on the deck.

Mr. Raymond had been anxiously watching Scott's face. Now he saw a strange light break over it, and tears glisten in his eyes, as he left the secluded spot where he had been standing, and, hurrying forward, knelt beside the forsaken little boy, and put his arm about his neck. Mr. Raymond turned away, and went aft alone. It was two hours later when Scott came into the saloon, but a single glance assured his friend that at last the boy had forgotten himself. From that moment he was another person.

"I am very fortunate to have my father still," said he: "and it is much better that little Paul should be stolen than dead; for we may find him, and bring him back."

"I am sure we shall," replied Mr. Raymond earnestly.

The remaining days went by rapidly enough, for Scott was busily engaged in comforting the little orphan among the steerage passengers.

The steamer entered the Irish Sea, and stopped only an hour at Queenstown; for which the two travellers were very thankful, as the sight of land made them all the more anxious to be on the way across the Continent without a moment's delay.

"We shall be in time for the royal mail," said Mr. Raymond, carefully studying his watch and chart, and the time-table of the North-Western Railroad. "We shall reach Liverpool this afternoon; and, if all only goes well, we shall take the evening train for London. We shall get there about daylight; and, as soon as the Peninsular and Oriental S. S. office is opened, we will secure tickets to Brindisi if possible."

"Where shall we go then?" asked Scott.

"If we are successful, we shall take the train that leaves London every Friday night at nine o'clock."

"Why do you say if?" Scott asked again.

"Because I am very much afraid that we may find the seats all taken. I shall telegraph from Liverpool, but this is a new thing. It is a weekly mail for India. On Friday night, at a quarter before nine, an engine and mail-van, with only passengers enough to fill one American sleeping-car, leave the Charing-Cross station. At Paris the sleeping-car is attached to the mail-van, and no one without a seat is allowed to go. It is the fastest express, and has nothing to do but get to the south of Italy as quickly as possible."

They were late in entering the River Mersey, for the tide was wrong for them to cross the bar; and Richard and Scott stood anxiously leaning against the chain that was stretched across the prow to prevent the passengers from going too far forward, when the great port of Liverpool appeared in an enormous half-circle before them, with Birkenhead upon the other side.

Oh, those interminable miles of wharves!

"Shall we never come to the end?" asked Scott, as he nervously watched, while the steamer slowly passed one after another of those world-famed, solid piers, from which merchandise is sent all over the wide world.

"Patience, patience, my boy!" replied Mr. Raymond, smiling. "You will have many lessons in patience before you have travelled long. We shall have to wait quietly hundreds of times, when it will seem as though every minute was worth a fortune."

At last, however, the company's tender came alongside, and the eager crowd hurried on board. They gave the good steamer a farewell cheer; and even Scott joined in it, though a little while before, he had felt any thing but grateful over the slow way in which she was creeping up the river.

Lamps were burning on the stage (or pier, as Scott would have called it), when at last they stood upon the solid earth again. The two had very little baggage,—only large valises, that they could carry in their hands in case of necessity,—and Scott supposed that they should start off at once.

"Which is the way out?" he asked eagerly, without noticing any of the strange sights about him.

Mr. Raymond only smiled, and again replied, "Patience, my boy, patience!"

"What! wait again? And are you in no hurry yourself?" he asked almost angrily, seeing the smile on Richard's face.

"I am in a very great hurry," replied Mr. Raymond; "but

ENTERING THE RIVER MERSEY. Page 27.

what good does it do? We have got to stand here till all those trunks are taken from the tender, and put into the custom-room; then we must go through there with the rest of the passengers, and have our valises examined. Then we shall be free, and can hurry as much as we like."

Mr. Raymond put his valise against the wall, and, leaning back, began to study the people about them, and call the attention of his little friend to interesting objects. It was not entirely in vain: but Scott had only an indistinct idea, afterward, of the lights burning here and there upon the stage; of burly British policemen, with beards under their chins, and red faces, and huge hats that looked like helmets, and reminded him so strongly of the stories he had read, by Dickens; of little bootblacks, with badges and numbers, that would cluster about them when the police-officers were out of sight, and run away when the officer approached again; and of how the officer would thunder at the poor little fellows, and push them about. Scott wondered what they were doing that was wrong, so long as they were allowed to be there at all. Here and there, too, were passengers from the steamer, hurrying about with anxious faces and angry words, as though they thought they could move the whole British Empire by demanding that it should hurry up for their especial benefit.

"They will get over that when they have tried it long enough," said Richard with a smile; and even Scott began to feel like an old traveller, and to gather patience from the anxiety of the rest. He became very nervous again, however, when the door opened, and again was almost angry with Mr. Raymond, at the quiet way in which he proceeded. It seemed as though every one crowded in front of him; yet Scott noticed with astonishment that those who were the most officious and noisy were still wrangling over their baggage with the officers, or trying to hurry others on, when Richard quietly

SCENE IN LIVERPOOL.

secured the attention of a polite official, and, without even opening but one of the valises, had them stamped with the customs label, and they were the very first of all the passengers to secure a carriage.

They saw very little of Liverpool, as they whirled through the streets to the great North-Western depot; but they were in time for the train, and that was the great object.

It was a curious sensation to enter a large hotel, on the way to a depot, and to find the uniformed officials everywhere; and, in the strange surroundings and bustle, it seemed to Scott that there must be confusion, and that they must surely lose their way. But he followed silently behind Mr. Raymond, and found every step so plainly marked before them, that out of the very multiplicity complete order was resolved. Very soon the two were quietly seated in a curious compartment of a long car, with the seats extending from one side to the other, facing each other, entirely shut off from the rest of the car, which was all cut up into similar compartments. The doors were at the sides; and, before the car started, a guard, or conductor, looked at their tickets, to be sure that there was no mistake; then he locked the doors on the outside, and the train started.

There was but one other passenger in the compartment with them; and, though the strange sights in the half-clouded moonlight were interesting for a time, Scott was very soon ready to roll himself up and go to sleep. England was not so very unlike America, after all, he thought then; for he was very tired, in the re-action from the anxiety he had felt all the afternoon. There was not so much noise about the road and at the stations as he was accustomed to at home, and he slept very soundly till he was roused by a particularly bad odor filling the compartment. He opened his eyes. Mr. Raymond was engaged in conversation with the other passenger; but, seeing that Scott was awake, he smiled, and asked if he was all right.

"What is this awful smell?" asked Scott.

"It is from a large extract-factory," replied Mr. Raymond.

"What!" exclaimed Scott, sitting up, "where they make perfumes?"

"Just that exactly," said Richard, laughing.

"And is that the way to make perfumes, by burning up the horrible odors, and saving the good ones?" asked Scott. But the stranger spoke to Mr. Raymond, and Scott received no reply. He lay and listened to the two till he fell asleep again. It was a strange language in which they were talking, and he gained but little information after all; but several times he was sure that he heard the name of Roderick Dennett spoken. When he awoke again, the light burned very low, and was smoking, as though the oil was out. The sky was growing gray in the east. He looked about the compartment. Mr. Raymond was asleep on the opposite seat, and the stranger was gone.

Scott watched the curious farms and houses that were now very frequent, till Richard looked up, and, taking out his watch, said, "We shall be in London in less than half an hour. Are you glad?"

"It is so much nearer India," replied Scott with a sigh, as he remembered that it was also so much farther away from home. And a moment later he asked, "Who was that man with whom you were talking?"

"He was a German, a civil engineer, who put through one of the India railways."

"I thought I heard you speak of Mr. Dennett," said Scott.

"Yes: Dennett worked on the railroad for a few months; and I obtained some information concerning native associates of his, that will help us, I think."

"It is very strange that you should have met that man," said Scott, much surprised.

"Not so very," replied Richard, gathering up the things that had been scattered about the seats through the night. "The farther you go, the more you will discover that the world is only a little thing after all, and you will be forever finding people who have been in the same places, and know the same people. But here we are! See! we are entering London."

"But it is not ten minutes yet. We must be early," said Scott.

"I think not," said Richard, sitting down by the window. "London is very large, you know. It would take you almost all day to ride from one end to the other in a hack."

"It must be a splendid place for criminals to hide," said Scott, as he looked down the interminable lines of dirty tile roofs, and, just as far as the eye could reach, saw the spires and domes and tall chimneys still rising, and wondered how it would be possible to keep the eye of the law on all the intricate lanes and by-ways that seemed to be everywhere.

"You are quite right there," replied Richard. "If there is a man outside of London whom the police are after, the thing that he often tries the hardest to do, and that they try the hardest to keep him from doing, is to get into the city. I was once in England in search of a famous criminal who had fled from India. We cornered him at last in a little town; and, if he did not manage to slip out, we were sure of him. We watched every train, and especially the express for London. I was sure I should recognize him if I saw him; and in all sorts of disguises, accompanied by a policeman or detective, I was at the station at almost every train. One day a young gentleman and a lady, beautifully dressed, came down, and took the express. As I was on the lookout for every one, I did not like to let the lady with a veil over her face go past me. I hurried to the guard-room, and borrowed a hat and coat of one of the officers of the train, while another went to the compartment where the gentleman and lady were sitting, and called the gentleman away to look to some baggage. Then I went up to the window, and suddenly spoke to the lady. She started; but, though her reply was very simple, I was sure, in an instant, that I had the man for whom I had come from India. I hurried back, and reported to the detectives. The train was held for fifteen minutes, till they could learn who the two were. Very soon word was brought by an officer that they were a couple who had just been married, and were starting upon a wedding-trip. The detectives laughed at me well, I tell you; and I had nothing left me but to give up. The train went on; but a half-hour before it should have reached London we found out, for a certainty, that the man had not only left the country town that afternoon, but that he must have left upon that very express train for London. The officers telegraphed forward, and had the station carefully guarded. It was about nine o'clock at night; and we all waited, sure of hearing of the arrest. But, when the train was about entering the suburbs of the city, the bell rang violently in the guard-van, and the train was stopped. Some one had pulled the cord, you know, that runs along just outside the windows there. The guard hurried down the line to see what was the matter, and at last came upon a compartment where an old woman sat all alone, with any amount of bandboxes and bundles about her. The old woman was deaf as a post, and the guard shouted a dozen times before he could make her understand that he wanted to know what was the matter. Then she looked up in surprise, and replied, 'I want some dinner. What did you suppose?' There was no use in swearing at her, for she could not hear a thing. She only pointed up to that notice there, and said, 'Don't that say when meals hare required, notify the guard? hand don't hit say to notify the guard pull the cord houtside the window? I 'ope you didn't stop the train hon my haccount.' There was a delay of fifteen minutes, so that it was three-quarters of an hour before the train reached the depot. Then there were the policemen all ready for it; and of course they went at once to the compartment where the young couple were. To their surprise, they found it empty. A bit of wet leather had been stretched over the lantern, so that no one could see when the door was opened; and, while the train stood still for the old woman, the two had escaped, and had had three-quarters of an hour to put themselves beyond the reach of the police."

"But the old woman!" said Scott.

"You are right, Scott," replied Richard. "And if the London police had only been as bright, and said so as quickly as you have, they might have accomplished something, at least, though it might have been hard to *prove* that she really had any thing to do with it intentionally. But, while they were vexing themselves over the fellow himself, the assistant, as the old woman doubtless was, left the train and the station without being suspected; and, before their attention was turned that way, she, too, was buried up somewhere in the great city."

"But that was not the end of it all, was it?" asked Scott anxiously.

"It was not really the end of it," replied Mr. Raymond,

"though the man escaped me, and I went back to India alone. But I expect to meet him again some day, and you may see him too. But here we are at last. Now we will go to a hotel, and have a bath and breakfast, and rest for two or three hours, before the offices are opened."

There was no confusion or turmoil; and Scott could hardly believe that they had reached the famous Euston station, when the door was quietly opened, and, following Richard, he went across a stone platform, and entered a curious sort of a gig. The driver sat behind it, and almost as high as the top of the carriage; and, having seated themselves where there was just room for two, they shut two little doors in front of their feet, boxing themselves in above the knees.

"I don't believe the driver more than half wanted us to ride," said Scott: "he never even spoke, till after you was close up to him."

"They would not be allowed to shout, and push themselves into one's face, as they do in America. But I fancy they have just as many passengers as if they were more noisy: for, if one wants to ride, he will ride; and, if he don't, I should not think the bullying fellows would tempt him to," replied Mr. Raymond. "I love America even more, perhaps, because I have not been there for so long; but there are some things that must yet be improved."

They were now rattling through dim, noisy streets, that were crowded, even at that early hour. Scott found, that, after all, it was not quite like what he had seen his life long, and began to feel as though he were one of the characters of some of Dickens's stories. The idea was very thoroughly taken out of him, however, when, a few hours later, he and Mr. Raymond left the hotel to find the steamer-office, and one of the first objects they met was a ragged little newsboy, who hurried up to them, crying,—

"All the latest news from New York! Only a penny!"

"How does he know that we are Americans?" asked Scott, chagrined, he could hardly tell why, to be so easily discovered.

"They all know it," replied Mr. Raymond, smiling. "Would you rather not?" Scott hesitated; and Richard continued, "You were ashamed of it, I fancy."

THE RAGGED NEWSBOY.

"A little," said Scott, blushing.

"And so are hosts of Americans," added Mr. Raymond. "I have seen gentlemen and ladies try in every possible way to hide the fact. They will buy English clothes the moment they land, and talk like Englishmen, and try to act like them, and then be very angry when they see how they fail after all. It is very strange to me; for America, of every land, is one to be proud of. I would rather be an American than any thing else on earth; and so would they, I think, if they really thought of it."

"I am not going to be ashamed of it again!" exclaimed Scott proudly; "and you shall see. The first time that any one thinks I am not an American, I will show him he is mistaken very quickly."

They hailed a bus. There was a winding flight of iron

INSIDE A BUS.

steps leading to the top; and, wishing to see all they could of London, they mounted, and seated themselves on the roof. A young Englishman was sitting there alone. He looked up as Scott took a place beside him, and pleasantly remarked, "A fine morning this."

"It might be more uncomfortable, sir," replied Scott; though he could not help looking a little incredulously toward the sky, for he thought it one of the most disagreeable, damp, and gloomy mornings he had found for months. It looked as though it would certainly rain in an hour; and evidently the Englishman thought so too, for he had an umbrella.

Noticing Scott's uncertainty, he added, "You've not lived long in town?"

"In town! What town?" asked Scott.

"Hereabout. You don't seem quite used to London weather," replied the Englishman.

"No, sir: I am an American," said Scott; and he blushed a little as he felt Mr. Raymond's hand touch his shoulder approvingly; "and I do not know much about London weather, if this is a fine morning."

The Englishman laughed. "You'll think it one of the best of the year, if you stop the year out."

"Then, I should hate to see a really bad morning in London," observed Scott, rubbing his hand over his pants, that were already quite damp with the fog.

"Ay, that you would!" replied the Englishman. "Sometimes they light the street-gas at noon, the fog is so thick; and I've seen more than one time when, in broad daylight, the driving was stopped in the streets."

"It must be interesting," said Scott, meaning precisely the opposite. But the Englishman thought him in earnest, and replied, "Right you are!" with an enthusiasm that almost made him laugh, in spite of his endeavors to keep a sober face.

They reached the up-town office of the P. and O. S. S. Company only to be disappointed. Every seat was taken; and there was no way in which they could reach Brindisi, in Italy, in time for the steamer.

"Let us walk over to No. 18 Cockspur Street," said Mr. Raymond. "It is only a little way, and there is a shipper there who has the agency for several Bombay steamers. It may be that one of them is leaving at once; and, if so, going by water will only delay us three or four days more than waiting for the next mail overland, and we should then be able to stop at all the ports where the Mediterranean steamer from New York stopped, and make sure that we are not following a wrong track, and that the passengers went right on to India."

"How should we go by water?" asked Scott, as they walked over to No. 18 Cockspur Street.

"We should leave either from Southampton or Liverpool, and go right across the Bay of Biscay, to Gibraltar; and from there we should stop at Algiers, Malta, and Alexandria, or Port Said; then through the canal to Suez, to Aden, and Bombay."

"I should think that would be better," said Scott.

"At any rate, we will make a virtue of a necessity, and profit by it," replied Richard, as they reached the office.

CHAPTER V.

OLD JOE, THE QUARTERMASTER.

TWENTY-FOUR hours later, the two were well established on a snug little steamer of the Clann line, and steaming away from England. They were the only passengers on board, and were consequently given the full range of the steamer, without restrictions.

"Two days ago we hardly expected to be here," said Scott, as they sat together on the deck.

"Hardly," answered Richard: "but life is full of sudden changes; and the more readily one adapts himself to them as they come, the more likely he is to make the best of them, and come out well at the end."

"You mean that for me, Mr. Raymond," said Scott; "and I begin to realize all that it implies. I have had a very wrong idea of what it was to be a hero, from reading about them in books. If all of this comes out right in the end, I think I shall know better how to be a man."

"All must come out right, Scott," replied Richard: "we will make it. We will begin by making the best of our position now; for, if we do not have a good time on this voyage, it is certainly our own fault. We shall have no one else to blame."

"You are very kind, Mr. Raymond. I was wondering last night how in the world it could have happened that you could have been in Beverly at just that time, and in the woods at just that moment, and then why you should ever have been so good as to do what you are doing."

Scott was going on to say more, but Richard interrupted him. "That is quite enough, my boy. In the first place, God does every thing in this world, and does it right. In the second place, you will learn, by and by, that men do very little that is not in some way for their own advantage. I am very anxious to find Roderick Dennett, and am only fortunate, if I can do so much more than find him for myself, in rescuing your brother Paul at the same time."

"You don't think he would hurt him, do you?" asked Scott for the hundredth time.

"Not a bit, Scott," replied Richard. "He is quite too great a coward to lay himself open to the charge of murder. He would do any thing in the world that was mean. He would do almost any thing for money, but he would do very little for revenge. I do not think that he would have gone to India, only that he was too great a coward to stay in America; and before long I believe he will of himself begin to see what ransom he can get from your father. He will be very careful of Paul; for it will be a prospect of money to him, if he keeps him safely. You may be sure, that, wherever Paul is, he is having just as good a time as is possible under the circumstances." And Richard believed this; though perhaps he said it a little more strongly than he really felt, in order to give Scott the courage that he lacked. "We are nearing the Spanish coast," he continued. "To-morrow night, or early the next morning, we shall be abreast the Cape. We must look out for ourselves that we don't bribe the wrong fortune here, and go on with what the sailors call the 'porter's portion.'"

"What is that?" asked Scott.

"Oh! it is only one of the thousand fancies that sailors have connected with every point of land that is often sighted by ships. I was thinking how a sailor told me the story when I went by here almost twenty years ago. I was a sailor-boy up in the fo'cas'le then. I had to do a little of every thing, all day long, and then spend my spare time in polishing up the brass about the ship, just as that little urchin is doing." And Richard pointed to where a little stowaway was busy rubbing up a brass knob. He had hidden himself away under a bunk before the steamer left Liverpool, and did not come out till they were too far away to send him back.

"You were not a stowaway, were you?" asked Scott.

"No; but I was the 'boy;' and a boy's lot, under any circumstances, is not an easy one at sea. I was very anxious to see all that I could of the strange countries; but there was little chance of my being able to go ashore anywhere. There were some of the sailors, and one of them was a particular hero of mine, who cared very little about going on shore, but were ready to give any thing to get a little rum. We had passed the Cape, and were looking forward and calculating the time that we should probably land at Gibraltar. We should be there during the night. This suited my seaman friend; and he made a proposition to me, that he should help me to escape from the steamer, and get ashore, so that I could go about and see every thing, if, in return, I would bring him back a bottle of rum." Richard laughed. "I was thinking of old times, and wandered away from the 'porter's portion.' It was the bargain he made with me that brought out the story. A young fisherman on the coast over there had made a haul of two of the finest fish he ever saw. He determined to present them to the king; and, just as he was,

THE PORTER'S PORTION.

he made his way to the court. The palace porter who was on guard objected at first to letting him in, but at last made a compromise with him, that he should go in and sell his fish to the prince, but that, in exchange, he must give the porter just one-half of what he received, his regular commission. The prince, passing through the court, and seeing the two splendid fish, at once ordered his butler to take them, and pay the fisherman whatever he asked for them. 'If it please your Highness,' said the fisherman, 'I should like to receive one hundred lashes.' This was the most severe punishment ever bestowed with the whip. It often cost the criminal his life. The prince turned in surprise, and demanded his reason for asking such a reward. 'Because, your Highness,' said he, 'the porter at the gate is in the habit of demanding one-half of what we receive from your Highness, before he will let any of us enter; and I know of no compensation that I would rather share with him than one hundred lashes.'"

"It was good enough for him," said Scott decidedly.

"Yes: it was good enough for him, and does very well for a story," replied Richard; "and it gives the sailors something to say whenever they hear any one making a bargain while they are in the neighborhood of the Cape. You must make the acquaintance of the quartermasters on board; for, when they are off duty, you'll find them full of interesting stories."

"They're a sorry-looking set of fellows," said Scott, as one of the quartermasters of the ship approached that part of the deck where they were sitting. He was a tall, gaunt, awkward fellow, with a wrinkled face, and sharp eyes, and hard, brown hands. And Scott added, "I should hate to have any thing to do with him."

"Sailors are always rough to look at; but they may have kind hearts, after all. You'll find the flowers growing wild in India are more beautiful than the best hothouse blossoms in America; but you'll hardly find a flower in Hindoostan so sweet as the yellow daisies and pink roses that grow by the side of the road in Beverly."

The old sailor came up, and began to work on one of the steamer's boats, close to them, stretching a canvas over it, and binding it on with a strong cord.

"What's up, Jack? Will she catch a blow in Biscay?" asked Richard.

"Bit of a brush, maybe," replied the sailor.

"The barometer has held low ever since we started," added Richard.

"Why, I heard the captain say, an hour ago, that it was going up fast!" said Scott, who had begun to study the prospects with a nautical eye.

"Sudden rise after low indicates a harder blow," muttered the sailor in a sort of singsong as he worked.

He was quite correct in his prediction; for before night it began to blow, and the waves not only ran high, but seemed to run in every direction. It is a peculiarity, in that Bay of Biscay, that every one who ever crossed it knows. They did not see the coast of Spain and Cape Finisterre at all, and were down where the Tagus River flows by Lisbon (the capital of Portugal), and empties into the sea, before they again ventured into sight of land. It was a wild and fascinating coast, with its ragged ridges of rock extending to the very water's edge, its white cliffs gleaming here and there, and now and then a green gorge, where a little stream wandered down from the mountains. The villages along the coast were all of white, and looked like drifts of snow along the sand, till Scott went up on to the bridge with the captain, and, taking his telescope, brought the shore under the very bows of the steamer.

"That town is Peanno, over there," said the captain. "Do you see the little steamer just making into the harbor?"

"Are those towers all along the coast, lighthouses?" asked Scott.

The captain laughed. "They are Moorish watch-towers," he said. "It was only a few years ago that the Moors ruled all the south of Spain and Portugal; and they had their strongholds all along the coasts, even after the entire interiors were given up. Those towers, and the castles about them, are impregnable, even now, to any mode of warfare but that of our heaviest cannon."

"I should like to visit them," said Scott, fixing the telescope on one of them with fascinated interest.

"So you would," replied the captain, giving an order to slightly change the direction of the steamer, that she might run a little nearer in, and give a better view. "There is many a wild romance connected with those Moorish towers, of battles and sieges, and tyrants, and lovers, and misers, and all kinds of every thing that went on there years and years ago. Now raise your glass a bit, and on the highest hill, to the right of Peanno, do you see a great castle, all towers and every thing, and a hundred times bigger than the Moorish towers down below?"

"Oh, yes, I see it!" exclaimed Scott. "What an enormous thing it is! What is it?"

"It's the summer palace of the king of Portugal. And just down at the foot of that hill, on the other side, is the capital, Lisbon. You cannot see it now; but in half an hour we shall be below the mouth of the river, and you can look back, and see the shipping, at least, just below the city."

"The king of Portugal must like to read novels," said Scott with a sigh of envy. "Living in such a romantic place would make them all seem real, I should think. I never liked to read stories, because they never seemed true, except Dickens's works, and I have read all of those. I felt as if they were true when I read them; and when I reached England, and saw it for myself, — just a little of it, I mean, — I was sure of it."

"He does like to read novels better than he likes to fight," said the captain, laughing; "and he's got the waxiest little doll for a wife, and she likes to read novels too. They're a pretty little couple; but they're too small for that castle, and they spend most of their time in a beautiful palace in the city, at the foot of the hills."

"And is that all the vacation they have? It must be very tiresome."

"It's hard work being a king," replied the captain. "I'd rather be the captain of a good steamer than that king of Portugal, this minute; and I fancy he's got the best berth of any of the crowned heads of Europe, so far as taking comfort is concerned."

"Why is that?" asked Scott.

"Oh! he's plenty of money to live upon, and he's nothing in the way of a throne that any one wants bad enough to try and get it away from him."

Just then the first officer came up, and spoke to the captain; and he turned away, saying, "You must excuse me for a few minutes, for I want to see if my chronometers are keeping good time."

Scott watched the operation without understanding much of it; but when the captain returned, he explained, "You see, we have three or four ways of taking reckonings now; so that, if we make a mistake in one, we correct it in another. One of them is to carry two chronometers with us, giving the time at Greenwich. Then we know just how much the time at Lisbon, for instance, differs from Greenwich time; and we take an observation when we are just off the point yonder, and find out the exact minute, and the distance we are away, and compare the result with the time. But there goes dinner. You'll lose nothing, for we shall not see land again till we sight Cape St. Vincent, and that'll be in the night. Then the next thing is the Straits and Gibraltar."

Taking Mr. Raymond's advice, Scott followed the old quartermaster down into the little sailor's room, in the very prow of the steamer, when he knew that he was off duty.

"Can I come in and call on you, sir?" he asked, bowing a little timidly.

The old sailor looked around, leaned back against a beam; and, resting his hand on the mess-table, he smiled pleasantly, though it wrinkled his face into all manner of criss-crosses, as he replied, "Drop anchor where you will, my lad. It's a free harbor, this voyage; but it don't do to 'sir' a craft like me."

"You're older than I am, and I should say 'sir' to every one who is older," replied Scott.

"Thet's by American reckonin', an' here ye stand on British plank," said the sailor.

"But I am an American, and I am not ashamed of it!" exclaimed Scott.

"Steady as ye go!" cried the old quartermaster in a firm,

OLD JOE, THE QUARTERMASTER.

enthusiastic voice, giving the call of the wheel-house, when the steamer is headed right. "But there's a difference in the water, that'll git ye out o' your bearings, if you keep that tack. You say 'sir' to an Englishman, an' he don't know no better than to think you mean to say that he's a bigger craft than you. That's what the word means in his signal-book. You Americans, who don't drop your ensign to nobody but in courtesy, can afford to go sirrin' round as ye will, in your own waters. But put it in your log, my lad, if you're an American, an' proud o' it, ye are as good as God save the Queen! And don't go drop your ensign to any Englishman that lives."

"Thank you, sir—I mean, thank you," said Scott with a laugh. "I'll put it in my log, and remember who told me; but I shall have to read it over every day or two for some time, I think. Now, I came down to ask you if you had time to tell me a story about the sea."

"Spin a yarn?" asked the old quartermaster, pushing back his heavy hat.

"Well, I suppose it's the same as spinning a yarn," said Scott. "But, for mercy's sake, don't spin it in sailor-talk, for I cannot understand. If you haven't time now, I'll come again."

"Time enough, time enough!" said the old salt. "But how's the tide? It's forever agin me when I try to yarn. I'm tongue-tied, instead o' high tide, when it comes to talking. And ye ask me to talk like a landlubber, too, when I don't know a goat from a turkey. But make fast aft there, my lad: I mean, sit down, and—what? no place to sit? True with ye! And whatever do I do when I heave to? Why, I never stopped to think, but must be I make for the mess-table, or ground her on the shoals behind you there." Scott sat down on the step. "And come a brush and blow, I lay to, and hug the coast." And, suiting his actions to his words, the old fellow sat directly down upon the floor, his sharp knees on a level with his sharp chin, and his back against the beam. "Whatever to talk about, now, is the next thing, and however to say it in landlubber's lingo. It's bad as a fog and a gale, bow and stern. You'll have to give the sailin' orders, and start me off, my lad; and ef it come thick weather, an' I drift away from shore, why, give the word, put to, call the points, and we'll right up agin."

"Any thing, any thing about the sea," said Scott, his eyes fixed upon the old sailor's mouth; for, in spite of his endeavor to talk like a landsman, it was still hard to understand, and it seemed to help the matter a little to watch the working of his lips.

"Any thing about the sea! Ugh! It's an awful place," said the old sailor with a shiver.

"What? You say so? How long have you followed the sea?" asked Scott in surprise.

"Just fifty years and two, my lad, which is since the day that I was launched upon life's ocean; which, agin, was mor'n a thousand mile from port."

"You were born a thousand miles from port!" cried Scott. "And did you never think of leaving the sea, if it seems like an awful place?"

"I've left it mor'n twenty times, and wus always back agin afore I could get my sea-legs off. Ugh! it's an awful place."

"Why?" asked Scott.

The old man was silent for a moment. His head dropped down between his knees. Then he went on as though he were talking to himself. "My father and mother lie under the sea. My grandfathers were both drowned in salt water. My wife—my—my little boy—ay, ay, they've hove to under the lea o' some ugly rock, too deep down for the breakers to shift 'em. It's calm water there, they say, till the end o' the voyage. But up here! Ugh! When the sea's on, and lumpy, it's an awful place."

"You must have been shipwrecked," said Scott, his eyes bright with tears for the old sailor. And he could not help thinking of what Mr. Raymond had said of the hearts that were sometimes hidden under the weather-beaten faces of sailors.

"Shipwrecked," said the quartermaster with a shudder, "just as often as ever a seven came into my years. Seven time seven is forty-nine, and from out o' them I came with my mast-head above water. But that fills up the landings. Next time is four year yet to come, and that's the last. It'll be a stiff 'un that shivers the last timber in old Joe's keel; but it's comin' at fifty-six, sure as the sea is salt."

"I hope not," said Scott earnestly. "Was it steamers, or sailing-vessels, that you were on when you were wrecked?"

"Never pressed a steamer plank afore this voyage," replied the sailor.

"Do you like it?" asked Scott.

"Ay, ay! Give me steam," said the quartermaster enthusiastically, forgetting his gloomy thoughts. "I've been master of a sailor for twenty year; but they'll have to take the wake water, or drop aft, now. Yarn about sail! Why, the last time I went ashore, she scooped me clean, with rocks ahead, not a stitch o' canvas drawin'; while we a-looking in the eye o' destruction, and not a power could lay her to."

"I hardly understand," said Scott faintly.

"True with you. Shiver me, lad, but I wus back aboard that vessel, and forgot about you and this fo'cas'le. When I am on land, I forget myself now and again, and it seems as if the street was tossin' like the ship, and I haul up, and put out a spar, sailor fashion, to keep her steady; and it's

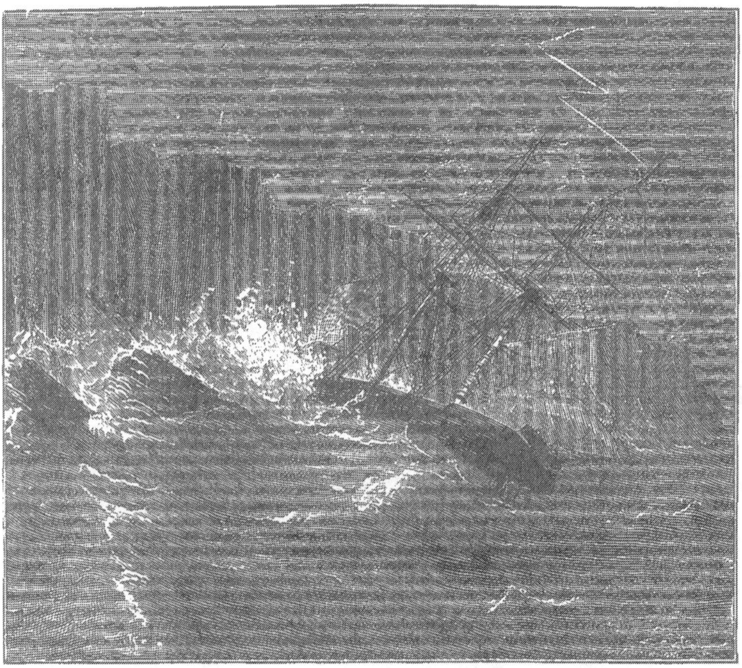

ROCKS TO STARBOARD, ROCKS TO PORT, AND A CLIFF DEAD AHEAD.

just so talkin'. But this wus the drift of it. We wus round the Cape, and swimmin' like a fish. The night wus black as burned coffee, and blowing like — however the wind blows according to land lingo, I don't know, my lad; but 'twas mor'n a gale. Every thing was fast but a gib for'ad, and a bit aft, just to steady her. 'Twas a dirty night, I tell you, and my seven years wus out. I knew I must come to anchor on a rock in that twelvemonth some time; and, feeling sure 'twas that night, I couldn't turn in, but held by the lookout. I knew there were islands and ugly rocks about us, but for my life I couldn't tell where; and through the Straits the sea wus running so hard with the wind, that no anchor cables could 'a' held us. It was go on, or go down; and we did both. Of a sudden I looked up, for something wus wrong. I heard the gib flapping against the stays just by my head. The wind wus gone, and nothing but a ledge o' rocks could 'a' cut it off. Then come a flash o' lightning. Holy Mother! There wus rocks to starboard, and rocks to port, and a great ledge dead ahead, and we making for it full fifteen knots. Quicker'n thought I looked aft. The lightning shivered a mast, and I saw the two men at the wheel drop. I started for it. Heaven knows 'twould 'a' done no good! but I started, when the ship careened, and I wus thrown fair afoul the deck-cask, and knocked almost senseless. Afore I could right myself, she struck. Holy Mother!"

The old quartermaster shivered, and seemed to shrink into himself, as he sat there on the floor. But Scott was too excited to wait long, and in a moment he asked, "And you?"

Old Joe started. "Ha, lad, I'd forgot myself again. Oh, 'twas awful! The next thing I knew, I wus clinging to that deck-cask, and wallowing among the rocks. Not another man wus saved, I think; and all the money I'd laid by in the nine and forty year wus in that hold as cargo. Mary, my wife, ay, and my little Joe, they two were asleep down in the little cabin. God knows, I'd risked every thing on that voyage, and promised Mary that it should be the last. 'Twas her last, but not mine. No. But had it 'a' been a steamer, she'd not 'a' got into a place like that."

Scott was so thoroughly sorry for the poor old man, that he even forgot his anxiety to know how he escaped at last; and, trying to make him forget the sad thoughts into which the tale had drawn him, he took the best way in the world, by "setting him off on another tack," as the sailor would have said, in asking, —

"Were you ever in a war?"

"I've been in mor'n one," replied the old man thoughtfully.

"I wish you would tell me something about them," said Scott.

"I wus once in a privateer, just off this coast," said Joe. "I wus skipper, and running for a tenth of the prize. The British held Gib, but there wus no communication with 'em."

"Gibraltar, do you mean?" asked Scott.

"Ay, ay! Gibraltar. We'll be there early in the morning. Better turn out about daylight, for the coast of Africa's worth seeing."

"So I will," replied Scott. "But go on, and tell me about the privateer."

"Well, the fleet had orders for Gib, and wanted news, and offered well for carrying a mail, and bringing back despatches. I heard of it, and shipped the cargo. We could sail within fifteen miles of Gib; and the first black night I took my best boat, and my best man to row, and one good rifle, and the despatches. Rowing thirty miles in one night is nothing to laugh at; but the sea was calm, and the wind blew just enough to make a noise, and hide the dip o' the oars. We reached Gib all right, in spite of the enemies' fleet. We went right under the nose of some of their big ships."

"Were you frightened?" asked Scott.

"Not then," replied the old salt; "for, like other big things, they never thought o' looking under their own noses for a bit of a cork with two men on it. But when we put about, the sea wus up a bit, and, worst of all, the lightning began to let loose. We saw a big ship ahead: there were no lights out, but we gave her the way. We were just abreast, when two or three flashes all together let the lookout have the sea; and he sighted us. The wind was agin 'em. They did not even hail us, but we heard 'em lower away a boat. They had our points. We lay to our oars for life; but it wus six to four, and a dead sure, that they were on us. I dropped my oar, and, taking up the rifle, I rammed down another ball. Then I lay down in the stern, and rested the rifle, aimed it as nearly as I could by the splash of the oars, and waited till I could sight by the lightning. In a minute there wus an awful flash. 'Steady there, captain!' cried my man at the oar; but it wus too late. I fired. Shiver me! I had never fired a gun before in all my life. I could handle a pistol or a cutlass, but that rifle handled me." Old Joe laughed, a low, chuckling laugh, as though it was a very good joke.

Scott was more anxious to know what the muzzle of the rifle accomplished than the butt, and asked,—

"Did you hit any one in the other boat?"

"Came nearer hitting the man behind me," replied Joe. "The old gun lamed me for a month. But when I came hoisting myself up from the bottom of the boat, I heard a voice a little way off, calling, 'Captain Beer, ahoy!' That wus me; and when I heard the voice I knew it wus my third mate."

"How came he there?" asked Scott.

"Why, lad, 'twas my own ship we passed. They were afraid we would swamp in the sea that wus rising, and had come nearer than was safe, and we had rowed faster than we thought."

Scott was tempted to smile at first, and think he had been listening to one of those proverbial sailor's yarns; but the next moment the tears came into his eyes again for the old sailor, as Joe continued,—

"I had a fair wind aft, and a clean sky, in those days; but now I'm old. My keel's all barnacles. My tackle's out o' gear. I'm Old Joe now, the quartermaster; and nobody hears a command from Captain Beer. Captain Beer's dead. He died when his last ship went on the rocks, with his wife and—ay, ay—when his little boy went down. And Old Joe will go down too, in four years more; only four year, my lad. And the rock's growin' sharp in the sea now, that will be Old Joe's gravestone."

CHAPTER VI.

WHALING OFF GIBRALTAR.

IT was hardly daylight the next morning when Scott came on deck; but the coast-line of Africa was clearly defined along the southern horizon, and the course of the steamer was entirely changed. The sun rose in front of them, instead of coming into his stateroom window.

As soon as Scott appeared on the deck, the captain, who was on the bridge, sent for him to come up there, and giving him the glass, with a hearty good-morning, asked,—

"How does she head, my boy?"

"First-rate, thank you, sir!" replied Scott cheerfully. "It seems good to see the sun forward."

"Why's that?" asked the captain.

"Oh! because, so long as we are going toward the rising sun, we are so much nearer India."

"What!" exclaimed the captain, slapping him on the shoulder, "tired of the sea already? It's not all like the Bay of Biscay: that's a dirty pond at the best. Look there, now: see that sand-mountain rising up? The big desert's behind there. See the caravan-paths winding down the sides of the hills this way. And that big peak there is Ape Hill."

"Ape Hill?" responded Scott. "What a name for a pile of sand and rocks like that! No ape would be fool enough to live there."

"That's what you think now," replied the captain; "but, if you should climb that hill, you'd find gorges with shrubbery, and the shrubbery would be full of apes. And there's something out of the common trade in the course of those monkeys too; for old Gib, over there, — you'll see it plainly when you come up from breakfast, — is the only spot in Europe where there are monkeys, and those monkeys are precisely the same as the monkeys on Ape Hill. They live in great caves on the south side of the Rock of Gib; and there are caves there that no one has ever found the bottom of. Now it may be all a yarn, or it may not; but they say that those apes have a subterranean passage under the Straits, between Gib and Ape Hill."

"I shouldn't think that would be any thing so very strange," said Scott, looking over the masts for the great Rock of Gibraltar at the left.

"Well, there you have it," replied the captain. "Then, you're just the one to believe the story, and chances are, you're right. And then, again, we come across one who will laugh at the very idea. But it's no use looking for Gib yet. You'd be disappointed, even if you could see it now. Wait till after breakfast, and have your first sight when it looms up dead ahead."

While Scott was at breakfast, the captain sent for him to come on to the bridge instantly. He dropped his fork, and sprang bare-headed for the deck, expecting to see the great rock, fourteen hundred feet high, right before him; but as he mounted the bridge he looked about in vain. Every thing was much as he left it.

The captain, with a rifle in his hand, was giving an order to slow down. A moment later he turned to Scott; and, pointing to a little floating foam on the water, he said, —

"See there! — just starboard the beam!"

"I see some foam," replied Scott.

"Keep your weather-eye on it," said the captain. "Look alive now!"

After watching for a moment, a glossy blue-brown mound seemed to rise up in the midst of the foam. Scott was on the point of asking what it was, when two jets of spray shot into the air, and he cried, —

"A whale!"

"Ay, ay, my lad! Now keep a sharp lookout. The fellow's coming across our beam, and if he don't change his course he'll pass close in on the port side. You may get a shot at him." And he handed Scott the rifle.

With trembling hand Scott took the piece, and watched the lumbering fellow as he slowly plunged along, spurting the water above him, and seeming to have no idea that a steamer was in the neighborhood.

"I didn't know that there were whales down here," he whispered.

"Plenty of them in the Straits," replied the captain. The tide runs hard in the Channel and the Narrows, and there's any amount of little fish here for them to feed on; but they see so much of steamers, that they have learned to be careful. That's a young fellow, though, and he may not have his weather-eye out."

The captain was right. The steamer floated so silently on the water, the engine being still, that the huge creature did not take the least notice of her. Scott waited impatiently till the whale was just by the steamer's course. He rested the rifle on the rail, and his finger twitched nervously upon the trigger. The sea was perfectly calm. There was no motion

THE ROCK OF GIBRALTAR.

to disturb his aim. He felt sure he could hit it the next time it rose. Up it came, slowly, wallowing, as though enjoying its breakfast and morning swim. Up went a dash of spray. All was ready.

"What will he do if I hit him?" asked Scott excitedly.

"Dive," replied the captain.

Scott began to press the trigger.

"Will he come up again directly?" he asked.

"Not if he is badly hurt, or scared," replied the captain.

Again Scott bent forward, and took deliberate aim. But he hesitated.

"What's the use?" said he; and, with a sigh of real regret at the sacrifice, he loosed his hold on the rifle, and stood erect.

"Right you are," said the captain enthusiastically. "I said to myself that that was the timber you was built of, but I didn't know till I had tried." And Scott was prouder, after all, than if he had made a good shot, only to see the poor creature leap from its pleasure into the waves, and dive in agony.

As soon as the whale was out of sight, Scott went down and finished his breakfast. When he came on deck again, he found the Rock of Gibraltar in plain sight. The captain was eating his breakfast on the bridge. The harbor was so clearly visible with the glass, and all seemed such plain sailing, that Scott asked in surprise the cause for his keeping on watch.

"There are more dangers ahead than you think for," he replied. "And many a ship has gone on the rocks when trying to enter of a bad night, before the signals were placed as they are now."

"How is it now?" asked Scott.

"Why, there's one of the best lights there in the Mediterranean Sea. And there's just one channel where any ship can enter, and be perfectly safe. But if she gets out of it, she's gone. Now, that light is red from every direction except when you ride dead in the channel, and then it's white. So we sail due east till the red disappears, and the light is white. Then we put her right about, and make for the light."

"I don't wonder that it is a strong fortress," said Scott, looking up the perpendicular ledge of rock to the fortifications built on the top, and then down to the little town nestling at the base.

"Those works up there are fourteen hundred feet high, and they command every thing but themselves. They've changed hands as often as an old packet. See the green hill as it falls away behind!"

"It's a beautiful spot!" exclaimed Scott. "And grand too. It must be very healthy there."

"So you might think," replied the captain; "but many's the British soldier and merchant that has had to leave the place, or die. They have a peculiar fever there that is nowhere else in the world. They even call it the Gibraltar fever; and it takes the strength out of a man like nothing else in the world."

They only made a short stop at Gibraltar; for there was little cargo to ship, and the captain wanted to make Algiers and Malta by daylight, which, in the common course, would be the case if he left Gib early in the day. Scott went on shore with Mr. Raymond, and wandered for an hour through the old town; but they did not venture to climb the hill. In the bazaar he bought a little African ivory box, beautifully carved on the cover with the figure of one of the old Moors in full battle dress.

MOOR READY FOR ACTION.

"We should very likely fall into their hands, if we went far beyond the walls of Algiers, where we shall stop next," said Mr. Raymond.

"Then, I think I'll stay inside the wall," replied Scott. "He's an ugly-looking fellow, a perfect walking arsenal.

Look at those pistols and knives in his belt. And what a gun! Do you suppose it's good for any thing?"

"I do, indeed," said Richard. "It is beautifully ornamented with silver, and some of them have jewels of great value inlaid; but that is all outside. And I know, from experience, that those guns can fire."

"You have tried them?" asked Scott.

"I have felt them," replied Richard.

"Oh, tell me about it!" exclaimed Scott.

"Wait till we have nothing better to do. At Algiers you will have a chance to see some of these fellows and their guns. They will not look so bright as this, perhaps; for the Moors are poor now, and even the robbers do not have such magnificent arms as they used. But the work on some of those old guns is simply magnificent. You thought, because it was so beautifully ornamented, that it was not good for any thing for work."

"I know my plain double-barrel shot-gun is a deal better than Bobby Brackett's fancy one; and father said it was only ornamented in that way to make it sell."

"That's very true," replied Richard. "They've grown into that way of doing business in America; because people will pay their money for any thing showy, and not care a straw whether it is worth any thing or not. But these fellows' guns are their very life to them, just like the lances and swords and shields of the old Saxon and Norman warriors. You remember those beautiful shields that we saw in England, in the window of the old curiosity shop?"

"Yes, indeed, I do!" exclaimed Scott.

"Well, did it make them any weaker to have all that carving on them?"

"Of course not," said Scott.

"It's a bad habit the people of America have grown into," replied Richard. "Half of them go in so much for show, that the other half go as far the other way, and think that any kind of show is an actual sin. It doesn't make these fellows' guns any worse to ornament them, after they have made a good gun in the first place, any more than it makes a real gentleman a fop to dress in the fashion, if he is a true and brave man to put the clothes on to. Don't you see?"

"Indeed, I do, sir," replied Scott. "And if I do not know what it is to be a true hero before long, it will not be because I've not had a good teacher: that's sure. But what made me think that those guns were not good for any thing, was because I had read about the fellows that carried them being unable to fire them off, and being such cowards whenever there was any real danger."

"Those things do very well for travellers' stories," replied Richard, "and make people laugh when they read them. There is some ground for them, too, according to our ideas; for these fellows are not the same kind of people that we are. Their ideas and ours are very different; and, while we judge them by our notions, they are acting according to theirs. What we call bravery they think is bravado, and what we consider cowardice is really more discretion with them. There have been some very valiant deeds done by Mussulman warriors and brigand robbers. It is a regular profession with them, and nothing to be ashamed of. And, in spite of all that the brave travellers say to the contrary, I should be very slow to put myself into their clutches, without some necessity. They fight like mad tigers when they are cornered."

"You say they are not ashamed of being robbers?" asked Scott.

"Not a bit of it," replied Richard. "I have talked with an old fellow over there in Algiers, who was constantly telling stories of old times, and saying, 'When I was a robber.' And there are many like him, — the Bedouins of Syria, for instance, — who consider it one of the most honorable ways of getting a living."

"They must be horribly wicked people," said Scott with a shudder.

"I don't know about that," replied Richard. "They are not civilized Christians, of course; they would be very much better if they were: but we think it all right to take any thing from our enemies when we are at war, — it is not long since the days of privateers; and they only go a little farther, and consider themselves always at war with every one."

When the steamer left the harbor, they had another passenger, a military officer, going over to Malta; and, though it was an unusual appendage for a soldier, he was closely followed, everywhere he went, by an enormous hound. He was a good-natured fellow; and as Scott was fond of dogs, and the hound very soon discovered it, they became intimate friends at once. But no matter how familiar they grew, the hound could not be induced to remain a moment if his master was out of sight.

"He is very fond of you, sir," said Scott to the officer, as he vainly tried to induce the dog to go below with him.

"And I am very fond of him," replied the officer in good English, though he was not an Englishman. "We have seen hard times together."

"Has he ever been in a battle?" asked Scott.

"That he has," replied the officer; "and in more than one. He saved my life once at least, and I don't know how many more times. I was a petty officer in the ranks, and was wounded. At night I crept away from the field, and tried to make my way to camp. But it was too far. I crawled up into the hills, and there I fell exhausted. The poor fellow tried to help me, but it was of no use. I thought I was dying, and for several days I lay unconscious. When I came to myself, there was the old fellow, thin as a starved rat, licking my hands, and barking at the vultures and crows that were waiting for my corpse."

Scott shuddered; but he was beginning to become accustomed to all sorts of people and ways.

"How did you escape?" he asked.

"Why, the beast no sooner saw that I was up and awake, and able to keep the ugly carrion-flies off for myself, than he started away. It was an hour before he came back. I was faint and hungry and thirsty and every thing else. I thought if I could kill one of the vile birds it would be better than nothing; and I tried to load my rifle, but I was too weak. I lay down on the rocks to go to sleep again, when a beastly crow came and sat down on my foot, and gave a fiendish cry to the rest that were lying round in ambush. I would not have moved my foot to shake him off; but old Zigg came tearing up the hill, and away he flew. I opened my eyes as Zigg came up. He had a hare in his mouth, that he had just killed. I ate a half of it raw, and he ate the rest. He was colonel of my commissaries, division-surgeon of my hospital, captain of my picket-guard, field-marshal and sergeant-at-arms, father, mother, and best friend, for eight days, till I was able to crawl on and find some help. He's old now, and beyond the limit of most dogs' days. He'll die pretty soon."

Scott looked up, for the officer's voice trembled. He was stroking old Zigg's head gently, and the dog was looking

THE FAITHFUL DOG.

into his master's face with a low whine. Scott saw that tears were glistening in the soldier's eyes, and wondered how it was that a moment before he had thought the officer so rude and hard-hearted.

"Has he ever been at sea before?" he asked.

"Not long at a time," replied the officer. "He doesn't like the salt water, and I don't blame him. But he took a trip with me a little while ago that very few dogs ever took, and he seemed to enjoy it."

"What was that?" asked Scott.

"I was ordered to carry despatches to Paris during the siege, and return with replies in ten days. I went along as a blind beggar, and Zigg carried a string that was tied to my wrist. He took the cue like an old actor; and not a living soul suspected that I'd not been blind and led by that dog all my life. In three days I was in Paris. But how to get out again was harder. I tried three times, and failed. At last it came to where I had to go. There were only three days more. There was a balloon in Paris, and they offered me that. I didn't think much of flying, especially when the fellows outside knew the joke, and only waited to see a balloon in the air, to make a target of it. The only man who knew how to run the engine was afraid to go. But I took lessons all the afternoon, and at night I started. There was a full moon; but clouds were coming up, and I waited till they were almost over the moon. Then I got in, and Zigg with me, and away we went. Heavens! how we shot up! It took my breath away, but I let her go. Zigg began to howl till he found that it was all right, and then he enjoyed it. We shot into the black clouds and out of them again in an instant; and then all was bright above us, and nothing but a fog-bank beneath. She was running

THE DESPATCHES MUST GO!

away with me. I caught the rope, and began to pull. But suddenly I felt sick, and before I knew it I had fainted away. When I came to myself, we were whirling along right in the clouds. We must have come down a long way, I thought, and wondered why, till I looked round, and there sat Zigg, with the rope in his mouth, pulling for dear life. He must have seen it drop from my hands when I fainted, and taken the matter in mouth himself, because he could not take it in hand. I had no idea where we were; but she was dropping, and I let her drop. We made bad work of landing; but we were all right when we got out, and we left the old man's balloon hanging tangled up in a grove of trees." The officer turned to the dog again, and, laughing, said, "Old boy, your teeth are all gone now. You couldn't hold a string in those old jaws; but your will's as good as ever it was." And getting up, he walked away, with Zigg following close at his heels.

CHAPTER VII.

ALGIERS AND ENGINEERING.

"ALGIERS is a horrible place!" exclaimed Scott, as he came on deck in the morning, and examined the little African town that they were approaching.

"That depends upon how you see it, and where you look," replied the captain. "Point your glass up the hill there, port a little. There you are! What do you think of that?"

"Beautiful! beautiful!" exclaimed Scott. "What pretty little houses there about the grove! And what is that big building? What makes them have those great white fences all about every house? Oh, I know! It's to keep the robbers off."

"Right you are," replied the captain.

"And what splendid broad roads! The street commissioners of Boston should come over here, and find out how it looks to have their work properly done. They have done it just half way for so long, that they begin to think that that is really the right way to do it. And those are splendid wharves there too. Well, Algiers is not so bad, perhaps; but that's a miserable little town down under the hills, on the water."

"It's a little odd at first, like all heathen places; but, when you get used to them, you'll like them, I warrant you. Every one does; and, after you've been back in America for a while, you'll begin to sigh for another sight of the horrible places, as you call them now."

They made a very short stop at Algiers, to ship a small amount of cargo; but Mr. Raymond and Scott took advantage of the two hours to go on shore. And Scott began to feel that fascination of which the captain had spoken: every thing was so wild, so strange, so intensely interesting, in spite of the bad smells and dirty streets, that were so narrow that sometimes they could almost touch both sides at once.

There were such strange people as he had read of in "The Arabian Nights." There were Arabs and Moors and Turks, in all sorts of strange dresses, — some with fancy turbans on their heads, and fancy little jackets on their backs, and bagging breeches. Then there were fellows with cloaks all over them, even around their heads, bound there by a smaller turban. Some were very light, and some were very dark; but there were none so black as the negroes of Boston.

"These are not Africans, are they?" Scott asked Mr. Raymond in surprise.

"Indeed, they are," said Richard. "Why did you think not?"

"Why, the Africans are very black," replied Scott.

"The Africans that we see in America are black enough, surely; but they come from a very little corner comparatively, — chiefly from the coast, far down to the South. The people of Zululand, or Zanzibar, are black, with thick lips and curling hair. But there are many Africans who are almost as white as we are, and all shades between."

The booths, or native shops, of the bazaar, which itself is only a street of these shops, are not large stores, such as one finds in America; and Scott stopped in wonder before the

IN THE BAZAAR.

little things, hardly larger than his stateroom on the steamer, filled up with all sorts of wares, beautiful cloths, jewelry, and the pottery that is so precious in America. He recognized some bits very much like ornaments in his own home.

They stopped for a moment before one of the largest shops in the bazaar, where a very pretty young woman was having some silver ornaments fitted to her arm. She had a thin veil over her face; but she was almost white, and through it her pretty features could be very plainly seen.

"She is a Mussulman woman," said Richard. "It is the custom for all of them to go veiled; but she is so pretty, that she hates to hide her face, so she makes the veil very thin. The old fellow standing behind her there, smoking the cigarette, is her husband. See that beautiful rug behind her, hanging on the wall."

"I don't call it beautiful," said Scott.

"Never mind, your mother and sisters would," replied Richard, laughing. "You could buy it for a song here, if you took the right course with the white-bearded old fellow; but in Boston it would cost thirty or forty dollars, at the very least."

At that moment some one slapped Mr. Raymond on the shoulder, and a hearty voice exclaimed,—

"Speaking of Boston reminds me that I came from there myself a long time ago. It seems like a lifetime; and I'm overjoyed to find any one else in the same box."

They found themselves greeted by a Boston artist, there in the bewildering and dirty bazaar of Algiers, where Scott had thought himself surrounded by nothing but heathendom. The artist had been living there for several years, sending his pictures back to America for sale. He was disappointed when he learned that they were to leave in an hour and a half, but insisted on their coming with him to his house, just in the outskirts of the town, and having breakfast with him.

It was a pretty little place, on the verge of a hill, with a garden of brilliant flowers all about it, at one end of which Scott was amazed to see a tangle of dandelions and buttercups.

"Do they grow here?" he asked, while his heart seemed beating in his throat, as his eyes rested on those little blossoms.

"No, indeed!" replied the artist, tenderly picking one for each of his guests, and presenting them as though they had been the choicest of moss-roses. "I brought them with me from home. I had some daisies too, but I could not make them live. I know of nothing in the world that carries the heart back to dear old New England, when it is weary of being away, like the dandelions and daisies and buttercups. This is the most precious part of my garden. And it is a little peculiar; but my neighbors, the natives living about here, think there is nothing so beautiful in the world, and almost all of them have roots growing in their gardens. They say, 'What a wonderful country yours must be, where such beautiful and fragrant flowers as the *dadelean* grow wild!' and, now that I am away from it, I am tempted to agree with them."

"Then, why don't you go back?" asked Scott more abruptly than he thought, he was so busy caressing the little yellow flower.

The artist smiled. "I am making my fortune here," he said; "and I expect to go back when that is made perhaps. But, after all, I love this place. There is something very fascinating in Oriental life. I think we are too far from it in America. We are too rigid and straight there, and make life too much of a burden. There is Russia, for instance: it is much colder, and harder to keep comfortable there, than at home; but they are perfect Orientals, — the wealthy I mean, of course. I love America; and, if I were not an American, I believe there is nothing in the world that I should long for so much as to be one. And yet, after each time that I have gone home for a vacation, the first sight of these long-robed, dark-skinned fellows, their dirty streets, their curious customs and melodious languages, have thrilled me with a pleasure that I cannot express. I hope that fortune may never place me where I shall be unable, at times, to revisit the Orient."

The artist turned away from his bed of buttercups, and conducted his guests to his little breakfast-room. After breakfast he opened his studio at their request; and, as Scott was particularly pleased with a painting which the artist had made of his grandfather, — who was one of the famous sculptors of London nearly a century ago, — in the act of making a clay model for a marble bust of the lord-mayor, that now stands in the Council chamber of the Houses of Parliament in London, he presented him, when he left, with a little medallion of the painting on a piece of ivory, that, about the outside, was beautifully carved, to form a frame.

"I shall keep it as long as I live," said Scott to Mr. Raymond, as they were being rowed out to the steamer; "and I shall press this dandelion, and keep that too. He was a first-rate fellow, and I never thought half enough of our buttercups at Beverly before."

To occupy the time while on the voyage, Mr. Raymond succeeded in interesting Scott in the engineering of the

IN MEMORY OF A PLEASANT HOUR.

steamer, among other things; and here he had a valuable assistant in the chief engineer, who was an enthusiast in his department, as every man should be to succeed. Economical consumption was the order of the day; and economical consumptionists had to give the palm, thus far at least, to this chief engineer.

"You see," he said to Mr. Raymond and Scott one day as they came into his cabin, shortly after leaving Algiers, and caught him figuring, — "you see, the coal costs so much, that it is really one of the greatest items of the entire voyage. Why, I am going to save as much in coal, over what this same steamer consumed three years ago, as the salaries and feed of the whole crew for the entire voyage, including the captain and all."

"What makes the coal cost so much?" asked Scott.

"Transportation, my boy," replied the chief. "It has to be shipped from England to Gib and Malta and Port Said and Aden and Ceylon, and so on, to the end of navigation. Every mile that it is carried costs so much more coal to carry it; and then it has to be stored and reshipped, and there's the insurance, the loss, the interest, and every thing else."

"Why don't you carry coal enough to last?" said Scott.

"Take mor'n the steamer could carry, to last her the voyage. But look at here! See what I have done this voyage. We've three thousand tons dead freight."

"What's dead freight?" asked Scott.

"It is the solid, paying freight down in the holds. We have averaged over ten knots an hour."

"I call that very slow time, especially when one is in a hurry," interrupted Scott; for he felt every delay and detention more keenly than he might under almost any other circumstances. "Our American steamers go it at fifteen knots and over, and then the passengers complain."

"They are English steamers, after all, that take you so rapidly across the Atlantic," replied the chief a little gruffly, for economy was just then his hobby. "But even they could not do that in this water, no matter how much coal they burned."

"Why not?" demanded Scott, ready to fight for any thing that was even so much American as a steamer leaving an American port.

"There are several reasons. The density of the water is one. It is harder making time in this water than in the Atlantic. Then, the temperature is very much against us. The steam is condensed, you know, by constantly pumping water from the sea over the steam radiators. If you take a bottle half full of hot water, let the steam rise till it has filled the other half, and driven out the air, then cork it securely, and pour cold water over the half that is filled with steam, you will make the water boil; and the colder the water is that you pour over the outside of the bottle, the harder the water inside will boil. It is on precisely the same principle that we magnify the heat of steam produced by the fires. When we are in water that is as warm as your blood, you can see that we get less benefit." Then he turned to Mr. Raymond, as though he were a little tired of talking to an unappreciative listener, and continued, "What I am proud of is, that we have made such time, with this burden, at an expense of actually less than fifteen tons of coal a day. Why, when 'The Great Eastern' crossed the Atlantic in 1867, she only made fifteen knots an hour, and she actually burned over three hundred tons of coal every day."

"Yes," added Mr. Raymond: "the steamer that we have just crossed on consumed over a hundred tons a day, and they thought they were doing very well."

"They can afford it," said the engineer. "In the first place, it costs them comparatively little. Then, their celebrity in opposition depends, in great part, on their speed."

"I wish there was more opposition here," interrupted Scott, who did not intend to let the chief go too easily. But he only smiled, and continued,—

"They carry large lists of passengers, and set expensive tables; and one meal even is worth saving, even though at cost of a little more coal. It is just the other way with us."

Scott was on the point of saying, "I should think so:" but he decided that he had already said too much; and though the table of the steamer, like that of all the English steamers for India, was very poor, he laughed with himself over the little joke, and let the chief go free.

"But I should think, that, if you can go ten knots so very cheaply, you might at least add another knot or two, which would save a deal of time at the end of the voyage."

"That is just it," replied the chief pleasantly. "It is just that last straw that breaks the camel's back; and that is where I am making the greater part of my saving. If you are walking down street, at home, on a warm day, and you walk leisurely, you can go a great way without being very warm."

"I might in Boston, but I could not here," replied Scott, wiping the perspiration from his face.

"Well, I am talking about Boston now, my boy. If you hurry, you become heated and tired before you have gone half as far."

"I know that that is so," replied Scott. He was taking

Old Joe's advice with the greatest care: and, of all men on board, he did not mean to "sir" the chief engineer; for he could not but feel that in some way he was a little to blame for the slow progress that they were making.

"Very well. It is just so with the engine."

"If you keep the engine greased well, it should not get heated," said Scott, a little doubtful about the propriety of the engineer's logic.

"Not exactly. But while it is very easy to drive the steamer at a moderate rate through the water, when we go faster the friction begins to tell, and the wheel, of course, has to turn much faster to produce the same effect. And every mile that we increase on the easy speed takes an increasingly larger quantity of coal. Many of the engineers who are trying to reach this economical plan do not think of this," added the chief with a chuckle; and Scott said, with a shrug of his shoulders, —

"I hope we shall go back on a steamer where the chief has not found it out."

CHAPTER VIII.

SIGHTS IN THE SUEZ CANAL.

IT was night when the steamer reached Malta, in spite of all calculations to the contrary. Mr. Raymond went on shore to learn of the steamer from New York, and was assured that the two passengers whom he sought had transferred to the Indian steamer at that port. He was sure of it in advance; but now additional weight was added to his theory, and all that was left was for them to reach Bombay at the earliest moment possible.

All that Scott saw of Malta was the high walls of natural rock rising up out of the water, all about the steamer, with little houses built on the cliffs, and forts and fortifications on all the prominent places overlooking the almost land-locked bay. But he would much sooner have left without seeing even that than have waited an hour longer than necessary.

With the first gray light they were again under way. All sails were set; and, in spite of economy of coal, they were able to make the great light of Port Said as the sun went down on the evening of the fourth day. There they were to coal up; and a gloomy place it made of the pretty saloon of the steamer, to close it up fore and aft, and shut all the ports of the state-rooms, and draw the Venetian blinds and latches. But it had to be done, for a dirtier place can hardly be found on earth than one of the Indian steamers when they are coaling.

Very slowly they worked their way up the harbor, till they

lay within a stone's throw of the cafés and dance-houses that are so abundant in Port Said. Instantly the steamer was surrounded with small boats of all sorts and sizes, with all kinds of passengers. But they were an ugly-looking set in the night, and Scott was not particularly enchanted with the terrible racket that was kept up. He went into his stateroom, but it was very warm and close. When the ship's papers were signed, and the crowd of agents was allowed to come on board and make their bargains for supplying the coal and provisions that were needed, the steamer became a little more quiet, and Scott went up on to the bridge to watch the operation of coaling.

Huge flat-boats — lighters, they called them — came alongside. The coal is piled up in cubic blocks fifteen or twenty feet each way, with little alleys between them. One after another, the lighters are pushed up beside the steamer, one on each side; and a narrow plank is run on the steamer's deck from each end of each of the lighters, and one from the middle if the steamer has four shoots to the coal-bunks. Then a multitude of vile Arabs, who are covered with the dirt of years at this business, with coarse blankets on their heads, upon which they carry baskets of coal, start on one never-ending line up the two planks at the ends of the lighters, dumping the contents of the baskets in the shoots, and meeting in the middle to come down the plank there in solid file for fresh basketfuls.

The officers of the steamer usually weigh this coal in some way, to avoid deception. This time the chief engineer went through the lighters; and, picking out several of the blocks, he measured them carefully, and weighed them on large scales fixed over the shoots, as they were brought up. Then he measured all the other blocks, and estimated from those he had weighed. Then the work began in good earnest. The lines were formed. The Arabs began to sing a horrible nasal song, and to climb the narrow plank, one close behind the other.

Port Said was a dirty little town, made up only of such people as could earn a living or a fortune out of the steamers that were continually stopping there; and after an hour's stroll the next morning, through the damp streets, vile smelling, and teeming in the heat of the sun, that was something terrific, the two travellers went back again to the steamer, perfectly satisfied to be under way again.

The Suez Canal was a sight that Scott had looked forward to ever since starting for India. He was disappointed, and yet it was wonderful. It was only a narrow river of salt water, not half as wide, at the most, as the steamer was long. There were low banks on either side, of the whitest of white sand; and now and then there was a station, an official building, and sometimes two or three hovels about it. The officials at these stations managed the progress of the steamers by telegraph with the other stations, to prevent any accidents; for the channel was not wide enough for two steamers to pass, and the first steamer to pass a station had the right of way to the next. Sometimes a steamer was unfortunate, and had to keep tying up all day long, to let others pass, and was three or even four days in getting through the canal; but usually it was not more than two, and in the long days steamers have been through in a single day. But this is not often the case: for, at the best, they are only allowed to go at the very slow rate of five knots an hour, except in the Bitter Lakes; and they can only move between sunrise and sunset, except with especial permission, which is hard to obtain.

It was rather monotonous, but Scott did not mean to lose any of it on that account. The pilot of the Canal Company

THE SUEZ CANAL.

stood on the bridge, so that the captain was not so much confined as he had been; and Scott always found his company interesting. Now and then, too, there was a sight that was well worth seeing in a little oasis, or a little native village as gray-white as the sand which was all about it, or a caravan, or a pilgrim winding his way along the banks.

"Whatever possessed those natives to build a village there?" Scott asked the captain, pointing to a little town they were passing. "There is not a green thing anywhere about it."

"There is nothing green just now," replied the captain; "and at the best there is not much to boast of, though in the winter and spring there is a little grass about the houses. But they certainly find something to live on, or they would not be there. Caravans always stop there, for one thing. There is a ferry a little lower down, and we shall very likely see a caravan crossing. But there's always something to do wherever there is a village: you may depend on that, no matter where you are. Were you ever in the north of Norway?"

"No, sir," replied Scott, surprised that the captain should ask him such a question, forgetting that Norway was really much nearer his home than the Suez Canal.

"Well, when you go to Norway," said the captain, "you will see, along the northern coast, a hundred villages with less show for a living than yonder town. Every thing is bare rocks there, and icy cold ocean. They have a legend, that when God had completed the world, and made every thing beautiful, he lay down to take a nap, and that the Evil One was so outraged that he had succeeded so well, that he took up a tremendous rock, and threw it with all his strength at the world. It struck near the pole, and was shivered to small pieces. It would have sent the entire hulk into kingdom come, had not God waked up at that moment, and put his hand on his trembling world, to keep it where it was. But it tipped the earth a little way, and that is why the poles are inclined, to this day. There was but little of the material left from which God had made the earth; and that he spread, as best he could, in a few of the cracks between the ugly splinters of the rock that the Devil threw. That was all he could do, and to this day that barren splintered rock remains; and that is Norway. And yet there is a whole nation of people living up there, and making, not only good livings, but such fortunes, sometimes, that many from Denmark and Germany are tempted up into those frozen, rocky deserts, in a desire to get rich."

Scott made up his mind that one of the first things he did, when he became a man, would be to go to Norway, and see that strange land that the Devil added to the beautiful world that God had made. But he had no time to ask more about it then, for just ahead appeared the ferry of which the captain had told him; and to his delight he discovered that a caravan was in the very act of crossing. He left the bridge, and went as far forward as possible, to obtain a better view.

Thirty or forty camels, with curious bags upon their backs, and some of them with a man or woman balanced between the bags, were huddled upon one bank, and as many were forming into a new line of march on the other. Between the two, a broad, flat-bottomed boat was slowly moving, with its long-necked burden. There were white and black camels, and almost all shades between. But they were shaggy, dirty creatures, and not the handsome, graceful animals that Scott supposed the real camels of the real Orient must be. Old Joe was beside him, holding a rope, for they had been signalled to tie up; and Scott gave vent to his disappointment in words.

The old quartermaster did not move his head, or hardly his lips; for it was against the strictest orders to speak to passengers when upon canal duty; but he answered him nevertheless.

"Mind how you look at things, my lad," said he. "A ship comin' out o' a long voyage, her masts and spars all black, her riggin' ragged, her canvas dunned, the paint knocked off her keel, and barnacles a-hangin' to her water-line,—there's nothing purty about sich. And them ships o' the desert is built on the same stocks."

"Very well," said Scott, laughing, and apparently speaking to himself; for he saw that he had made a mistake in breaking the rules: "I will wait till I see them under better circumstances."

"Wait till ye overhaul a camel that's not been loggin' sand for three months, and ye'll see as neat a ship as ever sailed the sea. They hail from Bagdad, those camels, and they're headed for Cairo."

Scott began to look at them with new interest, and to think them a wonderful sight, after all. All the way from Bagdad! No wonder they were dusty.

Several very small steamers passed them, carrying passengers up and down the canal,—steamers made for canal travel, that drew only a few inches of water, and could go close up to the banks. There were other small craft, too, in the canal,—native sailing-boats, creeping along from one station to another with loads of fish and melons. They were curious melons, yellow as gold, and shrivelled like a summer squash. Scott thought they were pumpkins, and bought three of them, and, carrying them in triumph to the chief steward, asked him to have some American pumpkin-pies made of them.

The steward replied that he would find them better raw, and began to cut a piece from one of them.

"That's because you Englishmen don't know what an American pumpkin-pie is," said Scott with a toss of his head. But when he saw the steward really begin to eat the piece he had cut off, and as though he enjoyed it, he cut off one too, and, to his astonishment, found himself eating one of the coolest, sweetest, and most delicious cantelopes he had ever tasted. He did not say any more about pie; but the first time that the steamer stopped again, and he had an opportunity, he bought a basketful of those pumpkins, and Mr. Raymond very willingly assisted him to dispose of them raw.

The fish that the fellows had to sell were caught in the canal. They were large and very good. It gave Scott an idea; and, when the steamer was still at night, he tried his luck over the stern. Some of the boatmen had clams for sale too: they were a little odd in shape; but Scott's home was New England, and he knew the peculiar virtues of clam-bakes and oyster-stews, and again went to the chief steward.

"Can't we have some fried clams for breakfast?" he asked.

"Certainly," replied the steward: "any thing that the ship has, or can get, you are welcome to; but you must agree to eat them, if they are cooked expressly for you."

"Of course I will," said Scott, but a little doubtfully, for he remembered the pumpkin-pie. "What is the matter with them?" he added, as the steward smiled.

"Oh, nothing much! Only they are full of sand."

"Never mind the sand!" Scott exclaimed. "I guess I can go them for all that." And he honestly tried to, when the tempting little dish was set before his plate at the table: but it was inexpressibly worse than eating Beverly strawberries before they were washed; and, boy that he was, he had given that up years ago.

It was very hot in the canal. The sun beat down with nothing to break its force, and the sand returned good interest for all that fell upon it. The glare, too, was terrible; and, long before they were out of it, Scott had to borrow of the captain a pair of colored glasses, for his eyes began to suffer. At night the heat seemed even more oppressive. The breeze that blew from the baking sand-banks was almost hotter than the sun. Scott opened his port window wide, on going to bed, in spite of the steward's warning, that, before morning, he would be nearly eaten up with sand-fleas. The steamer was so still that he did not go to sleep at once, and was only drowsy when he heard Mr. Raymond come softly into his room, and shut the port. He thought it was for the sand-fleas, and, turning over, said,—

"I left it open on purpose. I'd much rather be eaten up than roasted."

Richard laughed, and replied, "You'll be neither roasted nor eaten up, but frozen to death before morning, if you leave your port open in the canal at this season."

Scott was too sleepy even to laugh at what he supposed was a joke of some sort; but he remembered it, and found it no joke, after all, when he awoke about two o'clock with a cold chill. He drew a blanket over him, but it seemed impossible to get warm; and at last he partially dressed himself, and went out to walk in the saloon. In a few moments the chill left him; but the re-acting fever set in, and he seemed burning up. At the end of the saloon was the cabin sideboard and a sort of pantry in a little room opposite the captain's cabin. The water-tank was kept there, and Scott went in for a drink. As he opened the door, there was a scurry of feet on the floor, a yelp, a flash from two greenish-yellow eyes, and a large, dark figure leaped out of the window, touched the deck, bounded over the narrow stretch of intervening water, and went howling up the sand-hill before he could either be frightened and shut the door, or be daring enough to think of some mode of attacking the creature. It effectually cured the fever, however; and, when he went to bed again, his knees were not precisely steady, and he was enjoying a healthy perspiration.

The steamer was under way again when Scott awoke in the morning; and, when he came into the saloon, the second steward was complaining to the chief that some of the sailors had stolen a cold roast that he left in the saloon pantry the night before. He said they must have taken it through the large sideport, which he left open to keep the meat cool, and save him the trouble of going to the ice-chest with it.

"You left the deck-port open, did you?" growled the chief in a surly way. "Did you never know that the jackals along these banks are tame as kittens? Take the price of the roast out of your pay at the end of the voyage. Go about getting the breakfast."

Scott smiled at the fright he had received the night before all from a frightened jackal.

"I did come near freezing," he said to Richard when he appeared on deck. "What makes it so cold in the canal at night?"

"It is always cold on a desert before morning," replied his friend. "There is a deep philosophy in it, which you will find out in the course of delving through college. Books will teach you every thing, Scott; and there are hosts of people who think their children should learn every thing from books, and would rather they would spend a year in college to find it out than to sleep one night on the Suez Canal. But you'll not forget it half so quickly as if you'd dug it out of a dog-eared book. The sun shining on the sand all day makes an oven of it, that sends up a torrent of heat. The whole of South Europe, you know, is kept warm by the hot wind from the Sahara; and, of course, to have that hot wind blow, a cold wind must be supplied from somewhere, to be heated."

"Oh, I see!" exclaimed Scott; "and after sundown the supply keeps on, and as long as the sand remains hot the furnace continues to run all right; but, when the heat is exhausted, it becomes colder and colder, till, in the re-action, it at last becomes colder than the surrounding air."

"I should think that that covered it," replied Richard, smiling, "though a philosopher would laugh at us, you may be sure."

Just before breakfast the steamer passed Ismalia, a little town upon a lake, with a beautiful stretch of blue water about it, and a dense green jungle behind. A palace of the Khedive was surrounded by a large garden at one end of the town; and a little farther down the bank was the palace that was built for the Emperor Napoleon, at the opening of the Suez Canal.

"It must be fun to have such a time made over you as that, and have a palace built for you, whenever you expect to stop over night where the hotels are not grand enough to satisfy you," said Scott, looking admiringly at the little gray sandstone palace.

"And it must be fun to be kicked out, as Napoleon was, when the people are tired of you, and not have them care a straw whether you have a roof to cover you or not."

"Perhaps it's just as well to go along sort of half and half, after all," said Scott.

"I am inclined to think it is much better," replied Richard; but Scott was eagerly watching a native craft that had been slowly sailing along the border of the canal, in the shoal water, with a heavy load of melons. When they had nearly passed her, the Arab at the helm veered a point toward the steamer, and suddenly the old craft began to increase its speed. Faster and faster it went, till it kept up with the steamer, and its prow was just ahead of the steamer's wheel. The weak and heavily-laden boat sagged and bent, and seemed ready to go to pieces, and the huge sail hung against the bamboo mast. Scott studied the matter intently. He saw that Mr. Raymond was watching him, and he hated to ask him to explain the curious sight. It was evident that something was dragging the craft along at a terrific rate for her, and that those on board were having a very good time over it. The propelling power came from the steamer in some way, for the boat neither gained nor lost after it had once come into position; but there was no rope, or any means of communication with the steamer.

"Do you give it up?" asked Richard, smiling.

"No, indeed, sir," said Scott stoutly. And just at that moment his eye fell on the water, and he began to see through it, or into it at least. In going forward, the steamer, of course, pushed just so much water out of place, or made a hole in the canal; and, just as soon as the steamer had passed, it left the hole with nothing to fill it, unless the water rushed up from behind, and down from both sides, to take the place. This made a current rushing in behind the steamer at precisely the same rate at which the steamer was going, and the Arabs had learned the trick of taking advantage of it.

"It is what they call stealing our wake-water," said Richard, when Scott had satisfactorily solved the matter. "There's another great principle of philosophy that you'll understand already, when you come across it, years hence, in some of those musty books."

About two-thirds of the way through the canal they came upon the Bitter Lakes, — enormous salt lakes stretching over the white sand, with a station or two and a green spot or two appearing here and there, and salt marshes everywhere.

Here they were allowed to go at full speed; and, the way being carefully marked by signals, even the pilot came from the bridge with a sigh of relief, and lit a cigar. All of a sudden Scott began to realize that it was no laughing matter to take a large steamer through seventy-five miles of that narrow path, where the least deviation in the course, or the least swerving to the current or the wind, or an instant's delay in giving an order to the men at the wheel, or in having it obeyed, or the slightest objection of the steamer to mind the helm, even a hand's breadth, would send the prow into the soft bank of the channel; and, of course, the motion of the steamer would then bring the stern round to the opposite side, and there the steamer would lie, stuck fast, fore and aft.

"Did such a thing ever occur?" Scott asked the captain.

"When the canal was first opened, and the pilots had not learned the new business, it often happened," replied the captain. "I have lain still in this water for four days, waiting for them to unload a large ship, that was stuck so fast that nothing else would get her out. There is a sort of suction in the sand; and the tendency is to draw tighter and tighter, when once a steamer has run her nose into it. But the pilots are growing brighter and brighter every year. You might have noticed,—but I fancy you didn't, after all,—a little while ago, the wind took us a bit, and I thought her nose was right in it, on the port side. Quicker'n thought the pilot gave the order to go ahead at full speed, and put her helm hard-a-port. In a couple o' winks that would have driven her square into the bank for which she was heading; but the jump that the engines gave her, and just the motion of the rudder in going round, sent her in a bit aft, like the push of an oar in skulling a fish-boat; and, before she could feel the helm, he had put it to starboard again, and slowed down, and we were all right in the channel. It's a wonderful thing, this handling a steamer," he added with a sigh, and leaned back against the rail in silent admiration.

By good fortune they made the rest of the canal without detention; and, in the dusk that so quickly succeeds an Egyptian sunset, they passed the station beyond Suez.

The city itself lay three miles back upon the bay; but Mr. Raymond assured Scott that he lost nothing in not seeing it, for, though larger than Port Said, it was upon precisely the same principle, supported only by the steamers that stopped there, and of no importance to the sight-seer.

CHAPTER IX.

ARABIA AND HER WATER-BABIES.

THEY did not leave the deck that night till the dim coast of Egypt on one side, and the shores of the arm of the Red Sea on the other, were lost to sight in the dim shadows.

"It seems as though the journey were completed," said Scott.

"Yes," replied Richard, as they went below: "we have passed the great gateway between the Occident and Orient. But what is the matter, Scott? you look pale," he added, as they came into the light of the saloon.

"I have felt queer," said Scott with a shiver, "ever since taking my bath this morning."

All the Oriental steamers are supplied with several bath-rooms, that are always popular, where the passengers can bathe in water drawn fresh for them from the ocean.

"Where were we when the steward drew the water for your bath this morning?" asked Richard.

"In the Bitter Lakes, I think," said Scott.

"That explains it," replied Richard, much relieved, for he feared the heat of the voyage might be proving too much for his young friend. "Those lakes are very broad, and rather shallow; and the great heat of the sun, and the porous bed, carry off such a vast amount of water, of the fresh-water part at least, that that which is left becomes the saltest, hardest, and, to speak plainly, the most electric water in the world, except, perhaps, the water of the Dead Sea. When you undress, you will find yourself all covered with fine white dust. You had better have the steward bring some hot fresh water to your room, and take a thorough bath in it. In an hour or two I will come in and see how you feel."

"That is another bit of philosophy that has come to me without the aid of books," said Scott, laughing, as he went to his room, and acted as Richard had advised, with perfect success.

"Do you think we have crossed the place where the children of Israel went over on dry land?" he asked Mr. Raymond, when they went on deck in the morning.

Richard smiled. "That would be a hard thing to say," he replied. "You know, there are a host of theories about the flight of the children of Israel, and just what the Bible means. I don't agree at all with people who think it is only a story. I believe there is truth in it, and that, when Moses wrote of it, he meant to tell a true history. But the question is, whether we understand it correctly. There was a book published only a little while ago, in Germany, which appeared to explain it very sensibly. The name that is used in the original is not that of the Red Sea, but the Reedy Sea. That was the name of this northern part of the Red Sea; but it was also the name of a long, swampy sea just north of what is now Port Said, and to the west of it. When the wind was strong from the east, this was dry land, and, when it came strong from the west, it piled up the Mediterranean till the water there was quite deep. That was just the course that the children of Israel would have taken in going into Syria, for the regular caravans all went that way; and, when they were in such haste to get out of the kingdom of Pharaoh, they would not have come way down here to the south, and struck for this Red Sea, when to do it they must go past several caravan tracks that would have taken them right out, and over dry land, where the Suez Canal now is. But this other route to the north, and past the other Reedy Sea, was the very shortest of all."

Scott's face fell while Richard was talking. "You may be right, but I hope not," he replied.

"Why?" asked Mr. Raymond.

"Why, because, if that is the case, I lay awake half the night last night for nothing."

"What made you do that?" said his friend, laughing.

"Because I thought we were going over the place where the children of Israel were, and I wanted to enjoy it," said Scott.

"And you enjoyed it just as much as if it were true, did you not?" asked Richard.

"I suppose so. But then"—

"I wouldn't 'but then' at all. You've had the fun. If you turn sceptical, you'll find you'll have to doubt almost every relic in the world. You'll have an opportunity to double the pleasure by going some time to the real sea, if the other one is real; and between them you'll probably hit the right one. I've seen three skulls of St. Peter, in different places; but it did not make them any less interesting. I called the old priest to account who was showing me the second one. Said I, 'Look here, I have just seen one skull of this man in Rome.' —'Ah!' said he scornfully, 'that was only when he was a boy.'"

"I guess it's something like the sailors' yarns: believe

every thing or nothing," said Scott, when the breakfast-bell sounded.

Two days later they were just off Jedda, the seaport of the great city of Mecca, the very holy city of the Mohammedans. They could see nothing of the land; but Scott fully appreciated the situation, for he was getting into that enviable condition of the professional tourist where even the proximity of any thing remarkable becomes a sensation.

A few days later the steamer dropped anchor off the rocky coast of the barren — terribly barren — Arabian town of Aden, another great coaling-port.

They took a little drive through the old town, with its historic tanks; but the most amusing sight of the day, and one that kept Scott by the steamer's side as long as she was in port, after returning from the drive, was the crowd of naked little Arabs that swarmed in the water about the ship.

They were thin, wiry little fellows, from ten to fifteen years old, and were in the water from early in the morning till three in the afternoon. Their hair was long; and many of them had it bleached with dye, till at the ends it was yellow, while at the roots it was the natural black. They seemed to enjoy the water as much as ducks, and all the time they kept up a sort of song: —

"Lemmedive, lemmedive, lemmedive,
Ever'day, ever'day, ever'day,
Tromershillin', tromershillin', tromershillin',"

sang the urchins, though it sounded more like a series of spasmodic grunts than music.

"What language is it that they speak?" asked Scott.

"English," replied Richard.

"English!" repeated Scott. "Why, what in the world are they saying?".

"They want you to throw them a shilling, and let them dive for it; but if I were you I would make it a threepenny bit, for they will dive just as quickly for that."

Scott threw a silver threepence into the water. In an instant every little head had disappeared, and twice as many feet were above the water. Then they, too, disappeared, and the water was quiet where before there had been such a crowd of noisy heads. There was not a sign nor a sound of one of them, till suddenly the water seemed full of yellow heads just below the surface; and then all the faces appeared, and the successful diver held up the piece of money with a grin that made his white teeth glisten; and then putting it into his mouth, as he had no other pocket about him, he began again the song that the others were already singing, —

> "Lemmedive, lemmedive, lemmedive,
> Ever'day, ever'day, ever'day,
> Tromershillin', tromershillin', tromershillin'."

When the silver-pieces came slowly, and it was growing an old story, they varied the performance by climbing up on to the steamer. Sometimes the sailors got after them, and they would run along the rail, and even up into the rigging; and, when they were hard pressed, they would jump into the water, no matter how high up they were, sometimes disappearing on one side of the steamer to come up on the other. And then, looking round, they would expect some silver to be thrown to them as reward for making the passengers laugh; and there was quite a company of these passengers now, for several had joined at Port Said, and several at Suez.

"Are they not afraid of sharks?" Scott asked of the captain, who was passing.

"Not when they go in that way," replied the captain. "They make that noise, and keep up that splashing, to frighten them. One of those boys alone would not come out here; and you'll find that one will not remain very long alone, even on the other side of the steamer. There are sharks all about them, but the fish are afraid of a racket."

When the steamer left the harbor, and the boys were turning back to shore, they threw kisses to the passengers, crying, "Goobbye, Englishman! Bergood, Englishman!"

"I don't believe there is an Englishman among us, except the sailors and officers," said Scott.

"We are all Englishmen in their eyes," replied Mr. Raymond. "After we pass the Suez Canal, and until we reach China, 'Englishman' is the name applied to every one with a white face."

They were now well out upon the open sea again, with a perfectly straight line between them and Bombay. The sun rose over the prow, and set directly aft. Scott had taken Richard's advice, and kept his watch at the same time as when he left his home; and this enabled him to tell very nearly what they were doing in Beverly, whenever he looked at his watch, without the necessity of calculating the difference of time, and also to tell of the progress the steamer was making, and her nearness to Bombay. While they were sailing eastward, the days were at least twenty minutes less than twenty-four hours long; for every day they approached the rising sun, and "met it half way," as the captain said.

While sailing down the Red Sea, they had made but little progress in time, for their course was nearly southward; but then there were continual appearances of islands and coast-lines to break the monotony, and Scott found the study of navigation something very exciting. Often the captain had let him lay out the day's course, and calculate the changes by the chart, while he stood by the table, looking on. They would take the observation, calculate the exact position, and then try

IN THE CAPTAIN'S ROOM.

and set the steamer so that the next land to come in sight would be over some particular object on deck, forward of the bridge, to see how near right they could hit it.

The names given to those points of land that fill the southern part of the Red Sea, making the navigation there very difficult, are as curious as the names of some of the Western villages in America. One of the last they passed before reaching Aden was a group of rocky islands called "The Twelve Apostles."

Scott was standing near where Old Joe was scrubbing one of the steamer's boats, as they passed The Twelve Apostles; and he counted the islands carefully, as every traveller does who passes them for the first time; and, after counting them several times, he made the remark, that thousands of travellers have made before him, "Why, quartermaster, there are only eleven islands there! How is it that they are called 'The Twelve Apostles'?" And the old quartermaster made the reply that every sailor who ever sailed the sea has learned, as a standing joke on the land-lubbers, while he smiled with one corner of his mouth and with one eye, —

"One of 'm — Judas, you know — went down."

But now that they were out on the Indian Ocean, all this excitement was over, and the great pleasure of the day was in marking the increasing difference in time. When Scott's watch told him it was just noon in Beverly, the ship's time had reached eight o'clock and after in the evening. And when he got up, at six o'clock in the morning, he found that it was only a little after nine the night before at home. It was a curious sensation that it was very hard to accustom himself to.

They were entirely out of sight of land now. To the north of them were the great pearl-fisheries of the Persian Gulf, and to the south there was nothing, — nothing but a few little islands between them and the frozen South Polar Sea. It had been almost impossible to wear any clothes at all in the Red Sea, where they had to have a double awning stretched over the deck and the bridge for protection against the sun; and even then it was necessary to protect the head against the piercing rays with great cork or pith helmets.

Mr. Raymond had procured one of these pith helmets for Scott at Port Said. He had one for himself in his trunk. They were almost like washbowls. The brim was very broad, sloping down over the shoulders, and was more than an inch thick, while the crown was three or four inches in thickness. But, being made of such light material, they were lighter, even, than an ordinary hat. The band that fitted about the head was lifted from the hat, to allow a perfect ventilation under the crown; and the crown was so thick that the sun could not penetrate it. Scott found it the coolest and most comfortable hat he had ever worn.

Another notion that Richard introduced, which Scott found decidedly agreeable, was a means of cooling drinking-water. Where the temperature was so high, it was dangerous to drink of the ice-water; but without ice the ship's water was warm and insipid. At Port Said Richard bought them each a Hindu *kuja*, or *chatti*. Scott laughed, and asked what in the world that sort of a thing could be good for; but he very soon found out.

The *kuja* were of plain, clay-colored earthenware, like large wine-decanters, and were very rough and coarse and ugly. Richard put some of the milk-warm ship's water into them, and set them in the hot sun, on the deck. The clay was so coarse and porous, that soon each *kuja* was glistening and wet over the outside. Scott looked on, more amused than really interested; for he was sure that the burning sun, falling full upon the little earthen jugs, must almost boil the water before long.

In half an hour Richard came on deck with a glass, and, turning some water from the *kuja*, gave it to Scott, who looked at it for a moment, and could hardly believe it the same as that which had been put in there. It was clear and sparkling. He touched it to his lips, and uttered an exclamation of surprise; for it was as cool and fresh as spring-water.

"How in the world can that be?" he asked.

Richard smiled, as he replied, "It is only another of those great principles of philosophy that you are going to learn by and by. The water is cool and wet: the air is hot and dry. The *kuja* is very porous, and allows the water to evaporate from everywhere at once. Of course, it cannot evaporate till it becomes as warm as, or warmer than, the air; and this rapid evaporation carries off the heat till it falls considerably below its original temperature. That is a rough way of putting it, Scott, rough as the *kuja* itself; but you will know all about it in real scientific language by and by."

"How long ago was it discovered?" asked Scott.

"Hundreds of years," replied Richard. "Necessity is the mother of invention; and, ages before our civilized world knew any thing about the principle of reducing heat by rapid evaporation, the Hindus were using these *kujas* to cool their water, just as they use them to-day."

"Is it any thing like the way that we manufacture ice?" asked Scott.

"The fundamental law is the same; and the art of manufacturing ice, too, is something that we borrowed from the Hindus. If we go to Calcutta I will show you, a little way from the city, where the natives are manufacturing ice, just as they have manufactured it for centuries."

"Well, what in the world has civilization done?" asked Scott almost indignantly.

"You'll ask that question oftener, the more you see of the

Hindus," replied Mr. Raymond. "Civilization has given us more elaborate and skilful and effective methods of accomplishing the same ends: that is all. You will be surprised to find that almost every thing we have is to be found far back in the history of some of these old nations. The Hindus were playing chess and whist on their marble balconies long before any other nation knew any thing about the games. They invented the decimal system, that makes mathematics so easy, and that will soon be used in every thing, as the standard of all calculations, all over the world. They were the first, too, to use figures, instead of letters, as in the old Roman system of computing."

"I thought it was the Arabs," said Scott. "They are always called Arabic characters."

"So they are," replied Richard. "But that is only because the Arabs introduced the figures to us Westerners, when all there was of us was a few barbaric and half-barbaric tribes in Europe, and a few half-enlightened and very aristocratic nations in Syria and Egypt, and Italy and Greece. The Arabs of Bagdad are the fellows that have the credit of this; for they were obliged to use the figures first, in their trading with merchants from over the Himalaya Mountains, who brought the new system up from India."

"But we have steam and electricity, at least, to boast of as modern discoveries," replied Scott, intent upon standing up for his own people, as every true man and boy should.

"That is what a great many of the wisest scholars of our day declare," returned Richard; "and yet they are beginning to find out that they are mistaken even there. It is not certain about electricity, though there are several evidences already discovered that the ancients understood and made use of it. But it is very certain that the Egyptians used steam-power in several cases; and, long before that, the Hindus lifted heavy weights, and did other wonderful things with steam, as you will see if we get well into India. But they never placed such importance as we do upon it, for there was not the occasion. Their requirements were very few. It took almost nothing to support a family; and it followed that there were a plenty of men to do every thing that needed doing, and they were ready to do it for a very small sum. As you see, even now, in coaling the steamers, and in a host of such things that are done by steam in Europe and America, the work is really done so much more cheaply by men here in the East, that, even though we have the improvements, they are not introduced."

"Did they accomplish as much in all branches as in these?" Scott asked.

"The very first work that was ever written upon language was a Hindu grammar. It is still in existence, written in India seven hundred years before Christ. There are eight large volumes."

"I'm glad I was not a schoolboy in India twenty-five hundred years ago, with those eight volumes to study before I could pass an examination in grammar," said Scott with a sigh.

"But wait till we arrive," added Richard, as with a smile he noted Scott's perplexed face: "you will see hosts of evidences of what those old fellows knew."

"But I thought they were heathen!" exclaimed Scott.

"That is surely what we call them," replied Richard: "and they are certainly far behind us to-day; for they have been almost standing still for hundreds of years, and for the last two centuries they have been falling behind, till they are not half the people now that their ancestors were. They did their discovering while our ancestors were savages; then we took it up, and have gone so far beyond them, that they seem almost like savages to us instead. But keep your eyes open, Scott, and do not be prejudiced against the Hindus by all the disagreeable things you hear. You may find, that, after all, these people are much better and wiser, even to-day, than the books and newspaper reports in England and America would have us believe."

The sunsets over the Indian Ocean were inexpressibly beautiful. Scott thought he had never seen any thing so grand, as he stood in the companion-way abaft the saloon, from where he could obtain an unbroken view of the magnificent display, as the sinking sun set the clouds on fire, flashed red on the water till it seemed like a sea of blood, filled even the air with its purple glow, tinged all the sky, and dyed the rigging and deck of the steamer. Then suddenly, as it dropped below the sea, a gray light put out the brilliant coloring, and the Tyrian cloud settled down over the opposite horizon, that forever hangs in the East, like a pillar, leading the pilgrim on to the mythic land.

Another diversion which Scott found in the Indian Ocean was watching and studying the flying-fish. They had swarmed about the steamer ever since she had entered the Mediterranean Sea; but he had never before had time to pay them much attention.

They would rise out of the water in large flocks often, and sometimes fly for a great distance, keeping close to the water, at last dropping as though they had been shot.

"What makes them fly so close to the water, and all the

while strike the top of the waves?" Scott asked Old Joe one day.

"To wet their wings, my lad," replied the quartermaster. "They've ne'er a feather, and can only flop out o' water while their wings is wet. When they dry, they stick, and then down the bird goes."

"Well, what makes them fly at all? Why don't they stay where they belong?"

"'Tain't the nature o' the craft, no mor'n 'tis o' any thing else that kicks, to stay where't belongs, if it can get somewhere else," replied the old quartermaster with a twinkle in his little eyes; "but these little skiffs ha' a better excuse than most. They strike for the air when some big fish is overhauling 'em that wants to take 'em in."

"Are they good to eat?" asked Scott.

"None better that swims the sea," said Joe decidedly.

"I should like to catch one, at least to look at," said Scott.

"Hang a lantern abaft the bridge there, where the deck's low to the water, and you'll have a boatload o' 'em, that'll beat their bulkheads against the glass and go aground there, before morning."

"They are curious things," said Scott, as a flock of large ones rose just before the steamer and flew away.

"There's many a wonder that's real, that beats the biggest yarn I ever heard afore the mast," replied Joe: "did ye never hear o' John the Scotch bye, my lad, when he come off the sea, to his old mother?"

"Never," said Scott. "What was it?"

"Why, ye see, he went to yarning the old gal on what he'd sighted in hot water. He told her how there were mountains all sugar, and how the rivers were running rum. And when he had pumped his bilge clean, and the yarn pulled taut, he slaked a little aft, and swung round afoul o' facts, and spoke a bit o' the flying-fish, and sich likes. 'Aha, thin, John!' says she, 'mountains o' sugar, an' rivers o' rum, I kin a weel ken how souch maun be; but when ye coum talk o' the fish that fly, John, ye maun na till that to me.' And it's many a like craft that I've logged, my lad. Haul your line where ye will, the bigger the yarn, the better. They'll take all you'll give 'em slack. But come to realities, and many's the craft I've seen kick over 'em like a ship in a lumpy sea, and never believe a word."

"There are a lot of wonders to be seen, and no mistake," said Scott enthusiastically. "There are many things that I have seen that I could hardly have believed if any one had told me. I believe I should like to spend my life upon the sea, just for the pleasure of it."

Old Joe turned abruptly, and looked at Scott for an instant. Then he muttered, "Who'll go to sea for pleasure'll go to hell for pastime. That's what we say 'fore the mast; but it's not the thing for an old tar to be saying to a lad from the first cabin. Don't stow it away in your locker, lad. 'Tis only Old Joe's way o' talking; and because it's Old Joe's way don't begin to make it right for him no mor'n it does with others."

This last Old Joe added with a jerk and a snap, like the firing of a potato popgun; and it contained a wisdom that Scott by no means despised. But the quartermaster was ashamed of himself, and hurried to change the subject, remarking, —

"It's a bit o' lovely sea that's on to-day."

There had been hardly any motion to the steamer since entering the Straits of Gib. It was like a river-steamer all the way, only that the machinery did not make so much jarring; and now the sea lay like a huge mirror.

"Is it always so smooth as this here?" asked Scott.

"Always at this season," replied the quartermaster; "but you should 'a' been here two weeks or even a week ago, to 'a' seen the old gal churning."

"How do you know?" said Scott, on the lookout for yarns now.

"It's the reg'lar monsoons, my lad. Here's the spot where a seabird can reckon to a certainty. One-half the year it's blow great guns, and steady as the binnacle from the sou'west. Then it's lay off a day or two, and begin again a purty little breeze like this for the nor'east monsoon. That's the way it should be: then a lad could go hang up ashore for the rough weather, and out again when it's calm."

"I thought sailors always like rough weather. They are always singing about it."

Old Joe shrugged his shoulders, smiled grimly, and walked away, singing as he went, —

> "Roar away the wild wind, aha! aha!
> Beat away the mad waves, oho! oho!
> My heart is happy, my arm is strong, aha! oho!
> I'll weather the gale, no matter how long, aha! oho!
> The mad waves beat, and the wild winds blow."

And then came the chorus, but Joe was out of hearing.

They were so near to Bombay now, that Scott could calculate within a few hours the time that they would arrive.

It had taken them ten days to go from New York to Liverpool. They were two days in England, and it would be twenty-eight days from Liverpool to Bombay; making just forty days for the whole trip. This could have been shortened by being but a day in England, and by going overland as they had hoped to.

CHAPTER X.

PAUL AMONG THE HINDUS.

A BRANCH road was being completed on one of the great Indian railways. Among the engineers was a half-caste. His face was dark and wild. He dressed in European style, but his clothes were ragged and vile. He smoked a pipe, instead of a *hookah*, or *hubble-bubble*, such as the natives used. His hut was like a European hovel, more than a native house. He kept a huge English mastiff, and was very proud of the fact that he was not wholly a Hindu. He was foreman over five hundred coolies, who were slowly accomplishing the construction of the road. A fiercer man was not to be found; and, as the Government usually upheld its subordinates, the half-caste foreman was feared, above even their gods, by the poor cooly men and women who worked on his division of the road: hence he was all the more valuable as a foreman. So his employers thought.

No one dared venture very near his hut, but left him to his own doings, undisturbed by prying eyes, whenever he chose to remain at home; for the mastiff was even fiercer than his master. He lived with a half-caste sister, but little more agreeable than himself, and with his old Hindu mother. She was a witch now, and made a fortune for herself in telling the fortunes of others, while she made every one shudder who ever came within the charmed line of her shadow. Her eyes were sharp, very sharp; and the eyebrows grew in bristles over them. Her forehead receded, only touched by straggling locks of draggling white hair. Her nose was hooked and long; and, as all her teeth were gone, her lips fell in. Her chin was hooked and long, and over her mouth it almost touched her nose. On her chin grew a coarse bristling beard, that stood out an inch and more, like the quills on a porcupine. Many were the reports, among the poor workers on the road, that this foreman and his witch of a mother were very rich, — that they had gold and silver buried in many a secret spot in India. But every one knew that in all India there was no one more ready to do any thing, no matter what it was, to make more money. It was for that reason that the old woman made herself so unutterably horrible to look at, and went about as a witch and a fortune-teller. When her two children were born, she was one of the most beautiful dancing-girls in the land; but now the beauty was gone, and she turned the scales, and still made a good living, only it was out of her ugliness.

For over a month there had been another member in the little family, — not a demon, like the rest, but a strange little being, as unlike them as sunshine and night, with a delicate little body, and a pale little face, and large blue eyes, and long brown and curling hair; with a skin as fair as the cream lily, and clothes as ragged as those of the half-caste.

It was little Paul Clayton; though who Paul Clayton was, the little fellow with blue eyes and brown hair could not have told. He did not remember any such child as Paul Clayton. He did not remember such a place as Beverly. He had only a very strange feeling, that grew stronger every day, that all was not just right, that the people about him were not true, and that he was not just what they told him. He had been very ill: he knew that; and every thing seemed so different from the pictures he remembered, as though they were the wandering dreams that had then flitted through his head, that he could not tell now whether any thing that he seemed to remember was real, or only some part of those dreams. He even supposed he had forgotten how to talk. His thoughts seemed to come in real words; but they were so confused, that he could not put them straight, and, when he spoke aloud, it was not in the same way that he thought. In reality, he was speaking in Hindustani, and thinking in English, and doing neither one perfectly.

Many a time, as he sat silently on the floor of the hut,—the only real thing that he was at all sure of,—he would try to grasp something that was only half-tangible in his mind, and come at last to the conclusion that he was still in that strange dream from which they told him he had wakened, and he would try to shake himself and wake himself, to find out where he really was, and what he was.

All the conversation that Paul heard was in Hindustani: it sounded strange to him, yet he generally understood what was said; and it seemed as though he had always heard it, yet as though he had never heard it before in his life. Every thing was so strange, so unreal, that, in a sort of stupor, day after day went by, till, in despair, he at last gave up trying to understand the half-idea of something very happy and pleasant, and so different from any thing about him, that ever and again would seem to come like a shadow before him, and then vanish as he turned to look at it. He did not remember how Roderick Dennett had worked for over five weeks, on the steamer, to teach him to speak Hindustani. He did not remember Roderick Dennett at all, or the steamer, except as a part of that dream that he had during his sickness, when he had seemed to be something beside the beggar-boy, who would have starved to death over and over again had it not been for the kindness of the old Hindu woman, and her son and daughter.

That was what they told him; and, as he had nothing else to believe, he tried to believe them. And he tried to be grateful, and not shudder and tremble every time they came near him. He longed for some one whom he could love, to whom he could fly for safety; but he looked and thought and wondered in vain. There was no one, absolutely no one, to whom he could turn. It was only one of the fancies of his dream that seemed to speak to him of some one. Every time he slept he dreamed it over again, and every time he woke he became more sure that it was only a dream; but there was just one thing that drew the past back to a reality, in spite of every thing: it was his long brown hair. It was never combed now, and lay in a tangled mat on his head; but, when a stray curl fell over his forehead and eyes, he seemed to see that something more clearly. He seemed to feel a loving hand — a hand as white as his own — caressing the little curl; and over and over again he would pull a lock down over his forehead, and laugh with himself as he looked at it, and felt so happy when his little heart was thrilled by the touch of that vanished hand.

The old witch caught him in this way more than once; and it was against her liking to see any one laughing. Being herself deprived of all that she had once considered happiness, she was bent on depriving every one else in the same way, and determined to make that hair so short that the boy could not see it.

She called him outdoors, and seated herself on a rough stool. This in itself was an awkward thing for her to do, for, like all Hindu women, she was accustomed to sit on the floor; but she wanted to reach the boy's head, and be in a position to carry her point, in case of struggle.

No sooner was she well seated, with little Paul before her, than she made a dive for his head, and, grasping a handful of his hair roughly with her left hand, flourished a long pair of shears in the other, and, with a fiendish grin, said, —

"Now, then! we'll have this off before you have a chance to laugh yourself dead through it."

With a shriek of fear, Paul seized the little lock that fell over his eyes, and passionately clung to it with trembling hands.

The old hag only struck him over the knuckles, and, with a hollow laugh, began her work. Zip, zip, zip! went those iron shears, pulling his hair at every cut, and each time wringing a cry from his very heart. And all the time the little hands were clasped more closely over that sacred lock. The back hair was almost gone, and in a moment more there would have been a struggle over the rest, when round the corner came the half-caste foreman, his pipe in his mouth, and his pants rolled up to his thighs.

Paul had had very little to do with him, and had little hope of mercy from him; still he was determined that that lock of hair, through which he could see the picture that seemed so real, of a happiness that now he could not even fully comprehend, should never be torn from him if any thing could prevent it.

A defiant fire flashed from his blue eyes as he looked up

at the half-caste foreman, but they fell again to the ground; and poor little Paul began to tremble, for a fiercer face few have ever seen or imagined. The eyes started from their sockets, the teeth shone fiendishly white through the black lips and beard.

PAUL AND THE HAG.

"What are you at, withered hag?" he cried furiously.

"At my trade. The hair's worth a pound in the market," she replied, though she loosed her rude grasp; and Paul gave a sigh of relief, but did not drop the sacred little lock.

"Haven't I sworn to the hairs of his head?" he asked.

"They'll grow again fast enough," replied the old woman. And again she laid her hand on Paul's hair, when her son darted forward.

"Drop it!" he exclaimed; and instantly the withered hand fell again.

"You're in a good mood to-day," she returned with a sneer. "I'll give my hairy chin but you've lost the worth of your pipe full of tobacco at some game or other."

"That I have," he replied. "There are men on the track of the kid there. They are already in Bombay. They have an eye, along the new line, for Dennett's old engineering friends."

"Ugh!" exclaimed the old woman, springing to her feet, and brushing the hair she was to sell for a pound in the market on to the earth, where she fiercely trod on it with her foot. "May their mouths be filled with dirt!" she cried. "May they be defiled, and the mothers that bore them! May the worms eat them, and the beggars spit upon their beards!"

"Che, che!" said the foreman fiercely. "Your curses are all very well to frighten these nunnies about here; but don't think that your tongue will drive off the English officers, if they come looking for the kid."

"Come here?" the old woman howled. "The wind will be in their bones before they see the second wall. May their eyes blister, and their tongues rot in their mouths! Never, never! Curse the kid! Never shall they come into this palace of"—

"Che, che! Keep your vile tongue to the beggars about you. I've a better plan. If I go down, Dennett goes with me," muttered the foreman. "He'll know it before dark to-night. And, if he kicks and runs his luck, I'll show myself, and offer to redeem the boy for a good ransom."

The old woman began to chuckle way down in her throat; and Paul looked up suddenly, thinking she must be ill. She was only laughing. She turned upon him as though she had forgotten him.

"Did you take in what that beast of a brute said to me?" she asked fiercely.

Paul started and trembled. He had not exactly taken in what had been said, though he had comprehended that in some way it referred to him, and it seemed to open his eyes a little to what was going on; though how, or what it really was that he began to comprehend, he could not tell. He had no idea of telling the old hag a lie, for instinctively a lie would have been impossible to him; but in utter fear and misery he looked at her with a bewildered stare, and shook his head.

"Guzzle the kid with your fury, and scare him out o' his wits, as though 'twould bring the truth out o' him!" shouted the half-caste. "But no fear: he's idiotic as an ape. Dennett took his senses away for everlasting, I'm thinking, in that long pull he gave him with opium, and the like."

"How is it we're to get rid of him for the time?" asked the old woman.

"Dhondaram will take him," replied the foreman, grinning. "I gave him a hundred rupees this morning, and promised him as much more when the kid was well placed. I've sent to Dennett for fifty, for doing the same thing."

"You're well for a turn, well for a turn," muttered the old woman.

"A cursed compliment. I came by it honestly," he replied, lighting his pipe again. "But do you put on the kid's good clothes,—not the dashedest ones in the box, but common good,—and make a bundle of some more. Don't you go to skimming the chest, and putting the cream under your own straw pile,—for, mind you, Dennett's sharper'n the sharpest, and he'd know,—but give the bundle and the kid to sister, when she goes to show her pretty face in the bazaar to-night. On the Boomal corner, by the well, and at the old Trimmal's fruit-booth, she'll see Dhondaram in holy contemplation. Let her send the kid to get some fruit, leave the bundle at Dhondaram's feet, and scatter herself so fine through that bazaar that there'll be no finding her."

"But suppose the young'n won't leave her," muttered the old woman as she turned toward the hut.

The half-caste gave a hoarse laugh, and shouted, "Never you fear! If he's got sconce enough to draw breath when he can't help it, he'll know better than to stick to you or yours any longer'n he's obliged to."

The old woman went into the house. The half-caste sat down upon the stool. He always sat upon a stool; for he would not have any one think he was a Hindu, and could sit upon the ground. He took the little trembling, half-stupefied boy on his knee, and almost tenderly he asked,—

"Well, my lad, would you like to go away?"

Paul nodded. He had comprehended much more than they thought, and, as the foreman had said, was not anxious to remain longer where he was. Any thing would be better than that; and yet he did not fully understand what it was to go away.

The rough man stroked his head for a moment; then, with a sigh, he set him down, and went into the hut, from which the old woman soon issued, ready to dress the boy as her son had directed.

It was a strange sensation that came over Paul as he put on the pretty and clean suit of boy's clothes. It was like the breaking out of the sunshine on an April evening, when, just before it sets, the sun pierces the rich auburn clouds that have been pouring down rain all day long. You may be in the house where you cannot see the sunshine; yet you know instinctively that the storm has broken, and that the cheerful light is again brightening every thing, and you feel happier for it. You cannot help it. Paul could not tell what made him happy. He could not tell why the pretty clothes were so much more real to him than the rags had been. He could not tell any thing, but that he was happier. He knew he was happier; but he dared not laugh, lest the old woman should take them away again. He thought of the name "Dhondaram." It was some one who was to take care of him; and instinctively he associated the new clothes and the delightful memories that they seemed to awaken, and the happiness in his heart, all with that name, and the man who bore it; and already he began to long for the time to come when he was to start for the bazaar with the foreman's sister. Then he wondered what the bazaar was. He had never been a dozen rods from that hut in his life, so far as he knew. But he did not care what it all looked like, if Dhondaram were only there.

The moon was already shining when the sun set; and he was soon taken by the young woman, and led away.

Every thing was very new to Paul in the busy streets that they soon reached, and the old ways down which they wandered; and yet he seemed to half-remember having seen it all before. He wondered if he were still dreaming.

The men did not wear hats and clothes, like the foreman; but many of them were naked to the waist, at least, and had only a light strip of cloth twisted about their legs as low down as the knees. Some had loose cloaks hanging over their shoulders, bound round the waist by a girdle, and falling in a sort of skirt over the legs to the knees. They all wore cloth twisted in different shapes about their heads, instead of hats.

The women were dressed in all sorts of fashions: some had light shawls all over them, with only one eye showing between the folds; and some were almost naked. Many of them had silver rings on their ankles, and many more on their arms. Some had rings in their noses, and large rings in their ears; and they all had silver rings all over their fingers and thumbs and toes, and colored glass rings on their arms.

Long before Paul began to grow tired, they had reached a corner by a well, and a half-naked native sitting behind some baskets filled with fruit. Right at the corner a very tall man was standing, all absorbed in thought. The young woman who was leading Paul stopped for an instant, and, without looking at the man, laid the bundle down at his feet, and went on a little way. Instinctively Paul seemed to know what it meant. He could not explain it, for the picture, more than the words, had been left upon his mind; but he was happier than he ever remembered having been before, and was not at all surprised when the woman told him to go to the fruit-vender, and ask him the price of some melons beside him.

Paul hesitated an instant at the last moment. It was breaking away from all that he knew any thing about in the world. He understood perfectly that he was not coming back again, and that he was to go away with the solemn man standing at the corner. He turned, and looked at him. There was something almost gentle in his face. It was very different, at least, from the faces that he already knew; and then the new clothes, and all the happiness! Little Paul left the woman, as she had bidden him; but, instead of going and asking the price of the melons, he went straight to the

DHONDARAM.

side of the tall Hindu, and, extending his little white hand, he said, in broken Hindustani,—

"Here I am, Dhondaram, to go away with you."

The muni started, frowned for an instant, and looked down at the tiny figure. But Paul had not been mistaken: little hearts rarely are in this world. No sooner did the muni's black eyes rest on the large blue ones turned up to him, and on the gold-brown hair, and the pale cheeks, and little extended hand, than the frown melted, and all that gentleness that Paul had detected came back again.

Dhondaram's plans for taking the boy were thoroughly turned upside down by Paul's greeting. It was that that had caused the frown; but, making the best of matters as they were, he took the little hand in his, and, picking up the bundle, said,—

"Very well. We will go." And they started off together.

For a while Dhondaram seemed to take no more notice of Paul. He almost thought he had forgotten him, and clung a little closer to his hand. The motion attracted the muni's attention; and, looking down, he said almost gently,—

"You are tired. I will carry you."

Paul did not understand precisely what he meant; but when the strong arm was about him, and he was lifted to the broad shoulder, he felt happier and safer, and put one arm around the muni's neck,—an action that pleased him much more than the gold he received from the half-caste.

They turned, very soon, out of the lighted street and into darker alleys; and Paul clung the closer to Dhondaram. He walked on now with rapid strides, and very soon approached a low doorway, where three women, dressed almost like men, were sitting and talking. They wore jewels; but they were evidently working-women, for two of them had baskets, in which they had been carrying something.

"Fie on you, daughters of Kali! to be out here hatching mischief at this hour. Go to your homes, and let Gunga come in and get me some supper," said Dhondaram.

"Gunga can go, if she will, at the beck of a monster like

you, who knows neither Kali nor Siva, and worships but Krishna," retorted one of the women; "but, as for us, we will neither leave this spot for you, nor a host just like you."

But Gunga rose; and, turning to the others with a laugh, she said,—

"Good-night till the morning, we'll meet in the temple;" and followed Dhondaram.

"Gunga knows who turns her *ghi* to gold," muttered one of the women so loud that all could hear; but Gunga made no reply, and soon had conducted the muni to a little room that she occupied, with screens here and there, dividing the cooking and sleeping apartments.

"What have you on your back?" asked Gunga, as she lighted a little wick, floating in oil in a cocoanut-shell, and turned to prepare some supper.

"A feringhi," replied Dhondaram.

"A feringhi!" she exclaimed, and turned suddenly to look at little Paul, who now rested on the muni's knee, as he sat on the floor. But a sweet smile broke over Gunga's face as she looked down into the tired blue eyes. She gently touched the soft cheek; and then, with a quizzical smile at Dhondaram, she said, "There must be a gold lining here, or the holy Dhondaram would be defiled."

"It is only a child," muttered Dhondaram, "and none of your business at the best. Get us some supper, and give us a bed for the night. Did ever you hear of a Feringhi Dennett? Roderick Dennett? Well, if ever you do, keep your eye on him, Gunga, and send me word, and till then keep your peace."

"That I will, as I have often done for you before," said Gunga merrily; and she began to sing a temple-song as she

DAUGHTERS OF KALI.

moved about behind one of the screens: for she was a sort of priestess in a Hindu temple,—a murli girl,—whose duty it was to dance and sing during a part of the service, and in her basket she had carried flowers to throw about the altar.

The food which Gunga set before them was of the very simplest kind,—only a dry meal-cake and cups of milk; but Paul was hungry, and thought it far better than any thing he had ever before tasted. On the whole, he was well satisfied with the change, and would not have gone back again for any thing.

After supper Gunga threw a coarse mat on the floor; and turning half toward Paul, whose eyes were very heavy, she said,—

"The little feringhi can have a mat yonder, between me and my little sister Prita, who is already sound asleep, if he would like it. It is a softer, better place than this."

Paul looked at Dhondaram, who bowed his head in assent; then he extended his arms to Gunga, who stood ready to take him upon her shoulder, as though he were light as a feather, though she herself seemed to him but a little girl. She kissed his cheek softly, as she carried him behind another screen, and there laid him carefully upon a rug on the floor, giving him her arm for a pillow, where he fell asleep before he had hardly time to realize how happy and comfortable he was.

Before daylight he was awakened by the little sister Prita, who was kneeling beside him, kissing his hand.

"You are a very pretty little Ingrij," she said. "Can you understand what I say?"

Paul rubbed his eyes, and answered, "Yes."

BOATS AND BOATMEN OF THE GANGES.

"Where did you learn to talk like me?" asked the girl.

Paul wondered where, and rubbed his eyes again; for it suddenly seemed to him that he had not always talked like that.

"You must get up, and let me wash you, and comb your hair; for you must eat breakfast soon, and go away," she added sadly.

"I don't want to go away," sobbed Paul. But he got up; and the little girl began to bathe him as he had never been bathed before, so far as he could remember. She gathered up all the mats, and left only the smooth stone floor. Then she brought a jug of water, somewhat like a *kuja*, only larger, and, after taking off his clothes, began turning it over him, a little at a time, and rubbing him gently with her soft hand. Then she wiped him, rubbed his body with something that smelled so nice he thought he would like to drink it, and then dressed him, and carefully combed his hair.

"I'm very sure I don't want to have you go," she said; "but we must do as Dhondaram says, and perhaps he will bring you back again. If I were only a little older, so that I could go to the temple too, it would be better. But Dhondaram is very kind. He will never hurt you. Were you born in England? How long have you been in India?"

Little Prita chatted on, because Paul did not seem inclined to answer; and she forgot one question as soon as she had put it, and began another. But Paul did not forget them. They set him thinking, and thinking so hard that he had no time to answer. It had never occurred to him that he must have been born somewhere; and the more he wondered, the more confused he became. But the thinking was sure to amount to something in time.

They had rice and milk for breakfast; and, comforted by Dhondaram's promise that he should surely come back again, Paul once more mounted the broad shoulder, and left the little room and the low arched doorway, and, after a short walk, came out upon a broad river.

There were very few people to be seen till they came out upon the river-bank; for it was only the gray dusk before dawning, and the sky in the east was just turning red for the sunrise. Dhondaram wanted to get away without attracting attention, for he realized that he had undertaken a very difficult task. He could get the best of any Hindu or Mussulman that lived. He had often tried it, and always succeeded. The half-caste foreman had selected him to help him out of his difficulty, as the man of all men who was able to do it. But to carry his point against the English police, when to do it he had got to keep a little white boy out of their hands, was quite another undertaking. It had taken more than a hundred rupees from the foreman to induce Dhondaram to attempt it. The foreman had not dared to tell his mother it had cost him over a thousand rupees to get out of the fraud into which Roderick Dennett had drawn him. And he himself was ignorant of the fact that it was not at all his gift of a thousand rupees, and promise of as much more, but something entirely outside of that, that had induced the Hindu muni, Dhondaram, to undertake the difficult engagement.

There was a score of boatmen on the river-bank when they reached it. Some were cooking their breakfast, some eating it. All were preparing for a fresh start, for boatmen will not sail at night in India unless it is absolutely necessary. There are several reasons for it. The Hindu rivers are very hard to navigate, and the Hindus very superstitious. Beside this, they are never in a hurry. If time and tide will not wait for them, they are satisfied to let time and tide go on without them.

Paul was a little frightened at the sight of the rugged, almost naked boatmen, with their smoothly shaven heads, where only a little tuft of hair was left on the very top. That tuft was never cut at all, but twisted up in a little knot. They were singing and shouting and praying and eating and cooking in a terrible confusion; but when Paul looked down at the man upon whose shoulder he sat, to find him taller and stronger than any of them, and when he saw how those rough boatmen knelt and touched their foreheads to the ground as he and the muni passed them, he lost his fear, and only realized a still greater confidence in Dhondaram.

"What is this water?" Paul asked, as Dhondaram was preparing to take him on to a boat that seemed to be ready for them.

"It is the sacred Ganges," replied the muni solemnly, setting Paul down on the bank for a moment, and making an humble obeisance to the river. "It flows directly out of the mouth of the incomprehensible Bramha," he added; and Paul drew a long breath, and tried to understand it.

The sun was just rising as they passed the city proper, at the outskirts of which they had embarked. The boat in which they sailed was a curious contrivance. Paul was sure he had never seen a boat before; yet as they pushed off from shore, and began to rise and fall on the little waves, there was something so natural, that again and again he looked out of the little window and over the dancing ripples, as though he could almost see something there, almost hear some one speak to him, almost discover something that he had begun very seriously to long to know.

There was one mast to their boat, and a huge triangular sail attached to it. There was a little house with curious doors and windows in the stern; and there they were destined to eat and sleep for many days, while slowly making their way up the Ganges and one of its branches, stopping every night by the bank till the morning.

A CURIOUS CONTRIVANCE.

As they passed along the border of the city, the boats became very numerous in the river; and Dhondaram drew the blinds, or bamboo awnings, before the window where Paul sat. It did not prevent his looking out, however. There were beautiful towers rising up almost from the water's edge. But, when they had passed the city, they seemed once more to sink into the mists, that there had not fully risen from the river. Once more Dhondaram opened the bamboo blinds; and, leaning out of the window, Paul watched the water splashing against the boat, till suddenly his attention was drawn to strange figures along the bank, just discernible in the mists, moving slowly up and down, or lying still in hideous piles.

CROCODILES.

"What are they?" he asked, eagerly pointing toward the shore.

"Crocodiles," muttered Dhondaram; and, with a peculiar smile, he added, "They are very sacred animals. We make sacrifices to them; and sometimes little children are thrown into the water, for those crocodiles to eat them up."

Paul started, turned pale, trembled a little, and looked up into Dhondaram's face. The muni looked quietly into the blue eyes for an instant; then, with scarcely a perceptible change of countenance, he lifted his hand, and stroked the golden-brown hair. Paul nestled closer to him. He was not afraid of being thrown to the crocodiles. Oh, no! — not so long as Dhondaram was near.

CHAPTER XI.

WILD LIFE ON THE RIVER, AND A HINDU FEAST.

UP the sacred Ganges and one of its great tributaries they sailed; and it seemed to Paul that they must be going a long way off from everywhere, especially from the city where the little Gunga and her tiny sister Prita lived. He did not know the name of it: but he grew brighter and clearer in his mind each day, and comprehended more of what he saw; and, to his own surprise, he seemed to understand a great many new things without asking. He had learned, too, the way to the stern heart of the muni, and had not the least fear of Dhondaram. When he awoke in the morning, and found him out on the river-bank, engaged in a sort of fierce devotion, his eyes flashing, his body writhing about in terrible contortions, while he placed fire in his open palms, and cut his flesh with little knives, Paul would go right up to him, and, putting his arms fearlessly about his neck, would kiss him, and cry, "Stop, stop! don't do that!" while the boatmen, who would as soon have had a hand cut off as to have disturbed him, would look on in horror, till they found that the frown disappeared, instead of gathering deeper on the dark brow of Dhondaram, and that, taking the child in his arms, he would go back to the boat, to wait till some other time to finish his terrible devotions.

The water of the river was very yellow with mud as they

went up, and every day they passed bodies of dead animals that were floating down; yet at every little village that they passed, and at every encampment, there were many people bathing in the water, especially at sunrise in the morning. And while they bathed they prayed, and threw the water over

"THEY ARE COMING TO BATHE THE IDOL."

their faces. "They think it sacred. They believe they are washing their sins away," said Dhondaram.

One morning, just after they had started for the day, they heard a loud noise of singing and shouting on the banks, beyond a little jungle ahead of them. Dhondaram drew the awnings over the windows, and sat on the floor by the side of Paul. Soon they passed the cause of the noise. In the lead was a band of girls, whirling about each other, singing and dancing, with soft, white cloth wound gracefully about them, and garlands of flowers upon their necks and round their waists. Behind them came Bramhan priests, shouting, and waving heavy wands in the air, and bearing an image on a litter.

"What is the matter, Dhondaram?" asked Paul, alarmed more at the serious face of his protector than at any danger he could conceive of from the happy throng upon the bank.

"They are bringing the god of the temple down, to bathe it in the Ganges. If the boatmen say I am a muni, they will stop us, and I shall have to help them. But we must not stop: we cannot. If I stop, I shall tell the boatmen to go on with you."

Paul caught Dhondaram's hand, and shook his head. The muni smiled, and continued,—

"You shall not fear, for it will only be for an hour. I shall hurry up the river, and meet you. But they will not stop us," he added, as the boat was pulled past the point where the murlis, or dancing-girls, were approaching the river, and no one paid it any attention.

They made slow progress up the river, especially when the wind was against them, so that they could not use the sail, or the current ran fast. Then the boatmen were obliged to take the oars, which they did not fancy, and sometimes even to take a long rope, and go on shore with it, walking along the bank, and pulling the boat after them, which they disliked still more. And the worst of all was when the banks were so covered with jungle, or forest-growth, to the very water's edge, that the only way they could do was to start on in a little boat with the rope, and, fastening it to a tree as far ahead as was possible, draw the large boat up to it, and then go on again.

When they came to anchor at night, Paul would run and play upon the sand, while the boatmen built a fire, and Dhondaram, with his own hands, prepared the supper. Like the breakfast, it consisted of a simple preparation of rice, made hot with something like mustard, that they called curry, prepared from several kinds of green leaves and spices mashed, and ground to a soft pulp between two stones. With this they had fruit, — bananas, plantain, dates, tamarinds, pomegranates, and, best of all, sweet limes as large as oranges, of which Paul was very fond. He made an exclamation of delight the first time that he tasted them, and from that day there was always a bamboo tray of sweet limes lying on the floor of the little cabin.

When there was a jungle near their stopping-place, Dhondaram always warned Paul not to go near it; and even Paul noticed, that, wherever he went, and no matter what the tall, grim muni was doing, he never looked back without finding his two piercing black eyes fixed upon him. The old witch used to watch him in that way, and it made him tremble; but he only felt the safer now, to know that he was not for a moment out of the sight of his friend. Richard Raymond would have shuddered had he known, Scott would have trembled could he have been told, that little Paul was laughing in the face of the terrible Dhondaram.

Once when he had wandered too near to a jungle, Dhondaram hurried toward him, and, catching him in his arms, went back to the boat with him.

"There are ugly tigers in there," he muttered. "You do not want to meet one of them."

"Why not?" asked Paul.

"They would kill you," replied the muni.

"What would that matter?" asked Paul, very little understanding what it was to be killed, or what he was saying, and yet half realizing after all.

The muni looked at him silently for a moment. Then, brushing a tear from his eyes, he said huskily, "Your little lips have kissed Dhondaram. You neither hate nor fear him."

"No, indeed, I am not afraid of you!" exclaimed Paul, throwing his arms around the muni's neck, and kissing him again. "And I shall never be killed while you take care of me."

Dhondaram looked about him hurriedly, to be sure that none of the boatmen saw.

One night they had eaten their supper, and were at anchor a little way out in the stream; for the current was slow, and the jungles were close upon the bank. The boatmen had usually built fires at night, to keep the wild beasts from coming to the water near where they were anchored; but there were villages within sight of the boat to-night, and Dhondaram did not want to attract the attention of the villagers, who would be sure to come down and make them a call. So they only pushed out farther than usual; and the sun went down, and the moon rose, and the boatmen lay stretched over the deck, sound asleep. Paul had been asleep, but was wakened by Dhondaram, who was praying, and fiercely beating himself. Getting up from his mat, Paul went to the muni, but had hardly reached his side, when from the distant bank there sounded a shrieking whistle. Dhondaram started to his feet. He listened intently for a moment. There was a sharp cracking and swaying of the branches on the other side of the river, that there was not a quarter of a mile wide. Some large body was forcing its way through at no easy pace. Suddenly the muni disappeared in the cabin,

THE MAD ELEPHANT.

but re-appeared in a moment, carrying a bundle. Paul had not time to ask what it was; for his eyes were fixed on a huge, dingy form that loomed up on the opposite bank.

"It is only an elephant," said Paul, who had seen them carrying burdens along the river-bank.

"A mad elephant," muttered Dhondaram, watching him intently.

"What makes him mad?" asked Paul.

"I don't know. But he is alone, and a wild elephant never goes alone unless he's mad. Ha!" he exclaimed, as the huge elephant seemed to have noticed them, and at once dashed into the water, and began to swim rapidly toward the boat.

"Not yet, not yet," muttered Dhondaram, catching Paul in his arms, and setting him on his shoulder, while he balanced the bundle on his head. "It is not written in Dhondaram's forehead that he die at the will of a wild elephant, or a tame one either." And with his burden he slipped silently over the edge of the boat, away from the approaching animal. Fortunately, being able to wade, he moved rapidly toward the shore. When the bank was almost gained, and the water not more than waist deep, a sudden splash sounded a little way up the river; and Paul, whose eyes had been fixed on the approaching elephant, turned with a cry of fear to see the great glistening jaws of a crocodile opened wide, less than ten feet away. But Dhondaram was strong and supple. His lithe body sank into the water to the shoulder. Then he sprang forward. The lumbering crocodile swung about, and his great jaws came together with a resounding click that would have made a stronger heart than little Paul's stand still. The maddened creature turned about, and opened the horrible jaws again; but Dhondaram had gained on him. In a moment more he was bounding along the bank, now with a foot in the water where the trees crowded him, now flying like the wind on the sand. But the signal had been given; and all up and down the river, with many a grunt and snort, they heard the sleeping crocodiles awaking, and swinging their heads back, to open the terrible mouths ready to close like a vice on any thing that might fall into them. But holding Paul firmly on his shoulder, and the bundle on his head, without a sound the Hindu bounded on, seeming hardly to touch the earth, resting his foot for an instant against the very nose of a crocodile, to be ten feet away before the animal could close his glistening rows of savage teeth.

Then there was a terrible splashing and crashing behind them; and, looking back over the moonlit water, Paul could see the boat flying into a thousand pieces under the wrath of the mad elephant, and hear the cries and groans of the boatmen, suddenly aroused from sleep to find themselves doomed to death. And the little hands clasped the muni's neck more closely, as Paul realized the terror from which he had saved him.

They were well away from the river, and in a broad, open plain, before the muni paused, and, looking cautiously about him to assure himself that there was no other danger at hand, laid his burden tenderly down, and asked, —

"Has the little feringhi had a pleasant ride?"

"The poor boat Wallahs! They are all dead," replied Paul, thinking of the boatmen.

"It was written in their foreheads," said Dhondaram indifferently, "but not in mine."

"But if you had staid there you would have been dead too," said Paul, with a logic so simple, that the greatest theologians are only just finding out how full of force it is.

"But I did not stay," replied the muni. And, after waiting a moment to gather strength and breath, he untied the package, which Paul now saw contained his bundle of clothes and a bamboo sack of sweet limes. Giving the boy two of the sweet limes, he replaced the bundle on his head; and, taking Paul again on his shoulder, he said,—

"You can eat those to keep you awake when you are sleepy. We have a long way to go. We should have reached

THE LONG ROAD.

the end of our journey to-morrow night. Now we must reach it to-morrow morning instead, for there are two villages that we must go past before daylight."

So they started on; and all night long the muni kept at a steady, rapid pace, never flinching or swerving from the track that he seemed to be as sure of as though it were his home. Before the sun had risen, they passed the last of the villages that Dhondaram wanted to avoid. But the people were already engaged at the morning worship, and were lying on their faces, falling on their knees, beating their foreheads to the ground, and crying and howling before a rude little temple, where Paul could just discern a hideous image, that

THE GODDESS KALI.

reminded him so much of the old witch, that instinctively he tried to shrink away from it.

"What is it?" he asked timidly.

"The goddess Kali, the wife of the great Siva,—the powerful Mother of Destruction. She kills every thing."

"How do they dare to be so near, and pray to her?" asked Paul again.

"They are praying to her to keep away from them," replied

the muni, smiling in a peculiar way, as he pressed a little nearer to the jungle to escape observation. "Her hair touches the ground behind her. She has three red eyes. Her lips and tongue are dripping with blood. She has dead bodies for rings in her ears. Once she had only two arms; but, when her husband was in trouble, she sacrificed an arm to save him, and now she has four. She is standing on the body of a god, and has the head of a mortal in her hand. Her girdle is made of the hands she has cut off from the arms of her enemies, and her necklace is skulls."

"I would not pray to her," said Paul with a shiver.

"You would, if praying would keep her away from you, I think," replied Dhondaram.

"You do not pray to her, do you?" the child asked.

"There are so many gods, that it is impossible to pray to all," said the muni.

"How many gods are there?" asked Paul.

"About three hundred and thirty millions," replied the muni, a smile of derision curling his lips again, for all the fact that he, too, was among the humble devotees at the altars of those innumerable gods.

"Why don't I pray, Dhondaram?" the boy questioned, after vainly trying to gain any idea of how many three hundred and thirty millions might be.

"You are an Ingrij," returned Dhondaram.

"And what is that?"

"You were not born in India. You are different."

"Where was I born?"

"I do not know," replied the muni almost impatiently.

"If I had been born here, should I pray as you do?"

"No: you are white."

"Does being white make me different?"

"No: being different makes you white."

"I wish I were not different. I wish I were like you, Dhondaram."

"But you would not be, if you knew me well. And you could not be, for it is not written in your forehead."

"What is it that is written in your forehead?" asked Paul, rubbing his little white hand over the furrowed brow of the dark Hindu.

"Nothing good, nothing good. There is nothing good in Dhondaram," replied the muni with a shudder.

"There is! there is!" cried the boy sharply. "Who wrote what is bad?"

"The God of Fate."

"I will kill him when I am a man!" said Paul fiercely.

"Che! che!" whispered the muni: "say it softly;" for, although he had smiled in derision, he was yet fearful that there might be some evil following such a remark.

"Are there many people who are white?" asked Paul.

"Some," replied the muni briefly; for he had been walking hard all night, and was not only tired, but very anxious. Little Paul did not dream how he, sitting so comfortably on that broad shoulder, was making the strong man tremble.

They turned now along the river-bank; and, in the gray mists that lay there just before morning, they saw little flickering lamps floating down the stream.

"What are they, Dhondaram?" cried Paul. "They seem like"—Paul almost said, "Fourth of July." It was on the very tip of his tongue; and yet, when he stopped and wondered what it was that he was about to say, he could not remember. Some happy thought had flashed before his mind: he was sure of it. He laughed even then under the bright influence; but what it was, was like all the rest,—hidden just beyond his reach. "It must have been some dream," he said to himself, as Dhondaram replied,—

"Those lamps are offerings to the river, by the women of the city just above. They are little wicks floating in oil, in wooden boats."

But Paul cared less about the boats than the problem he was solving concerning himself. And as they turned down a broad avenue lined with magnificent palms, and with beautiful flowers in an endless profusion everywhere, he began again,—

"Are there many white people, Dhondaram?"

"A few," replied the muni, hardly knowing what he said; for the city was yet two miles ahead, and the sun was almost rising.

"I never"—Paul hesitated. He was about to say that he never had seen any, when it suddenly seemed to him as though he had seen many. "Do they live far from here?" he asked.

"White people live everywhere," said Dhondaram with a frown; for far in the distance he saw several people coming down the way from the city. And the domes and minarets were now plainly visible through the trees, a half-mile away. He began to realize, that, after all his struggle, it would be impossible to get into the gate, and down the by-ways, where he knew many a hiding-place, without attracting attention to the little boy upon his shoulder. Paul's questions about white people added to this fear; for, in truth, he knew that there were many white people living in the city.

Just then an owl gave a farewell hoot to the dying night, from his perch in a banyan-tree not far away, and an ass brayed in the field to the left. They were two omens that were the worst that could have been given to the anxious Hindu; and while he waited for a moment, wondering if he had better disregard them and go on, a wild hare ran across the road in front of him. Had the voice of God sounded, telling him in so many words to go no farther with the child, he could not have been more sure.

"What are you waiting for?" asked Paul.

"I am thinking you must be tired," Dhondaram replied. "You have been riding all night. You shall not go into the city till evening. You shall stop at this house here and sleep, while I go in and find a good friend, where we will live for the present."

"I would rather go with you, Dhondaram!" exclaimed Paul, clinging to the muni's neck, and beginning to sob; for he was very tired and sleepy, though he did not realize it.

"I shall not go away at once, and I shall be back before long for you," said Dhondaram, turning boldly up toward a little hut that lay half hidden in the verdant jungle that bordered on the road.

It was a beautiful little spot, and at the first sight Paul was delighted with the prospect of waiting there. Dhondaram set him upon the ground, and let him run beside him. The house was built in two separate parts. At the left stood the working-part, without any front wall, but a sort of booth arranged in front, as though the owner sold something through the day; and at the right was the sleeping-hut, with only one very small door and a very small window.

Dhondaram approached the working-hut, but it was empty. There was nothing on the booth, and only the pots and *kuja* standing behind, and a smouldering fire in a round hole in the centre of the room. The family were evidently Hindus, judging from their pots and the arrangements of the hut; and, seeing several empty tobacco *bunniahs* lying about, Dhondaram at once determined that the owner of the hut was a tobacconist.

Knowledge is power. That is the muni's motto; and, not

NATIVE HUTS.

to be wholly without knowledge, and seem too much like a stranger, Dhondaram called aloud, —

"Ha! you *biri* wallah" (tobacco-dealer), "come out and show yourself if you are an honest man."

A woman's head was thrust a little way out of the door of the other hut.

"Who calls? There's nothing to sell to-day. Go on to the festival." But, seeing that it was a muni who spoke, she put her head a little farther out, and made an obeisance, putting her hands to her forehead. The muni returned her salaam, and, without waiting for any further introduction, said, —

"Look to what I tell you, mother of an evil-doer. It is ill that you bid one of the gods' selected to leave your house, and go his way. I want no purchasing from such as you, and I will go my way to the festival when it pleases me. Mark what I say: it is ill for you that I go without leaving you indebted to me for an opportunity, well accepted, to serve the Mother."

Of all this the stupid woman understood as little as did Paul; but she realized that she had offended a wandering muni, which is not a very safe thing, for the poor at least, to do, and she hastened to reply, —

"Ask what you will of me, and in the name of the Mother I will do it, and do it without pay."

"Do it you will, and do it without pay; and woe to you or any one who would not! But that it may be the better done, if you do well I will pay you well."

The woman touched her forehead to the ground. The muni continued, —

"This little feringhi who is in my care has the Bramhanical blessing. He is weary, and before we enter the city he must rest. Give him the best you have, and let him sleep. I will lie and rest me in the shop, and later I will come for him."

"We are not outcasts," said the woman, trembling; for she feared that she should lose caste or defile herself by taking the little white boy into her dirty hut. Dhondaram was instantly angry, or appeared to be. He turned suddenly, and, with his back to the woman, he threw dust at her with his foot.

"Lower than the lowest! viler than the vilest! eat dirt and be defiled. Go hence a beggar. Thus saith a Bramhan of the Bramhans."

It had the desired effect. The woman fell upon her face with a wail.

"Let him come in. Let the feringhi have all and more than all. Come in and find the best, and give it him. Let me sit by him and keep ill from him while he sleeps. Let me be his slave, but keep thy curse."

"I'll see how you perform yourself. Come out of the house. I will not defile myself by going in till you are out."

Creeping on her knees, the woman came out of the low door; and, leading Paul by the hand, Dhondaram entered. There were only two rooms, and very simple; but he soon prepared a comfortable mat, and, assuring Paul that the woman would not dare to do any thing but the very best for him, he left him lying on the mat, with no ornament or piece of furniture to attract his attention (for there was nothing of the sort in the little room), and with several sweet limes to eat when he should wake up. The boy was so used to strange surroundings, that he hardly paid them any attention; but before the voice of Dhondaram had ceased to sound, in conversation with the woman outside, he was fast asleep.

Creeping in to see that all was well, the old woman crept out again to talk over the event with her nearest neighbor. There was to be a great festival in the city; and the neighbor, owning two bullocks and a cart, was going to carry into the city all of his friends who could get on, to participate in the very holy festival and merry-making. The old woman's son, who kept the tobacco-booth, had already gone to the city, and she did not propose to be left out.

Regardless of the promise she had made to the muni, and the boy who lay sleeping in her hut, she took the advice of her neighbor, and made herself ready to go in the cart. It came rattling to her door, with its two noisy wheels and no springs, the long pole resting on a sort of crossbar, that, in turn, rested on the necks of the two bullocks, just in front of a huge hump growing on the fore-shoulders of each, almost like the bump on a camel, and effectually doing away with the need of a yoke.

NATIVE CART.

Once more the old woman crept in, and looked at the child. Paul was soundly sleeping. Then again she crept out, got into the cart, and was gone.

It was past noon when little Paul awoke, rubbed his eyes, sat erect, and wondered where he was. He had had so many strange impressions of late, that it was some time before out of them all he resolved the present, and was sure of what had happened just before he went to sleep. But there were the sweet limes, at least; and he ate one of them while he waited for some one to appear. No one came; and he got up and went out. Every thing was deserted. He called Dhondaram, but received no answer. He remembered that he had said he should go to the city, and the city was plainly in sight. He must be coming back by this time, Paul thought, and at once made up his mind to go toward the city, and meet him. He put two sweet limes in his pocket, and began eating a third, for he was very hungry, and started on. On the way he met a little naked Hindu boy with some bananas, and he gave him a sweet lime for two of them. Paul thought he had made a good trade, and the Hindu was sure that he had. The two bananas satisfied his hunger, and kept him busy till he was very near the gate of the city.

Every thing was so strange and interesting to Paul, that he forgot about Dhondaram, and forgot about himself. He never thought of being alone, or of being afraid. It seemed more like one of the old dreams than any thing real; and at last he reached the gate. Inside there was a dense crowd, but outside there were very few. It was a gloomy gray wall that surrounded the city, and a gloomy gateway. Inside he could see all sorts of bright costumes and bright colors, and hear the music and shouting, that betokened the happiness of every one engaged in the religious feast. It drew him like a magic spell. He was hurrying in, when his eye fell upon an old beggar sitting beside the gate, and a little boy close to him.

Paul was not sufficiently versed to know by the dress and position what the old man was: indeed, he hardly looked at him a second time. But a cry of joy burst from his lips as he saw the boy beside him. In his own boy's heart he thought it the prettiest face he had ever seen. That tantalizing picture that had so often come almost into his mind, and then slipped away again, once more appeared; and he seemed to half remember merry times that he had had somewhere, with merry children all about him. He ran across the road; and, sitting down on the mat close to the little black-eyed, black-

BEGGAR AND BOY.

haired boy, he touched a lock of the curling hair with his dainty little white finger, and, looking into the child's face, in a spasm of joy he kissed the dark lips that were half open over the tiny white teeth. The child shrieked, and sprang upon the old man's knee, rubbing his lips furiously, to wipe away the kiss.

Paul stepped back, and watched him doubtfully.

"I didn't mean to scare you, little boy," he said apologetically. "But I don't believe I hurt you like that. My lips are not dirty, are they?" he asked, suddenly remembering that he had been eating. He wiped his mouth carefully on his sleeve. "You can put mud on your mouth, and kiss me to pay, if you like. I'm sorry; but I don't think I am like you, for I was made white."

Paul had mingled some English words with his Hindustani without knowing it; and at best the boy did not understand much Hindustani either, for there are many languages spoken in India. But he understood enough to know that it was an apology; and, pouting, he slipped off the old man's knee again. Paul was disheartened, however, and was turning away, when he bethought him of the last sweet lime that remained in his pocket; and as he took it out, and held it up, the boy's eyes brightened, and his little hand was extended instantly.

"You like sweet limes better than you do kisses," said Paul a little sarcastically, as he turned away, and entered the gate.

Throngs of people crowded the streets. Every one was talking and shouting. On almost any other day there would have been swearing and terrible cursing by people who were so used to it that they really did not know that they were

THE HINDU FEAST.

cursing at all. There would have been venders of all sorts of every thing, and every one would have been hurrying in his own way. But to-day was the great festival, and every one was good natured.

No one seemed to notice little Paul, as he bent his steps this way and that, catching glimpses of pretty things that pleased him as he slowly worked his way toward where he heard the loudest music, intent upon reaching the spot if it took him all day: and it seemed very likely to; for, if he had thought of it, the sun was sinking very low, and the air was growing red with the approaching sunset.

Soon, however, the music helped him out by beginning to come toward him. There were huge elephants as far as the eye could reach, with magnificent golden *howdahs*, or cars, upon their backs; and flags were flying, and priests, with all sorts of instruments, were making all sorts of noises; and everywhere the boys, and even the men too, were firing fire-crackers to make more noise. There was little in harmony; and, as for the music, it was horrible, there is no doubt of it: but Paul had not an educated ear; and the excitement was so new and grand to him, that, for a little time, he seemed in the seventh heaven. But the procession was very long, and the crowd was very rude, and little Paul was jostled about in every direction.

The first of the long line of elephants was out of sight in one direction, and still there was no end to the line in the other. Some one stepped heavily upon Paul's foot. The pain brought tears to his eyes. He struggled to get out of the crowd. He wanted to go home, when it suddenly occurred to him that he had no home. He would go back to the place where Dhondaram had left him. But where was it? He had no idea. And where was Dhondaram? It came upon him, in all its force, that he had lost every thing, just at the moment that he had begun to have something worth keeping. What could he do? He was too miserable to cry. It would only have clogged his throat, when he was choking already.

While he was uncertainly yielding to every pressure of the crowd, not caring what became of him, he had been pushed nearer and nearer the path of the elephants; and now, as he looked up, the gloomy shadow of one of those great blue-black creatures was right upon him, with all its bespangling gold and silver, and beautifully embroidered blankets, and a little temple on its back,—all of glistening gold.

The driver, with a pointed iron bar in his hand with which to guide the elephant, was sitting on his head, and saw Paul in the path. He shouted to him to get away: but Paul did not see or hear either the elephant or its driver; for suddenly his eyes were riveted on the figure of a man, tall and broad-shouldered, towering above the other Bramhans, walking before the elephant, playing on a native instrument.

"Dhondaram! Dhondaram!" cried Paul in a shrill voice; and rushing before the elephant, whose great trunk must have struck him and knocked him down, had he not carefully lifted it out of the child's way, Paul sprang into the arms of his muni friend.

A sharp, bitter contortion distorted every feature of Dhondaram's face, as he recognized his charge, and heard his own name shouted in that throng. He had made discoveries that had horrified him on reaching the city; and, thanking Heaven that the boy was safe outside, he had bearded the lion in his den, and, to throw off suspicion, was marching there in that procession, under the very eye of officials who were searching for him, when "Dhondaram!" rang from the lips of the little boy, and Paul leaped into his arms. For an instant the black eyes rested on the little figure. It was a moment when life and death were but a hair's breadth apart. He could drop the child there, and possibly escape alone. The arms relaxed. Whatever his original motive had been, in taking charge of Paul, it evidently would not stand this test.

"Dhondaram! Dhondaram!" rang from a hundred voices in that crowd, as that magic name sounded, sending a thrill of fear into many a heart, and making many a coward quail. Paul did not even wonder why.

In an instant that horde might fix upon him, and tear him in pieces. Dhondaram knew it well. It was growing dark. The procession had already begun to light torches here and there, and all was an uncertain mass in the conflicting cross-lights. The momentary hush was simply because the crowd were waiting to know just where and which Dhondaram was.

The muni looked steadily into the large blue eyes. They were laughing and happy. In that instant the arm tightened again about the little figure. "He is not afraid of me. He kissed Dhondaram!" the muni muttered; and, bending forward with his burden, he sprang under the elephant beside him just as a hand was laid upon his shoulder.

All that Paul realized was that he was wrapped beneath the robe of his friend, who hurried one way and another. He was painfully crushed sometimes; but he only realized that there was danger of some sort, and heroically ground the suffering between his little teeth without uttering a sound that might hinder his protector's escape, till finally the cries became more distant, and the pace of Dhondaram slower and more regular. When Paul opened his eyes again, through the folds of the priest's robe he saw that they were in a very narrow street, where all was dark, except for torches that were smoking on occasional booths, where there were people without any bright-colored clothes, and where there was no room for elephants. Sometimes a calf or a cow stood in the way, or a donkey with his burden almost filled the breadth of the path, and there was shouting and wrangling; but no one was shouting the name of Dhondaram now, and a moment later they turned into a still narrower alley, where the houses rose up above their heads till they seemed to touch the sky. Here hardly any one was passing, and there was very little noise. Here, too, Dhondaram walked still more slowly, and soon turned into a narrow doorway, and entered a small room opening from a court.

A NARROW STREET.

There, with a sigh, he laid the burden down upon a coarse mat, lit a taper, and looked long and earnestly into the pale face and large blue eyes.

"The little Ingrij was frightened," he said, gently touching the golden-brown hair.

"I was frightened till I found you, Dhondaram, and now I am hungry," said Paul, sitting up, and patting the dark hand.

Dhondaram hurried out, locking the door behind him; but in a moment he was back again with rice, cakes, and milk, and Paul noticed that his little bundle of clothes and the bag of sweet limes were already in the room.

CHAPTER XII.

SCOTT IN THE MYSTERIES OF INDIA.

IT was growing dark when the steamer on which Scott Clayton and Richard Raymond had so long been passengers came in sight of the beautiful harbor of Bombay. In the distance they obtained a fine view of the clusters of islands upon one of which the city of Bombay is built. But the gray dusk of night lay over the harbor, and the flash from the new Colaba light dazzled them as they passed it.

The steamer made slow progress, for the water was literally filled with fishing-craft. Scott could see the quaint outline as they crept through the forest of boats, and at last he was interested in every thing. This was the land toward which all his hopes were turned; and he eagerly drank in every item, that he might the more rapidly become acquainted with it all.

The steamer was delayed in waiting for a pilot, for the pilots of Bombay are a very independent set of fellows.

"They'll come when they get good and ready, and not before," remarked the captain gruffly, as he stood watching for their light.

"Why is that?" asked Scott. "I should think they would want the job."

"So they might," said the captain: "but there's a club of them; and they all get their percentage, no matter who takes in the ship."

"Then, why don't you go in yourself, and cheat the whole of them?" said Scott. "That's what I'd do."

"I'd have to pay the pilot-fee all the same, as soon as I came to anchor," replied the captain. "And then, if I did any damage to myself or any one else, I'd be well punished for it by the court. That's all."

COAST OF BOMBAY.

"And quite enough," observed Scott. Then the pilot-boat appeared.

"They've stocked their lockers, and now they'll take us in," said the captain as he went on deck, meaning that they had waited to finish supper before coming out.

Slowly, very slowly, the steamer crept up, and rounded the point, when suddenly all the lights of the circling city came into view, extending for several miles away in the distance. All over the water, too, were the lights of almost innumerable ships; for Bombay is the great importation port of India.

No sooner were the papers signed than the decks were swarming with all kinds of natives. There were half-naked boatmen, *dingi* wallahs in scores, wrangling for an opportunity to carry them ashore; for the tide rises seventeen feet sometimes in Bombay, and it is impossible to make the fine stone wharves available for the larger steamers. Mingling with them were very polite and loquacious hotel clerks, with the dark Hindu faces, but dressed as Europeans, pressing the claims of a half-dozen of the best hotels of the city. There were several Hindus and Mussulmans, who spoke English well, as they thought, urging the passengers to engage them as *kitmutgars*, or servants; for, as Scott soon found out, every one in India has to have at least one native servant. When they were out of the bustle, Richard explained to him the necessity. These fellows were shoving in their faces numberless letters of recommendation from former employers. They were the neatest set who came on board, with white or colored turbans twisted tightly about their black hair or smoothly-shaven heads, long white cloaks bound about the waist with soft girdles, very small white breeches clinging about their ankles, and feet thrust into pointed slippers. But the most insinuating and the most unpleasant class of all were the Parsis, in all kinds of dress, most of them aping, in some respect, the clothes of the Europeans, but all wearing the curious shining black hats, looking like bishops' mitres turned sideways. They were money-changers, looking for opportunities to purchase English gold with Hindu rupees. They are lighter in complexion than the Hindus.

"They look as though they had a bilious turn, and had it bad," said Scott. "I should like to push the whole lot of them overboard."

"It would hardly do," replied Mr. Raymond; "for they are the Jews of Bombay. They have the money. They are very serviceable sometimes. You will meet them everywhere."

It was so late when they landed, that as they rolled away in an English cab, driven by an apish-looking Hindu, Scott obtained but a faint idea of his surroundings, except that every thing was very strange. They went to the Byculla Hotel as soon as they landed on the Apollo *bundar*, or wharf; and early in the morning they started for a walk.

Just outside the court of the hotel they came upon one of the great sights of India,—a band of jugglers.

"They are bound to initiate you early," said Richard. "Here are some fellows that are almost the trademark of Hindustan. Wait till I set them going. They are lying around here, waiting for the people in the hotel to wake up." He threw some coins into the midst of the crowd, saying in Hindustani, "What are you about, you lazy fellows? Don't you think we want to see any thing of India?"

It was like throwing corn to a flock of hungry chickens. Instantly the whole crowd sprang up, and all together began operations. One fellow began beating a drum, and moaning and howling as if in his last agony.

"Can't he stop that noise? I can hardly see while he is making that racket," said Scott.

"You would see nothing if he should stop," replied Richard; "for it is that delightful music that inspires the whole of them."

And, sure enough, as soon as he was well under way,

they all grew excited, and their bodies and voices joined in the hubbub. In the front, just under their eyes, sat a fellow who drew out two thin swords twenty-six inches long; and,

JUGGLERS.

after insisting that they examine them, he deliberately put the points into his mouth, and pushed the entire length down his throat. Then he wanted them to put their hands over his stomach, where they could feel the points. Another put a stone into his mouth; and a moment later, fire and a dense cloud of smoke issued from his nose and mouth, which at last completely enveloped him. Then he suddenly turned a somersault, and, opening his mouth, calmly took out the stone, and threw it on the ground. One fellow took some iron hoops, one after another, on a pole, where he set them spinning, till he had eighteen in a line; then, sticking the pole into the ground, he deliberately sprang through the whirling hoops, and, landing on his feet, he turned about, picked up the pole, and still kept the hoops whirling. Another began throwing short swords into the air, till he had ten of them flying about his head; and, in all the confusion, little acrobats were performing all manner of antics, and a sleight-of-hand performer was endeavoring to attract their entire attention to endless little tricks he was dexterously playing. They set a basket down in their midst. It was about two feet broad, a foot and a half high, and two and a half feet long. They took a netting that was made in the shape of a small bag, and, after much ado, succeeded in crowding into it a Hindu boy. They tied the neck of the bag fast, and laid the boy upon the top of the basket, which was apparently much smaller than he was. A sheet was thrown over him; and in a moment the netting-bag was thrown out from under the sheet, tied as it had been, but empty. They drew the sheet away, but the boy had disappeared. Some one said that he was in the basket; and one of the Hindus at once took the cover off, and jumped in himself, stamping about in it furiously. He then put the cover on, and bound it. Then he took a long sword, and thrust it through the basket, and out of every corner. With the last thrust a wild cry of pain issued from the basket, and he drew the sword out dripping with blood.

"I have killed the boy!" he cried; and Scott shuddered, for he certainly thought he had. But the Hindu pointed to a crow sitting on a tree at a little distance, and said,—

"Heaven be praised! my boy was a good boy. He has only been turned into a bird; but I will soon have him back." He gathered the sheet up into a little ball, and threw it at the crow, which was frightened and flew away. But the Hindu only laughed; and, gathering up the sheet again, he cried,—

"I have him!"

Then he threw the sheet over the basket with one hand, while he drew it off with the other; and, behold, the basket was strained in every part, to contain the boy. The Hindu joyfully untied the knots, and the cover flew up, for the boy was apparently so large that it could hardly hold him; and, smiling, he crept out of the basket without a scratch.

One of the Hindus then began to play the famous tree trick,—making a man go grow from a little seed, blossom, and bear fruit, under a sheet, where there was absolutely nothing but sand before: but they had looked so long that it was time for breakfast; and, assuring Scott that he would see jugglers in India till he would wish that there was no such thing in the world, Richard turned away, and they entered the hotel court.

The guests had begun to gather on the broad veranda, where already there were two snake-charmers performing.

"These fellows are plenty just now: there must be something up in the city that draws them here," said Richard, as they approached the little group gathered about the charmers.

They were two wrinkled old Hindus, with eyes that looked like snakes' eyes, and motions that were so subtle and quick, that Scott thought there must be some affinity between them and their serpents. In little baskets before them there were several snakes coiled away; and each charmer was playing on a rude gourd flute to a huge cobra that was coiling and uncoiling and weaving before him in time to the music. They

SERPENT-CHARMERS.

would hiss, and dart their heads at the charmers sometimes; and the way the charmers dodged them showed that they did not think them entirely harmless, as they spread the broad hoods just below their heads, and displayed every symptom of anger. Then one of the charmers stood up, and, catching the snake about the neck with one hand, threw him three times about his head, and let him fall upon the ground. There he lay, rigid and stiff, at full length, and straight as an arrow.

"I have killed my snake," cried the Hindu; "but I have a good cane instead." And, taking the creature up by the tail, he pretended to walk about, leaning on him.

"Will any one buy my cane?" he asked, offering it to several of the bystanders, who shuddered, and drew away. He smiled; and, thrusting the head of the rigid serpent under his turban, he began to push up the rest of the body, till at last all but the tip of his tail had disappeared. Then he removed his turban, and there lay the poisonous reptile in a glittering coil upon his head

Scott gave a cry of surprise; and Richard asked, "Does that remind you of any thing in particular?"

"Of Moses before Pharaoh!" exclaimed Scott.

"You are not the first one who has thought of it," replied Richard. "Sceptics are using it as an argument, to-day, to prove that Moses was only an expert snake-charmer, after all."

"Well, he succeeded in getting the children of Israel away, and that was what he was driving at," said Scott.

Richard went up to the charmer, who was now waiting for his assistant to collect the offerings. The people who had been looking on did not pay half so much attention now as they had before, and were some of them so busy reading the morning papers that they could not even hear the assistant when he spoke to them. After a moment's conversation, Richard returned, with the information that that day was the great feast of Nag-Panchmi; and, on the way in to breakfast, he promised Scott that he should see serpents enough that day to keep him in snaky dreams for the rest of his life.

The breakfast-room was large and high, and full of windows,

opened wide and covered with kus-kus grass awnings, that Hindu servants in white costumes were continually sprinkling with water, to cool the light breeze that came through them. Over each long table something entirely new to Scott was suspended from the ceiling, looking like panels, three feet broad, as long as the table, and ornamented with fancy fringes. From the lower corner of each, that was only a little above the heads of those sitting at the tables, a small cord was attached, that, after passing through several pulleys, went down into the hand of a native boy, sitting close against the side of the room. Scott had noticed one of them in his room the night before, but he was too tired to wonder what it was. Now, before he could ask, the guests began to seat themselves; and suddenly all the panels began to swing vigorously back and forth, fanning every one at the table.

"You like the *punkas?*" said Richard, watching him.

"That is a name and a half," replied Scott: "I should like them better with some other name."

"There is nothing else that will do so well: '*punka*' is Hindustani for 'fan,' and these *punkas* are the saving of a fellow's life if he lives long in India."

"But it is not so very hot this morning," said Scott: "I noticed that the thermometer was only eighty-three."

"But did you ever know it to be so hot at eighty-three in Boston?" asked Richard. "It is a sultry, damp heat here, that tells on one. The blood gets hotter and hotter. After breakfast we will drive on Malabar Hill, and obtain a little sea-breeze for a change."

"I feel as if a breath of salt air would do me good," replied Scott, laughing. Nevertheless, after drinking a cup of hot coffee, and eating a plate of snow-white rice and curry, with chicken, and several bananas and oranges, he began to realize that eighty-three was certainly hotter in Bombay than it was in Boston, and that a sea-breeze would not be bad.

They walked down the street a little way, as Richard wanted to mail a letter at the Byculla station, which was just beyond.

Before the station-gate there sat an old man on the ground, and a boy stood beside him with a bamboo tray in his hands. They were ragged and dirty; and the old man, especially, had as ugly and unpleasant a face as could well be imagined.

FRUIT-SELLER.

"What in the world is that frightful fellow trying to do?" asked Scott as they approached.

"He's only selling fruit," replied Richard.

"But what a horrible face! It's enough to drive every one to the other side of the street."

"You don't buy the old man's face. You need not even look at it. Go to the boy, and get half a dozen of those custard-apples. You'll like them."

Scott obeyed; and when he was close to the old man, and looked fairly in his face, it was not so ugly after all.

While they were stopping by the gate, a curious vehicle was driven by, drawn, at a slow dog-trot, by a span of maltese bullocks, with humps on their shoulders, in front of which the yoke was laid.

"Look at there!" cried Scott. "Is that a man, or monkey, driving?"

"It's an argument for Darwin surely," replied Richard. "But the poor fellow is not half so much a monkey as he looks. He is only one of the poorest of workingmen. That is a native *gharri*. It belongs to his employer. The poor fellow will not receive ten cents a day; but out of it he

GOING TO MARKET

probably has a large family of children, and three or four wives, to support."

"But that was a regular buffer riding with him. What was he,—crown prince, or sheik of some sort?"

"Hardly," replied Richard, laughing. "What his ancestors may have been I could not say, for there are hosts of princes and nabobs working for their living in India now; but that fellow is only some one's cook or butler, going to the market to purchase the breakfast."

"I hope he's late enough about it," said Scott.

"Not very," replied Mr. Raymond. "At the hotel we

could have breakfast early: but, if we were living as every one lives in India, we should only have what they call '*chota hazri*,' or 'little breakfast,' of bread and tea and fruit, early; then we should sit about the house, and read and bathe, and about nine or ten we should have breakfast."

"See! He is stopping at that shanty. Is that the market?" asked Scott, still watching the *gharri*.

"It is the place where those fellows always stop first," said Richard. "It is a coffee-house. He will go in there, and smoke a *hookah*, and drink a cup of coffee, before he does any thing else; and then he will charge enough more for what he gets at the market to pay the bill."

"I'd go to market myself, if that's the way," said Scott, as they turned away.

"It wouldn't pay," said Richard. "In the first place, it is too hot; and then, when a European goes to market, they charge him so much more, that it is the cheapest in the end for him to pay for the cook's coffee."

"Ha, you! Buggy wallah!" he called suddenly, as a carriage something like a clumsy doctor's gig passed, with the driver sitting in front of the dasher. He obediently stopped, and turned up to where they were standing. As they got in, Richard directed him to drive them over Malabar Hill.

"What was it you called him?" asked Scott when they started.

"Buggy wallah," replied Richard.

"But is not that English?"

"Yes, the buggy part of it is; and this is supposed to be an English vehicle. At any rate, 'buggy' is the only name these people know it by. But eat your apples, and see if you like them. They have a wonderful history."

The apples were large and green; but, instead of a skin, they were covered with coarse green scales. Scott pulled out one of these scales, and a soft buff pulp followed it, that looked and smelled and tasted like a most delicious custard. But the moment he had put his teeth into it, they struck against a hard black seed that literally filled the soft pulp.

"It is splendid! what there is of it," said Scott; "but

TO MALABAR HILL.

one might almost starve to death while he was eating. What is the history?"

"Why, the real name is the apple of Eden; and the Mohammedans say that that is the apple with which Eve tempted Adam in the garden of Eden. They say that then it had a skin like tissue, and of a beautiful color, and that the seeds were almost invisible, and that the flavor now is the very faintest suggestion of the fragrance that it had in the garden."

"I don't wonder that Adam and Eve went for them, then," observed Scott, as he began a second apple of Eden. "How soon do we come to Malabar Hill?" he asked, looking up when it was finished.

"We are now driving on that illustrious spot," replied Richard, waving his hand ostentatiously. "We are in the midst of the residences of the aristocracy of Bombay,—Europeans, Parsis, Mussulmans,—the paradise of boobies and snobs, and some very good fellows too," he added with a laugh.

"But I don't call it much of a hill," said Scott, looking down a broad and certainly beautiful avenue; "though it was something like these apples,—very steep, what there was of it."

"It is the most of a hill that there is on the island," replied Richard, as the driver turned about, and in time was in the heart of the city again.

The streets were all crowded with people now, the booths were opened, and every thing in the bazaar was ready for business. There were all sorts of people, in all sorts of costumes, and doing every thing imaginable. There were nabobs swelling along with two or three servants about them, and beggars and merchants. There were women with their faces all covered with veils, and women with one eye exposed through the folds of a white *sari* that was thrown over them; and there were women very prettily dressed in gaudy little jackets and silk breeches, with only a fancy gauze cloak. There were children half naked, and children, hosts of them, with nothing on but a little string tied round their waists. There were porters carrying bundles, and sometimes half a dozen staggering along under the weight of a large box or bale hung upon a bamboo pole which rested on their shoulders; and as they went they grunted, "He, he, he! Ho, ho, ho!" to keep in step, and forget their burden. There were *bhistis*, or water-carriers, with large earthen jugs, or *kujas*, hung upon opposite ends of a long bamboo pole which rested over their shoulders, and women with all kinds of bundles on their heads. There were all nations there, and all seemed at home. There were British soldiers and native policemen; and during their ride they even saw the peculiar sight of two Hindu policemen taking a drunken English soldier to the fort.

No one seemed to fear being run over, or to be on the lookout for carriages; and the result was, that the drivers had to keep up one unending howl to men, women, and children, who were forever in their way; and one could have walked about as fast as the buggy was drawn through the bazaar.

"What makes every one walk in the middle of the street?" asked Scott.

"Because there is nothing but middle," replied Richard.

Scott had not thought of it before; but, when he looked, there was absolutely no sign of a sidewalk anywhere.

"They must get their shoes all dirt," he observed, "and have pretty-looking carpets to pay for it."

"In the first place, they don't have carpets, as a general thing, not even the rich fellows," said Richard; "and, carpets or no carpets, they never wear shoes into the house, any more than we wear our hats."

"But what an absurd idea to take off one's shoes!" exclaimed Scott.

"I don't know about that, Scott: they say, what an absurd idea to take off the hat, instead! for they say their shoes touch the ground, and are defiled, and will defile their friends' houses; but their hats do no harm on their heads. A host of things are right or wrong in this world, just according to who do them, and who judge them."

IN THE BAZAAR.

"I believe you are right, Mr. Raymond," said Scott. "But tell me some more about these fellows, and what they do. It is a deal more interesting than ever before, now that I am looking right at them."

"The best way to tell you will be to show you," said Richard. "And the best time to show you is right away now, for we don't know where we may be by to-morrow."

"How are you going to show me?" asked Scott, as Richard gave an order to the coachman.

"I am going to take you to call on an old friend of mine, — Esofali Hiptulabhoy."

"O Cæsar's ghost! what a name!" groaned Scott, as he sank back in the buggy. "What sort of a man is he?"

"He is a high official, and a very good fellow."

"He is a heathen, of course, to have such a name," muttered Scott.

"Yes, he is a heathen," said Richard, but in such a voice, that Scott instantly looked up, and realized that he had hurt his friend's feelings.

"I was only joking, Mr. Raymond," he hastened to add.

"That's all right," replied Richard, smiling. "I was only thinking how Americans enjoy calling these people heathen, while there is much to admire, and really not much to despise, in them, except the bad habits they have learned from the English, which are made a thousand times worse in the Hindus than they are in the English, because the Hindus do not know how to control them, and hide them."

"But tell me about this Mr. Hip — Hip — Hip — What was the name? Really, it was horrible, Mr. Raymond."

"Let me tell you what it means, and perhaps you will not think it quite so bad. My friend's name is Esofali.

His father's is Hiptula. The termination 'bhoy' is put on, making him Esofali Hiptulabhoy. The 'Eso' is for the word 'Esa,' meaning Jesus; and 'Ali' means follower, with a euphonious 'f' between. Then 'Hipt' means friend, and 'Allah' is God; so that the horrible name of this heathen is 'follower of Jesus, and friend of God.'"

"Then he is a Christian," said Scott.

"Not at all," replied Richard. "He is one of the strictest of Mussulmans; but the Mussulmans believe in Adam and Moses and Solomon, and in all the Old Testament, in fact, down to Jesus. Then they branch off, and believe that Mohammed was still greater, — the prophet of all the prophets of God."

"Then you keep speaking of the Hindus as though they were something else."

"So they are," said Richard. "It is only when we say Hindu very carelessly that we mean all the people that live in India. The Hindus are really the followers of the Bramhanical religion. There are one hundred and seventy-five million of them in India, and only fifty million Mussulmans, or Mohammedans as they are sometimes called. The Hindus are the people that the missionaries preach to principally, for the Mussulmans say that they are better than Christians already; and so it is the Hindus that we hear all the horrible stories about. They are the people that are so divided up into castes, where the Bramhans, or priests, are at the head, and the pariahs at the foot. It is very hard to deal with them, they are so full of whims; yet, after all, there is something very suggestive to our loose-jointed notions of strict Christian principles in the fierceness with which they stick to their religious peculiarities. I had two servants once, a Hindu and a Mussulman, who went with me on a trip into the mountains. We were all alone, and a long way from help, when they both became badly poisoned, and I feared they would die. I had a bottle of antidote with me; and, hurrying to the Mussulman, I put the bottle to his mouth without waiting to turn any out. Then I gave it to the Hindu; but the fellow refused to touch it because it had been against the lips of the Mussulman. I turned some out, but all in vain. Before I thought, I told him it was all I had, or I should have deceived him in some way. But he only shook his head, and said, 'I would rather die than defile myself to live.'"

"What a fool he was!" exclaimed Scott.

"I don't think so," said Richard. "That boy honestly believed that it was wrong for him to touch any thing from which one not of his caste had been drinking. Because we think it a foolish notion did not make it right for him. And he died up there in the mountains sooner than do what he thought was wrong."

"I don't believe a Christian would have done that," said Scott. "And I don't see the use of missionaries spending so much time and money in trying to convert fellows that are already a deal better than Christians. 'Twould be better to have them send missionaries to America."

"That's a mistake that I made too, and I did not get over it for a long time. It would certainly do Christianity a deal of good to imbibe some of the scrupulousness of the Hindus; but when it occurred to me how much better Christianity was, if really lived up to, than was this Hinduism, I saw at once the good of bringing such fellows as these Hindus into the line."

"Do they make as good Christians as they did Hindus?" asked Scott.

"Here we are already!" exclaimed Richard, calling to the driver to stop outside the gate. "This is a crazy sort of a gig to make a formal call on a great nabob in," he added with a laugh. "I fancy we might as well walk up to the house." And, suiting his actions to his words, he stepped from the buggy.

HINDU MENDICANT.

"I should not think he could be much of a nabob, to live behind a fence like that," Scott remarked, as he followed Mr. Raymond, and looked up at the high stucco wall, not in very good repair, beside a gate at which they had stopped.

"In America we spend every thing on the outside," replied Richard; "and we care comparatively little for the dust and dirty clothes behind the door, if our neighbor's eyes cannot see there. But in India they go on the opposite principle, and care very little what the outside is, so long as the inside is clean. It is only their way," he added, laughing; but Scott's attention was attracted to a figure at one side of the half-crumbling gate.

A fellow, the very picture of some of the idols Scott had seen in drawings, sat by the gate, covered with rags, and as dirty as mortal man could easily be. His forehead was painted with blue and red and yellow, in three circles, and there were stripes of yellow down each cheek. On his head there was a pyramid of beads as large as English walnuts, strung on a coarse thread, and wound higher and higher over some dirty sort of a turban, till they came to a point. Strings of larger and smaller beads were round his neck, and hanging down to his waist. The rags that covered him were fantastically arranged. In one hand he held a copper or brass plate, and in the other a sort of a globe.

"He is a religious mendicant," said Mr. Raymond, without waiting for a question.

"But what in the world is he doing there?"

"Waiting for alms," replied Richard, smiling.

"I hope he's waiting patiently enough! He don't seem over-anxious. He has not moved a feather since I first looked at him," said Scott.

"That's because he believes it is more blessed to give than to receive; and he thinks he is conferring a favor upon you by letting you have an opportunity to give him something."

"It's very good of him, I must say," said Scott a little scornfully.

"It is precisely what our Bible teaches," suggested Richard. "But never mind the theology of the thing. If you have a two-anna piece, like an English sixpence, hold it between your thumb and finger, by your side, and see how soon it will move him."

"The old reprobate!" muttered Scott. "I'd sooner give

him a slap in the face. He's the very picture of impertinence, sitting there like a statue. He's a hypocrite: I know he is."

Still he took out the two-anna piece; and, in an instant, the little dish came into position to receive it. Scott had a good mind to put the money back in his pocket. He even made a motion that way; but, seeing how willingly the beggar was withdrawing the plate, he decided it would not be so good a joke after all, and dropped the coin in the tray.

"Giving to the poor is purchasing mercy in heaven; and in the spirit that you give shall the mercy be delivered. Thank you, little gentleman," said the fellow, bowing and smiling, and speaking in very good English.

Scott shot through the gate as if he had been fired from a cannon.

"I saddled the wrong horse that time surely," he said, when Mr. Raymond came up with him; and his face was red to the temples.

"Yes," said Richard, "he had the best of you: there is no doubt of it. I never heard of but one of those fellows before who could speak English."

"Would you go back and apologize?" asked Scott.

"I think not. He would hardly know what you meant. But I would be careful in the future, and not take advantage of a fellow being deaf, to speak ill of him," replied Richard.

"So I will," said Scott decidedly. And now for the first time he noticed where they were going, and with a cry of delight paused for a moment to enjoy the beautiful picture. They were in the midst of a large garden, with brilliant flowers growing in profusion on every side. There were large trees, too, about the borders; and little green and red parrots were chattering everywhere. The flower-beds were not fanciful little things, like those Scott had seen in front lawns in America, but enormous affairs, without much regularity, with great flowering shrubs, like a little forest, and paths paved with white marble leading through them. Down the centre, through an open space, rose a large, and at least curious, mansion. There were little windows and broad balconies and domes and arches everywhere. The lower floor seemed to

ESOFALI'S HOUSE.

be only an immense pavilion of beautiful arches supported by carved pillars.

"Well," said Scott in astonishment, "he is something of a nabob, after all. But how in the world am I to act? Goodness me! I never thought of that. Let me wait out here. Please do. Do you keep on your hat, and take off your shoes?"

"How would you expect a Mohammedan gentleman to act, when he was calling on your father?" suggested Richard.

"Why, the best he knew how, of course!" said Scott.

"Very well: if you behave like a gentleman to the best of your ability, I don't believe that Esofali will find any fault with you." But here he was interrupted by two natives, who came running toward them with something made of beautiful peacock-feathers. But before they began to shield them from the sun, as was their evident intention, they fell upon the ground, touching their foreheads, and muttering something in which Scott could often distinguish the name of "Raymond Sahib." He knew they were greeting his friend; and he began to suspect that Mr. Raymond was of more importance than he had thought, from the generous way in which he had been his companion.

They entered the house through one of the beautiful arches. Several servants were formed in line on either side of the passage; and all knelt, and touched their foreheads, as Mr. Raymond and Scott went in. They were ushered into a large room with a white marble floor, and elaborately carved marble screens before the windows. There were fine tapestries and Persian rugs on the walls and floors, some very soft divans, or low sofas, and a little marble table; but otherwise the room was without any ornaments.

They had waited but a moment, when a very tall and fine-looking native entered the room, and almost running to Richard, clasped both hands in his, pressed them upon his lips and then on his forehead, held them there for a moment, then exclaimed,—

"Aha, Raymond Sahib! the sky has been black since you left, and now the sun breaks out again with your coming. But nothing has gone wrong, that you come so unexpectedly?"

"Nothing is amiss," said Richard pleasantly; and Scott

thought it precisely the way in which he would have spoken to him, and wondered how it could be, when in the presence of so great a man as he had described Esofali. Then he turned, and introduced Scott, and Scott felt his cheeks growing red, as the Mohammedan grasped his hand; but he shook it just as though he were an American, and, in very good English, said, —

"I am delighted to see you, my young friend. Any friend of the great and wise Raymond Sahib is welcome here." Then he went on in Hindustani with Richard, often addressing a question in English to Scott, till Scott felt so much at home that he began to examine him closely.

Esofali was magnificently dressed, yet very simply. He had a plain white muslin coat on, bound at the waist with a soft cashmere girdle. Over that was a long white silk loose coat, with a heavy collar embroidered with gold. It hung so low as almost to cover a pair of satin breeches that were very large, and, in turn, completely covered his feet. On his head he wore only a little cashmere cap as soft and white as snow, with a thread of gold embroidery about it.

He insisted upon their remaining to breakfast. Scott thought it nearly time for his dinner, but it did not matter much what it was called. He was so much in fear that he should do something wrong, however, for every thing was so strange, that he almost lost his appetite. Several varieties of sweetmeats were the first thing served to them, in as many little dishes. Then there were fish and fried eggs, with a curious flavor that he did not understand. The odor was delicious, as the dishes were brought upon the table; but the taste was so different, that, do what he would, he could eat but little. Then there was rice and curry and chicken; but the rice had cloves and cardamom-seeds boiled in it, and the curry was full of fruit. Scott knew it must be good by the way in which Mr. Raymond ate it, as he had never seen him eat before; but he quietly made up his mind that Mussulman cooking was not for him. He little dreamed what a very short time it would be before he would eat those dishes, highly spiced and curiously cooked, quite as ravenously as Mr. Raymond.

FIVE YEARS OLD.

Before they went away, their host brought in his old father, a gentleman with a very white beard. His hair was shaven close to his head, like that of his son. He could not speak English, but received Scott very cordially. Then Esofali brought in his little boy, a cunning little fellow of five years, who sat on the edge of the table, and pronounced a few English words very correctly, much to the delight of his father and grandfather.

When Mr. Raymond left, each pressed his hand to their foreheads, and bade Scott a cordial farewell, urging them to be sure and come to their home again.

"Is his wife dead?" Scott asked, as they rode down the street in their host's handsome English carriage. "I dared not ask him about her, for you did not; but it was very funny not to see any lady at all at the table."

Richard laughed for a moment, much to Scott's discomfort, then replied, "One wife died a year ago; but he has three, at least, left."

"Three wives! Why, how in the world can that be? And where do they keep themselves?" exclaimed Scott.

"Though you did not see them, I'll warrant they all saw you. I heard them chatting behind the screen at the end of the room while we were eating breakfast."

"Then it would have been polite for me to have asked for them?" said Scott.

"It would not have mattered with Esofali, but it is not the custom. The wives of the Mussulmans very rarely come into society where there are men, and one never asks concerning their health. It would be thought a great impoliteness here, just as it would be with us to ask a lady how old she was, or if she had the stomach-ache. It is simply something that they never talk about."

CHAPTER XIII.

SNAKES.

IN driving home they passed the great cotton-market, where bales of Indian cotton were piled in immense blocks. On rickety benches at one corner sat a few men, many of them Parsis, engaged in folding their hands, and smoking cigarettes.

"They are the famous cotton-brokers of Bombay," remarked Richard, pointing toward them with his thumb.

"Don't believe the board has opened yet, then," said Scott. "They are taking life easy."

"It's not much like a *bourse* in America certainly; and yet business is in full blast there, and those fellows literally control the vast cotton interests of India. They transact a tremendous amount of business, and do it all in that same solemn fashion."

"I should have called it a funeral," observed Scott.

When they reached the hotel, there were two natives waiting on the veranda, in clothes as white as snow, grinning from ear to ear; and, the moment that Richard stepped from the carriage, they were both upon the ground, kissing his feet. He stepped back, and made them stand up. Then each took a hand, and pressed it to his forehead, and knelt again. Scott stood back in amazement, till Richard explained, "They are two boys from my little place at Poona, whom I telegraphed to, last night, to come down and meet us. We shall need them as *kitmutgars*, and we can trust them better than the fellows we might pick up here."

"But what do I want of a servant?" said Scott independently. "I always waited upon myself."

"You'll find it very different here," replied Richard. "It is too hot to do every thing for yourself; and you will often be too tired, though you may have done nothing. Then, there are a host of things that will absolutely require a servant. Things that you could do in America, and be proud of doing,

THE COTTON-BROKERS.

would injure you in the opinion of natives, at least, to do here. One is obliged to cater to their notions somewhat, in living here; for he requires their respect and good will."

"It must make it rather expensive," said Scott.

"Not so very. These two boys, for instance, cost me eight cents a day apiece; and if we wished we could pick up boys for less. The hotels charge nothing for them; for they do our work, and wait on us at the table. And many of the railroads and steamers about India allow each first-class passenger to take one or two native servants."

By this time they had reached their rooms; and Richard said, —

"Neither of these boys can speak English, for I never employ one that can: they are apt to be unreliable. But they will either of them understand what you want, almost before you can ask them. You can take your choice. The one with the gold cap and jacket is Sayad, and the one with the turban is Moro. Sayad is a Mussulman, and Moro is a Hindu."

MORO.

The two boys smiled, as they already comprehended what Mr. Raymond was saying about them.

"I think I could get along with a Mussulman best," said Scott, to which Richard assented; and Sayad, with his pretty gold cap and vest, was turned over to Scott as his personal servant so long as he remained in India.

"He will sleep on a rug just outside your door at night," Richard explained. "He will attend to your bath in the morning; he will black your boots, and brush your clothes; take care of your trunk; see to your washing going and coming from the *dhobi*, or washerman; wait on you at the table; take care of your room; and walk with you whenever you wish him to, to carry your bundles, and do errands. You must let him do all these things every day, see that he does them well, and never do them yourself, or he will expect you always to do them. Be kind to him always, but never let him feel that you think him an equal. They are not brought up in that way here. There are just two things that you must be careful of. Foreigners often overlook them at first, and at once come to the conclusion that Hindus are the worst servants in the world. You must know just what you have in your trunk, and, if you miss any thing, tell him at once, and direct him to find it before the next morning, and never believe too implicitly what he tells you. As a rule, the Hindu idea of honesty is very weak in little things.

SAYAD.

They will steal and lie without thinking they are really doing wrong. If you charge them with it, and grow angry, they only become dogged, and you can do nothing with them; but, if you take it right, you will keep them right all the time, without their feeling it. That's a long sermon I've preached to you on the moral treatment of Hindu servants; but it took me years to learn it, and I found it very useful at last. Now we must be ready for dinner; and you'll be hungry, notwithstanding the hearty breakfast you ate at Esofali's, hey?"

Scott went into his room, followed by Sayad, who did not need an order to that effect, for his eyes had told him all about it; and he and Moro found it hard to tell which should be jealous of the other, — the one who was selected by the new comer, or the one who could remain with the old master.

Scott opened his eyes wider and wider to see how readily Sayad took his new duties in hand, and how he seemed to read his thoughts. The clothes for dinner were laid out at the boy's fancy, and correctly, without consulting Scott. They were brushed and put upon a chair in such a way that Scott could most easily reach them in the proper order. Then his slippers were given him to put on, while Sayad blacked his boots. Sayad even shampooed his head, and combed his hair for him, and did it as well as a barber, — an operation that Scott found very refreshing in the heat of that Bombay afternoon. Then he neatly folded the old clothes, and carefully packed the trunk, and locked it, giving the key to Scott. Thus, without a word passing between them, Scott was ready to go down, and every thing in order to leave. He had done absolutely nothing but move enough to take off one suit of clothes, and put on another.

"Why, it's like being a sultan!" he exclaimed to Mr. Raymond when they met. "He's the finest fellow I ever heard of."

"Well, don't let him know that you think so," replied Richard. "Nothing spoils a native servant so quickly as undue praise or blame. A new broom sweeps clean, you know; and, the first time you see that he has not done any thing just as well as he did it to-day, make him do it over again, no matter how tired he is. It is the only way to keep him straight."

"Isn't that rather rough?" questioned Scott.

"It sounds so: but that is the way I've brought these boys up; and you see they are not only good servants, but they love me."

After dinner Richard proposed that Scott should take a nap, while Sayad pulled the *punka* over his bed; "for," said he, "some friends of mine are going to give us a little dinner of welcome to-night, and it will be pretty late, as we must go first to the feast of serpents. It is a sight one sees but once a year in Bombay, and we must not miss it. You will be tired."

The sun was setting when they started. They went alone; and Sayad and Moro were allowed to go by themselves, to see what they wished of the festival.

"It has been going on all day, especially about the temples," said Richard; "but to-night we shall see the best of it. Look at that! See that bullock-team going by!"

Scott looked up, as, through the dense crowd that already filled the street, a curious wagon, drawn by a pair of nearly white bullocks, went crowding its way. The bullocks had really no harness on, but a strap about their necks to keep the unique yoke fast, and a ring in their noses, to which a sort of reins was attached; for the driver sat behind, as though he had a pair of horses. The carriage was the most curious thing, however. There were two heavy wheels, without springs, supporting a very clumsy body, that was nothing after all but a dome, very like a miniature temple, with four arches and four pillars, supported at the four corners of the vehicle. In the front arch sat the driver, and under the dome a woman reclined, wrapped up in a cloud of gauze, and wearing all the jewelry that she could pile upon her little face and neck.

"What is she?" asked Scott. "Upon my word, it's almost a mowing-machine!"

"A Bramhan woman, — one of the very highest caste of

CARRIAGE OF HINDU LADY.

Hindus," replied his friend. "It is their great day for showing themselves. It is really the feast of the god Krishna, whose great celebrity is his love for pretty women; and they make to-day the anniversary of his killing the great serpent Bindrabund, that was once supposed to be the spirit of evil on the banks of the Jumna."

"It is not simply the worship of Krishna, is it?" said Scott.

"No, indeed! It is a day of making offerings to snakes in general, — feeding them, that is about all, and praying to them not to bite them in the year to come."

"See those torches yonder!" exclaimed Scott.

"That is where we are going. That is the centre of the illumination. There is no hurry, though; for they will wait till it is quite dark before they begin."

"Look at these booths all along the way," he added. "They have images of the god for sale."

"Idols?" ejaculated Scott in horror.

"Yes, idols," replied Mr. Raymond, laughing. "And garlands of flowers, and milk, to offer to the snakes. You might purchase a can of milk, and take it with you; for the priests will be pleased with the offering, though they would not take the milk from you themselves."

"Do they really worship these things?" asked Scott in a sort of fascinated horror, working his way up to one of the booths.

"Not at all," returned Richard decidedly. "And that is where a host of our good people in America make a great mistake."

"I always thought they did," mused Scott, now taking one up, and looking at it for a moment, when, before, he would have loathed it.

"The Hindus who are at all educated would laugh at you, if you suggested that they were worshipping this piece of wood."

"What do they worship, then?"

"God," said Richard earnestly.

"Not our God!" exclaimed Scott.

"There may be a difference of opinion there," replied

Richard. "For my part, I believe they worship the same God that we do, and that he accepts their worship."

"Then, why should they be converted by the missionaries?"

"Because Christianity is so much the noblest and best way to worship God. The Hindus had, perhaps, the first idea of a Trinity; and their theology is something like that of very many scholars in enlightened lands. They believe that God is every thing, and that every thing is God. They say this little bit of wood, of which they made this idol, is a part of God, and that, in setting it before them when they pray, they are bringing the great God nearer, and more directly before their thoughts. That is all the use the educated make of idols."

MORE SNAKE-CHARMERS.

"I don't call that idol-worship," mused Scott.

"Perhaps not," returned Richard; "yet it is not the best way to bring God before the heart in prayer; and the quicker our missionaries succeed in their work, the better it will be for the world, even if it is no better for heaven."

Scott bought some milk, and turned away. While they had been waiting, a band of snake-charmers had gathered, with a crowd of boys who were anxious to see every new performance, around the posts of a fountain, or well, just opposite, and were meditatively twining their serpents around their arms, hoping for an opportunity to earn some money in performing for the foreigners.

They looked so patiently expectant, that Scott was on the point of giving them the milk he had bought, when Richard restrained him.

THE CROWD BECAME DENSER.

"They have had a good day, you may be sure," he said; "and, no matter how much they earn, they will spend it all before morning. You had better save the milk. It was the last they had at the booth; and, if you have an offering, they will let you through the crowd till you get a much better view farther on."

This was very good advice, as Scott soon found; for, as they approached the centre of action, the crowd became denser. And soon all that he could see, even when lifted up on Mr. Raymond's shoulder, — a position that his sea voyage had made him much too heavy to retain long, — was a crowd of dark faces and white turbans against the smoking torches.

It was a curious sight, however; and Scott declared that

even that was well worth coming for: but Richard insisted on getting him nearer.

A few minutes later a Bramhan bhat, with shaven head, went slowly past them. It was a difficult thing for a Bramhan to make his way through such a crowd; but they were not so boisterous or tightly packed as a crowd in America, and fell back sufficiently to give him room as he announced his approach.

Just as he was passing the two, Richard called,—

"Ha, Kashinath!" and added in English, "Will you pass an old friend in this way without speaking?"

The priest turned about, and, with an exclamation of delight, cried in English, "Welcome, Raymondrao Sahib! Welcome to India again! You could not stay away very long, thank Heaven!" And he touched his hands to his forehead.

"Come to the temple in the morning," he added. "We die if we do not speak with you."

"That's very good, Kashinath," returned Richard with a laugh. "But look you! Here is a young friend of mine, who has an offering of milk, and cannot reach your ugly gods to stuff them."

"Stand right by the corner here, Raymondrao, and I will send a *sapwallah* in five minutes to fetch him on his back."

"That's better yet!" exclaimed Mr. Raymond. "That beats all your Oriental compliments put together. Go on! Go on! Send the *sapwallah*, and we'll thank you in the temple to-morrow."

"Salaam, Sahib!" said the Bramhan, bowing as low as the crowd would permit, and touching his hands to his forehead.

"What is a *sapwallah?*" asked Scott.

"A serpent-charmer," replied Richard.

"Ugh!" was the comment. "Have I got to ride like a *cobra?*"

"Never mind who carries you, and brings you back," said Richard, laughing, "so long as he takes you safely where you want to go; and you may be sure of that with any one whom Kashinath may send."

"Well, what does Raymondrao Sahib mean?" questioned Scott, who was afraid, that, if he waited, the name would "slip from his mind," as he said.

"Rao is simply a title of respect, and so is Sahib. The old fellow felt good-natured, and put it on thick: that is all."

"Well, how is it that you know every one, and every one is so terribly good-natured when you are around?" asked Scott, determined to solve the question that was becoming more prominent every hour.

"There comes your *sapwallah*," was the answer, that was not at all satisfactory. "Now, twine around his neck, but don't go bury yourself under his turban."

A rather snaky but not altogether unpleasant looking fellow appeared through the crowd, and, making a profound salaam to Mr. Raymond, took Scott on his shoulder without a word, and, by wriggling precisely like a serpent, succeeded in rapidly making his way through the throng without apparently incommoding any one. He set Scott gently down in the midst of a scene that startled every particular hair of his head, and yet was so wildly grand that he stood enraptured.

All about nim torches were flaming and smoking. Grotesque banners were being swung back and forth by their

THE FESTIVAL OF THE SERPENTS.

bearers, as there was no breeze to do it. Men were beating curious drums, and wailing strange, weird songs, while others were blowing upon metal trumpets. From a circle in which Scott stood, the crowd had been kept back, by fear of the snakes perhaps; and all about the outer edge stood a line of women — that, in the cross-lights of the moon and the torches, seemed to Scott to be the most beautiful he had ever seen — in costumes as beautiful as they themselves. Some were dressed in tinsel and brilliant colors; some, only half clad, were draped in flowing white; all were bearing offerings of flowers or milk for the idols.

SAPWALLAH.

So far, the scene was so wild and beautiful that Scott would have stood there all night, an enchanted spectator; but, when his eye fell to the immediate circle about him, his blood ran cold, in spite of a lifetime of resolving not to be a coward. Directly before him there were two great bowls, each filled with milk; and around each bowl was a writhing ring of frightful *cobra*, drinking the milk, while their charmers, in a second circle, were making all the hideous moans imaginable, now and then catching one of the *cobra* away, to give another a chance. And the disappointed fellow would hiss in his madness, and spread his broad hood, that looked many times more hideous in the night than by day.

Scott deposited his can of milk, received the blessing of the chief *sapwallah* in a terrible contortion, that frightened him almost out of his wits. Then he signified to his particular *sapwallah* that he was ready to retire, and, with a shudder, was tenderly taken on the back where so many a *cobra* had been crawling, and a moment later was placed as tenderly by the side of Mr. Raymond.

"Did you see enough? You were only gone a moment," said Richard, as he dropped a coin into the *sapwallah's* easily opened hand.

"I saw enough. Indeed, I did!" replied Scott. "In fact, I think I have seen all the snakes I care to for a lifetime: am ready to go home any time you are."

"You are not hurt?" inquired Richard anxiously.

"No, indeed! But those snakes!" said Scott with a shudder.

Richard laughed outright. "If that is all," he said, "you'll soon be ready to do it all again. Snakes never lose their charm. But we will find a buggy or cab as soon as possible, and drive back."

CHAPTER XIV.

IN PALANQUIN AND ROW-BOAT.

THE evening dinner was a very grand affair. Scott had never seen any thing equal to it. And when the speeches began, he was hardly surprised, after all, to gather from the many words of welcome that his friend was a man of great importance in India, well known from Bombay to Calcutta, and from Madras to Massuri. He began to be afraid of him, and to wonder if he were not behaving himself improperly before a man to whom every one, no matter of what creed or nationality, seemed to offer esteem. When the dinner was over, however, he was altogether too tired to give the matter any serious thought; and the next morning, as he was very late, and his friend came to his room for him to go to breakfast, he found him the same Richard as ever, — just a kind, every-day friend. And Scott looked in vain for any of that dignified Mr. Raymond upon whom all the praises had been showered the night before.

Even had he tried, it would have been impossible for him to be any thing but his natural self with Richard Raymond, and he was very glad of it; for one of the hardest things for a real, true-hearted boy to be is an artificial, imitation gentleman.

When breakfast was over they started for a walk; but as the sun was well up, and was beating upon the city in a way that made it dangerous for them to exercise, Richard proposed that they take advantage of an offer a friend had made him at the dinner, and borrow his large palanquin for the morning.

"Then this afternoon we must go to the caves of Elephanta; for to-morrow is Sunday, and we should start for Puna the next day. I am anxious to have you stop for a day at my little home there, and we do not know how soon we may hear something that will send us from one end of India to the other. I have put the best agents right upon the track of Dennett; and we shall overhaul him in a little while, no matter what he is doing, or where he is."

"If little Paul were only safe with us, I should be perfectly happy," said Scott.

"Well, in time we shall have him. There is no human doubt of it," replied Richard. "I have had every outlet stopped. I don't believe the man can possibly escape from India. It is a big trap, to be sure; but he is here, and Paul was all right when they landed, about six weeks ago. Children rarely feel this climate the first year, and I don't believe Paul will."

After a short call, they accepted the palanquin, which was called to the court for them.

"One of those little carriages hanging on a pole," remarked Scott, laughing as he saw the palanquin.

"Yes, one of the handsomest and easiest ones I ever saw, except those belonging to natives," returned Richard. "There are not many palanquins to let in Bombay, at the best. They are not so popular as they are in the rest of India, and then the public ones would be so small that we could not both ride in one; and I want to keep you awake, and make you see the sights."

"A regular four-horse team, isn't it?" added Scott, as he seated himself in the handsomely carved wood carriage, that was, as he said, hung on a pole, — a long, ornamented pole at each end, — which was supported on the shoulders of four stalwart natives, who certainly seemed to enjoy their work, by the jovial way they started off, singing the great national song of the palanquin - bearers, "He, he, he! Ho ho, ho!"

THE PALANQUIN.

The palanquin was low: one could comfortably sit up in it, but that was all. There was a soft bamboo mattress over the floor, with embroidered pillows, so that one could lie down, and even sleep, very comfortably; and at one end was a little closet, where books for reading, or a lunch, could be carried. Before they started, their host slipped into this closet a little cask that contained some broken ice, and two bottles of soda-water.

"If you would only drink something, Mr. Raymond," he said, "we would put some champagne in there instead, that would make your eyes shine; but it's no use asking you."

"Not a bit," replied Richard, laughing, as they were borne away.

"Do you really never drink? I thought, till last night

at least, that it was only because you did not want to set me an example."

Richard laughed heartily at this remark of Scott's; for such an explanation had never occurred to him. But at last he answered, —

"It is a little over ten years since I have tasted a drop of any kind of wine or ale or liquor stronger than soda-water and lemonade."

"I thought people had to in this country," said Scott. "They say the water is very unhealthy, and that the heat is much more dangerous, unless one protects his constitution with stimulants."

"You heard some old toper say that," responded Richard, smiling.

"It was the captain of the steamer," returned Scott.

"Well, it is the sentiment of a great many; and possibly the water does not agree with all. Where it is not good, I do not drink it; but it does not necessitate my drinking intoxicating liquor. And, as for bracing up the constitution, I am very sure that ten Englishmen in India have to leave the country, broken down with over-drinking, to one that is broken down with the heat alone."

"But in emergencies you would drink, wouldn't you?" asked Scott doubtfully.

"Oh, I'm no temperance preacher, Scott!" said Richard quickly. "I never signed a pledge; I never talked on temperance in public; and, as for cases of emergencies, why, that's the same as with every thing else. One had better be his own lawgiver. I've noticed that fellows that carried liquor with them when travelling, so as to have it in case of emergency, generally succeeded in getting up an emergency before they got to the end of the journey; and those that did not have any very rarely needed it. I never take any with me, unless I am going far up into the mountains, or a long way from any possibility of obtaining it. But look at those three fellows down there! While we are talking temperance here, we are missing all the sights."

BEING SHAVED.

"What are they doing?" exclaimed Scott, as he saw the three men, — one sitting on his own heels, close against a low stone fence built out into a court; while another bent over him, and a third was standing near, and talking with them. "Is the man hurt?"

"Not at all. He is only being shaved."

"Shaved in the street?"

"Yes, right there in the gutter, or anywhere else."

"But the fellow is at work on his forehead," said Scott.

"The natives shave their heads and foreheads, and clip the eyebrows; then the barber washes the face carefully, and cleans and pares the nails on both hands and feet. He can't afford a shop; and, as the patrons often have no homes that he can go to, he attends to them where rent is the cheapest, which is right in the street."

"He makes an all-over job of it, and no mistake," said Scott. "But it must cost a fortune to be barbered like that."

"Yes, that is the worst of it," replied Richard solemnly. "It will cost that poor fellow nearly three cents."

"Starvation!" exclaimed Scott.

"Not at all," laughed Richard. "If he has three or four customers in the course of the day, the barber will be able to support a good-sized family, — say, three wives and ten children."

THE POSTMAN.

Scott groaned. But a moment later his attention was attracted to another curious individual.

"What sort of a fiend is that?" he asked.

"A very welcome one, I can assure you," replied Richard.

"Not with me," returned Scott decidedly. "He'd have hard work to make himself popular in my books. Look at that ugly coat, and that little round turban and big belt and little breeches and big shoes, and that regular base-ball club! And what a face! No, sir! I'll pass him every time."

"But, my dear boy, that is a postman," repeated Richard with mock gravity; for he knew how eagerly Scott was waiting their going to Puna, where letters from America that crossed Europe had been forwarded to his home, before their arrival.

"Ah!" said Scott, now watching him eagerly. "That makes a deal of difference. He's gotten up pretty well for a postman, after all. I wish he'd come round, and call on me. I should think our horses would get tired," he added, as the bearers of the palanquin, coming into a more open street, began to run at a rapid gait, passing several buggies that were going in the same direction, and shouting and laughing at the drivers.

"They are so used to it, that they would keep it up almost all day. The only thing they would not do would be to carry us an inch, if they found that we had a lunch in that closet that had a ham-sandwich or a bit of pork in it."

"I admire their taste!" exclaimed Scott. "They'll find no pork in my lunches."

"The taste is all very well, but not the extent to which they carry it. If they were our oldest and most trusted servants, and we were twenty miles from anywhere when they found it out, down would go the *palki* pole, and nothing would induce them to take it up again."

"I'd throw away the pork if it came to a pinch," said Scott.

"'Twould do no good; for the *palki*, once defiled, would be a long while in getting clean again. I once had a right troublesome native neighbor. A wealthy fellow owned a miserable hovel near my lawn. He did not fancy foreigners, and would not sell me the property, and would not turn out the tenant of the hut, though he was the vilest fellow imaginable. I tried every way to get him out, but in vain, till one day my butler, who was a Portuguese Christian from Goa, to do me a kindness I suppose, kept watch till the family had all gone out, and, stealing over there with a little pig he had secured for the purpose, he shut him up in the house. When the poor tenants came home, and discovered the pig, they turned about, and slept upon the ground outdoors, and in the morning left every thing just as it was, and went away forever. A year later the old owner sold me the property, for he could not either rent it or give it away to a native."

"That beats the piggest stories I ever heard," said Scott, laughing. "But what is this that we are coming to?" he asked, as the bearers, who had been running very rapidly, began to slacken their pace.

They had gone quite beyond the city, and were in open and grass-grown and palm-shaded streets beyond Mazagon. Far in the distance they could see the highest turrets of Malabar Hill; but it seemed as though they rose up out of a dense tropical jungle, instead of the heart of a great city. And close at hand, nestling in a little grove of almost impregnable green, lay a low Hindu temple, on the banks of a little lake.

"This is the temple where your Bramhan spends his time just now," answered Richard. "You know we said we should call on him this morning, and thank him for putting you through last night."

"That's an awfully pretty pond," observed Scott, as the bearers now came slowly up to the temple.

"It is the sacred tank, where they can bathe, if they wish, before going into the temple to worship."

"It would be some fun going to church on a hot day, if you could have a swim thrown in without breaking Sunday," observed Scott, calculating on his estimates between the religions of India and America. "Wonder if there are any fish

A HINDU TEMPLE.

in there!" he added. But before Richard could warn him that it would not be precisely in order for a Christian to go fishing in one of those Hindu temple-tanks, the fat Bramhan was beside the palanquin, making very low bows.

He did not attempt to assist them out of the *palki*, for there were too many humble Hindus looking on at that moment; though, if Richard had chosen to tell of it, he could have spoken of more occasions than one when his good friend had taken many a liberty: for the fat Bramhan was a very weak believer in the efficacy of what he professed; and, in less than a year from that time, he gave up his office at the head of this picturesque little temple, though he had to sacrifice an independent fortune to do it, and went with Mr. Raymond to the American mission-station, to be baptized, and taught the Christian theology, preparatory to becoming the exemplary and humble Christian minister that he is to-day.

"I knew you would come!" he exclaimed eagerly; "for no one ever spoke the truth who said that Raymondrao Sahib once broke his word. Come into the temple. I have a place saved for you in the outer court. I have a great treat for you. The beautiful Princess Nuna, the wonderful and celebrated Bramhan girl (whose mother Nuna was born to the noble Shastri Vias, and adopted by the Bramhan family of Yadaba, the rulers of Chandrapur, in the Deccan, and who is now the wife of the ruler), — this her remarkable daughter has been given to the temple service as sacrifice, and is the most beautiful dancer out of the paradise of Indra. She was in Bombay for last night; and, knowing you would be here to-day, I secured her to dance in the temple. Come quickly," he added, "for she is already dancing."

They followed him to the outer court and the position that he had kindly reserved for them, where they obtained a fine view of the figure, upon which all eyes were fixed, — a graceful young girl alone in the centre of the temple, with a bright-colored scarf, and gracefully trailing drapery, a few bright jewels flashing in her ears and about her neck (but less than most Hindu women wore), while her long, glossy black hair hung in light waves far below her waist. She was softly moaning a weird melody, and slowly whirling about, and gracefully bending her body in time with the singing.

It was not precisely what Scott had expected, but—

"It is beautiful, beautiful!" he whispered.

"Yes," replied Mr. Raymond, "just here it is certainly beautiful; but the murli dancing and the common nautch

THE MUSICIANS.

have been disgraced and degraded by the English in India, till they have lost the charms they once possessed, even for the Hindus; and, like all the other grand institutions of antiquity, they are rapidly becoming demoralized."

Sitting beside the altar, ready to take up the service when Nuna should have finished, were three or four other dancers of less celebrity, with their two musicians; but Nuna sang without even a native accompaniment.

"What has that old fellow got in his hands?" asked Scott, looking at one of the musicians, who had just risen to his feet as Nuna began to retreat, and was softly fingering the strings of his instrument.

"Which one do you mean?" questioned Richard.

"Why, the fellow that has the floor now," replied Scott.

"Oh! that is what they call a *saringi*. It is the model of the first violin that was ever made; for there, again, in spite of all that people say to the contrary, India led the world."

Just outside the temple, as they again prepared to enter the palanquin, Scott noticed a curious group of ragged men, two of them sitting on a sort of portable bed with their eyes shut, one of them counting a string of beads, while two stood up at the end of the bed. No two had costumes exactly alike, but they were all as dirty as could well be.

"The wind would blow it off, if they got any more dirt on them. What are they anyway?" asked Scott.

"Beggars," replied Richard dryly, as he tossed a coin upon the bed.

"They look like turtles basking in the sun," said Scott. "They don't seem very miserable."

"No, indeed! they are having a good time," said Mr. Raymond. "It is only a profession in India. There is no disgrace in it."

"Can any one be a beggar who wants to?" Scott asked.

Richard shrugged his shoulders. "I don't imagine one would have to try very hard; but the general claim is, that to pass the examination, and receive a diploma as a competent beggar, one must either have the right of birth (that is, his father and mother must have belonged to the class before him), or he must be a superannuated religious official, who is unable to support himself at the altar. But they stretch that a good deal, I fancy."

At a little distance down the road, they passed a small open square, where a dozen or more children were drawn up in line, and gravely saluted them as they went by.

"What is the matter there?" asked Scott.

SCHOOLBOYS SALUTING.

"The two men behind are teachers, and the boys are scholars of a private school," replied Mr. Raymond.

"A pretty set of scholars!" observed Scott. "There's not one of them a dozen years old."

"That may all be," returned Richard. "But I'll venture, there are not three among them that cannot repeat the multiplication-table up to twenty times twenty without a mistake, and as fast as their tongues will run."

"Are there no larger schools than that?" Scott asked, as they passed out of sight.

"Oh, yes, indeed! any number of them; and smaller ones too, where a few of the children of the wealthy are educated by a priest. They send the little fellows while they are very young; for they have a deal to learn, and but little time to learn it in. Many of the boys are married before

UNDER A PRIEST.

they are as old as you are; and the Hindu girls are married before they are ten, and sometimes even in infancy."

"Were there any girls in that crowd?" Scott asked.

"The girls don't often go to school in India, Scott. They are educated at home, in the branches that become a wife, as they suppose; and reading and writing are not fashionable for the women. They do not consider them lady-like accomplishments."

"I remember hearing mother talk about that," said Scott. "Mother's a great woman on the mission among the women and girls of India. But the missions have schools for girls, haven't they?"

"There are several large mission-schools for both boys and girls, and Sunday schools beside, where they are taught. If you like, we'll go to the mission services to-morrow."

"I should like it above all things!" exclaimed Scott. "And I must take notes on every thing, if it is proper; for I promised my pastor that I'd write him a letter about the foreign missionaries and their work. He's a little wild on the subject. It'll seem like 'The Missionary Herald,' won't it? But I can't help that. I think I can do it, if I keep my eyes open."

They started again at a rapid pace for the hotel; for it was approaching noon, and the excursion to the caves of Elephanta takes more than half a day, unless every thing is favorable.

"That Reverend Ka — Ka — whatever his name is, is a very obliging man," said Scott.

"Last night and this morning he has given you a chance to see the religious caste of Hindu women to the very best advantage. What do you think of them?" inquired Richard.

"Why, they're not bad-looking — females, when they're in full dress," Scott answered, hesitating as to whether he should call them girls or women, they were all so very small. "But I think it's more the fancy way they have of getting themselves up, and the very graceful motions, that make them seem pretty. When I get home I am going to rig Bess up something like this style. I think she'd make a stunning little Hindu. She has an awfully pretty way of walking, that ain't a bit like other girls that go bumping along like jumping-jacks. She moves all over, and nowhere in particular, just as these women do."

"Then, you don't like the Hindu faces?" asked Richard.

"The face is all right," replied Scott; "but they spoil it making so many holes in it. See that woman, now!" he exclaimed, pointing to a daintily dressed Bramhan woman going by. She had an unusual number of ornaments for one who is walking in the street, and proved a good example for Scott. "If she were my sister or my mother, I should want to kiss her sometimes, but ugh! Think of having to get round all that stuff before I could find her lips. Do they ever kiss in India?"

"I suppose they would take those nose-rings off, if they were going to make a real business of it," said Richard.

"There's a pretty costume!" exclaimed Scott, pointing out a woman with a snow-white *sari*, or Hindu shawl, thrown about her.

"She is perhaps in mourning," replied Mr. Raymond.

"White for mourning?" queried Scott. "What in the world is that for? Don't they *know* what is right?"

"Why do people in America wear black, Scott?"

"Why, because it is solemn."

"What makes it solemn?"

"Because it's mourning, I suppose," said Scott, laughing. "Didn't you say this was a temple?" he said to Mr. Raymond, as he stood that afternoon in the main gallery of the caves of Elephanta, with its corridors and arches, a hundred and thirty feet square.

"Yes, this is a temple. Many claim, that, ages ago, the Jains started it. It was literally excavated out of the mountain-side. Do you see, the floor and the pillars and caps and the arched roof are all of one single block of stone? And do you see that figure of Bramha there, behind the bas-relief of Siva? That is the marriage of Siva and the goddess Parvati; and that figure of Bramha, you see, has three heads.

CAVES OF ELEPHANTA.

If the Jain theory be true, it is one of the earliest records in the world, of any idea of a Trinity, or, perhaps better, a triad."

"How do they know that it is a marriage, if it was made so long ago?" inquired Scott.

"Simply because Parvati is standing upon the right hand of Siva; and no woman is allowed to stand upon the right hand of her husband, except during the marriage ceremony."

"They must have enjoyed picking as much as we do whittling, to have dug out all this," observed Scott, looking about him. "It's a big thing, but I wouldn't give a cent for it as a church. Did you ever attend a service here?"

"Just one," replied Richard; "but not the kind of one you mean. I attended the dinner given to the Prince of Wales here a little while ago."

MARRIAGE OF SIVA.

Scott drew a long breath. "Did they dinner that fellow here?" he asked, and, turning with a sigh, added, "I must make a note of that," and demurely walked out of the old temple.

At the ledge entrance, however, his gravity was somewhat shaken by looking up suddenly, to face one of the most peculiar specimens that had ever crossed his path.

"Great Cæsar's ghost!" he groaned, and sat down on the low stone wall.

Richard looked at the object that had caused the shock, and then, with mock anxiety, he asked,—

"My dear young friend, what is it that perplexes you?"

A KATWADI.

"What in the world was that?" asked Scott, helplessly pointing after the figure that had now nearly disappeared.

"A man," replied Mr. Raymond quietly.

"But, merciful sakes, what a man!" groaned Scott. "It was a walking skeleton."

"Just about as near it as one could come without hitting," replied Richard. "But you would be astonished to find out how far from a skeleton that fellow is in strength."

His skin was very dark, and it certainly looked as though there was nothing under it but bones; and over the joints where it must bend occasionally, it lay in dry, leathery folds.

"He looked for all the world like a rhinoceros," said Scott.

The man had nothing on but a dirty cloth about the loins,

and another twisted once round his head, leaving a mass of absolutely uncombed hair above it and below it. The hair was black at the roots, but dyed red at the ends.

"He is a full-blooded muni,—one of the kind that you have probably read about, who sometimes have held up an arm till it became stiff in that position, and could never come down again; who hung themselves up by iron hooks thrust through their muscles. They will lie down, and apparently die, and remain so for a month and more, with their flesh cold and hard, and their joints stiff. The heart will stop beating, for all that the most elaborate medical instruments can determine, and there is no observable breathing. But, when the time is up, they wake up, and go about their business. There are munis, too, who have fasted for forty-five days."

"You don't mean gone absolutely without any thing to eat!" exclaimed Scott, interrupting him.

"Yes, I mean exactly that."

"Well, I should almost think that man had just been doing it," said Scott. "But what was that painting on his bony chest?"

"That represented the two great principals of Hindu theology,—the Preserver and Destroyer."

"I thought there were three principals. Is it fair to be partial to the two, and leave out the Creator?" asked Scott.

"Bramha, the creator, is rarely worshipped or represented alone. There is no idol of Bramha in all India, and no prayer is ever offered to him. He is supposed to have no form, except when a part of the trinity, as you saw the three-headed god in the cave. He is in every thing, and every thing is Bramha."

"I should think they would be careful, then, how they

handle things in general," said Scott, as they walked on toward the boat that was awaiting them, to take them back to Bombay.

"You think just right, Scott. Even my little boy Moro will not so much as tread upon a bug in the street, no matter how much trouble it costs him to prevent it. They will not eat meat for that reason."

"Are all munis like that fellow at the caves?" Scott asked, as they stepped again upon the wharf in Bombay.

"Not by any means," answered Mr. Raymond. "They are of all varieties, from the gentlemanly soldier to such a vagabond as this one. Why, one of the fiercest leaders of the mutiny, one of the strongest soldiers of that Sepoy rebellion, was Dhondaram, a muni; and to-day he is an outlaw, for whom England offers ten thousand dollars. We have plenty of time, and on the way to the hotel we will drive round to the Hindu temple by the Byculla. You can see any number of them there. It is the great camping-ground for the munis that come on to the island in the course of their pilgrimages."

Mr. Raymond directed the driver of a buggy they engaged, and, seating himself, continued,—

"They are forever moving. They make tremendous pilgrimages. They never do a day's work, but they harden themselves to wonderful endurance. They torture and deform themselves, on the principle that suffering is meritorious, and then go about, and allow the public to support them, showing their marks as credentials. I saw a muni once, measuring the entire distance across India, from one side to the other, by lying down, and stretching his hands as far before him as possible, and making a mark with his fingers. Then, putting his toes to that mark, he would lie down again; and so on for the fourteen hundred miles."

Scott whistled, and stretched himself a little more comfortably in the buggy.

"It makes my back ache," he remarked with a sigh.

"Look there!" added Mr. Raymond, pointing to a group

WANDERING MUNIS.

of men in various costumes, resting about the roots and trunk of an old tree in the open parade-ground. "Those are munis, and they are not bad-looking fellows."

"They're a bad lot!" said Scott with a shiver,—"worse than our gypsies, I believe. But do they bruise themselves that way just to make begging pay?"

"They pretend that they do it for religion," replied his friend. "And I fancy a good deal of it is for the attention and glory they get. They very often make an oath of silence for some number of years, and refuse to speak a word, or pay any attention to any one, in that time. Some of them used to have a trick of going round stark naked, pretending that they were too holy for clothes; but the English Government has been arresting them lately for it, and now they are more careful."

"They must like something or other about it more than I do," remarked Scott.

"Well, here is an example; and you can judge for yourself what the fellow liked. There is a munï in North India, who, a few years ago, had gone through every manner of self-torture that he could hear of or invent. His name was so great, that he would draw dense crowds after him whereever he went. At last, to get up something new, he had a chair made, so that, as he sat in it, every part of his body would touch only on the points of nails; and in this chair he was carried about the country. A wealthy Hindu, who wanted to make atonement for his sins, and lay up a large balance in heaven, offered this muni a beautiful house and large garden, and agreed to pay all the bills that he would contract for his personal support, so long as he would live there. The muni accepted, and spent three months in the most luxurious seclusion. But that was all he could stand of it. He gave back the house, gave up the support, ordered his chair of nails and his bearers, and at once started upon a tour of the whole of India."

Just then the buggy stopped at the temple-gate; and, going into the court, they saw, as Richard had predicted, a most remarkable array of the holy men, in all attitudes, preparing their suppers, eating, smoking, drinking even, and sleeping. Some of them were as nearly naked as they dared to be. Some were covered with rags in an almost unlimited quantity. Some had gashes and scars all over them, and all sorts of deformities, and some were satisfied with fantastic painting.

"What a place this would be to turn P. T. Barnum into!" exclaimed Scott. "Wouldn't he have fun picking out specimens?"

They only stopped for a moment, for it was growing late; and in a short time they were seated at the supper-table, with Moro and Sayad behind them, and ravenous appetites urging them on.

"I believe I could eat Esofali's French cooking with cardamom-seed sauce to-night," Scott remarked; "and the cook into the bargain."

"You'd have to shut your eyes before you began on the cook, or you would never digest him, if he is any thing like the rest of the cooks of India," returned Richard, laughing.

CHAPTER XV.

A HOME AMONG THE HINDUS.

THE result of the Sunday among the mission churches and Sunday schools Scott reported to his pastor in the following letter, not re-written a dozen times, trying to make it falsely grand, but the result of notes, taken during the day, on what he thought his pastor wanted :—

"The mission chapel of the American mission among the Marathis in Bombay is situated in one of the busiest districts of the city. Along the street it fronts upon, there pours an incessant stream of Hindus of all castes, — Mussulmans of different sects, Parsis with their ugly hats, Jews of more than one tribe, Chinese with their pig-tails, Africans, and Europeans. The Christian service is conducted much as it is in our own church, only the congregation looks very funny. The church numbers about sixty-five members, and has a native pastor of Bramhan birth.

"The Sunday school meets at nine in the morning. There are about two hundred scholars. Most of the children are native Christians; but there are some Hindus, too, who go to the day-schools of the mission. They use the same 'International' series that we use at home.

"The language, both in church and Sunday school, is the Marathi. It sounds very funny to hear the children singing, both their music and poetry are arranged so differently from ours. At first they had to translate our hymns, and set them again to our music, and now there are many of these in use; but I can imagine how odd the arrangement must have seemed from the way that theirs strikes me. Some years ago, however, a young man was converted who had great talent in writing poetry, and understood music thoroughly. So he began writing Christian hymns, and setting them to Marathi metres. They are liked very much by the native Christians, and even people outside like them very much too. The superintendent in the Sunday school had them sing 'Come to Jesus' for me, first to the old music, that almost made me cry, it was so much like something from home: then they sang one of Sankey's pieces; but they did not do that so well. Then they sang some of their own poet's work.

"The classes went on just as we do; but some of the scholars were almost naked, and did not seem to have cultivated a very intimate acquaintance with soap and water. They were the Hindu children, — pupils of the day-schools. Their teachers go out on Sunday morning, and collect them, and bring them in. Otherwise, perhaps, they would not come at all; for they are very careless about time, and, even if they wanted to come, they would most likely be a half-hour or so late.

"The preaching is at four in the afternoon; then at five the missionaries and native teachers go out into the broad porch of the church, and there they sing for a few minutes, and then begin to talk to any who will stop and listen. They are very often interrupted by people with absurd questions, who only want to break up the meeting, and raise a laugh. Then they sometimes preach in the open air, and sometimes even in English.

"At one place in Bombay the missionaries began preaching in the street, near where there was a large public school, and just about as the school was to be dismissed. It was found that the boys would listen for about twenty minutes, and then begin to make such a noise that it was impossible to go on. Once a missionary asked if there was any one there who understood English. 'Yes, sir: I do,' resounded from different parts. 'Very well,' said the missionary: 'if you will keep quiet, I will talk to you in English.' — 'All right, sir! Go ahead, sir!' they shouted; and he preached there in English once a week for several months. They were tolerably well behaved and quiet.

"The missionaries tell a host of interesting stories. The Bramhan pastor I spoke of, while he was a rigid Hindu, was hired to teach in the mission-school. He taught because he received pay for it; but he hated the Christian books, till at last he broke down, and himself became the very good Christian minister that he is to-day.

"One day an old robber and murderer came into church when the missionary was talking on, 'The blood of Jesus Christ his Son cleanseth us from all sin.' After the service he came up, and timidly asked if that blood could cleanse from the sin of a murder. And when the missionary said 'Yes,' he went on, 'Of five murders? Of ten? Of twenty?' And on the spot he gave himself to God, and lived and died a good, honest Christian.

"The number of Christians has doubled in India in the past ten years; and a missionary told me, that, if the same rate were kept up that has been going on from 1861 to 1871, India would be a Christian nation in less than a century, but that, instead of going on at the same rate, the rate itself is constantly increasing.

"I'm afraid this is not a complete letter; but you know I have only been here one Sunday, and a few days beside; and oh, there is such a wonderful world to see, that I am thoroughly bewildered, and hardly seem to know any thing!"

"Mercy!" Scott gasped, when he had finished. "I feel like a missionary myself. I wonder if he will think I have been putting on airs! I hope not; but I've been using some long words, and stating facts like a newspaper."

He folded the letter, and, after directing the envelope, put it in, and was in the act of wetting the stamp on his tongue, when Richard stopped him.

"If you do that, you'll have to take it to the office yourself, Scott; for the boy thinks that saliva makes it unclean, and that he would defile himself to touch it."

Scott laughed, and wet the stamp with water.

Early Monday morning they were on their way southward into the mountains, and the cool, bracing air of Puna. The moment the cars started there was immediate relief; for the first-class carriages of the English trains in India have been made expressly to combat the heat, which is sometimes intolerable, especially when running through the dry and open sand-plains.

It was an endless delight to Scott to sit in the window, that was shaded from the sun by a wooden awning, and watch the constantly changing view. Sometimes they were dashing past old ruins, draped in parasitic vines, and sometimes beautiful hillsides lay about them, without a sign of human life.

"How many people did you say there were in India?" asked Scott.

"About two hundred and fifty million, — more than in all Europe and Siberia," replied Mr. Raymond.

"There's a good deal of vacant land, after all," remarked Scott.

"On these mountain-sides, yes, except as they use it for pasturage and hunting; but there are also broad plains to the north that support over seven hundred and fifty souls to the square mile, which is the largest average population in the world."

"Well, there are two things that I don't understand about India," said Scott reflectively.

"You are doing better than most, if there are only two," replied Richard, laughing. "But what are they?"

"Well, why do the women color their teeth and finger-nails, and what makes the butter so white?" Scott answered abruptly.

"One is because they want to, and the other is because they can't help it," replied Richard solemnly.

"Well, which is which?" asked Scott.

"They color their finger-nails and their toe-nails with red dye, chiefly because it is the fashion; and some of the women, but not all by any means, stain their teeth black when they are married, professedly because they say they do not wish to attract the attention of any other men: so they make themselves look ugly."

"I hope they succeed," observed Scott emphatically.

"They might," replied Richard, "but that so many do it, that the men become used to it, and think them just as pretty that way as any other. But in the case of the butter, that is so white, because it is made of Buffaloes' milk, as there are very few cows in India."

"I thought it was lard at first, and I did not eat any till after we went to Esofali's; and his was so much worse, that it made the hotel butter seem very fair."

"If you had tasted the butter at Esofali's, you would not have thought it bad. It was not our butter at all, but ghi, or clarified butter, that we had there, — a preparation made of the milk itself, instead of cream, that the natives are very fond of; and I quite agree with them."

"Perhaps I shall some day," thought Scott doubtfully.

It was night when they reached Puna; and Scott had little opportunity to see the beautiful, and at the same time miserable, mountain city. Mr. Raymond's large coach and two fiery horses were at the station, waiting to hurry them away as soon as the servants could finish falling on their faces, and kissing their master's feet. But Scott kept his eyes open, and saw all that there was to see.

"Look there!" he exclaimed, as a weird group appeared in the light of a torch held by one of the Hindus. "Is that a new-fangled bathing-tank, or is it only a moving drinking-fountain?"

"A little of both, and not exactly either," replied Richard. "That is the house of a Bramhan; and those fellows are

A BRAMHAN AND PILGRIMS.

pilgrims, who thought it best to stop on their way, wherever they are going, to get a touch of holy water; quenching their thirst, and washing their sins away, and washing their hands and faces, all at the same time. They have made up a small purse for the Bramhan; and, while his servant holds the torch, he is administering the blessing."

"Would he give me a dose, if I should go up there?" asked Scott.

"Go up and try," replied Richard, ordering his coachman to stop.

"I believe I'd rather be excused," said Scott; but, seeing Mr. Raymond laughing at him, he changed his mind, and, getting out of the carriage, made his way up to the platform upon which the priest stood.

Seeing a white person approaching, the crowd of pilgrims fell back in horror, lest they should be defiled while engaged in their ablutions. Scott hesitated for a moment, for the face of the Bramhan was not so re-assuring as that of Kashinath had been: but, gathering his courage, he went up as he had seen the native; and, laying a piece of silver on the platform, he knelt, and put his hands to his mouth in the form of a cup.

The priest looked at him in astonishment for a moment; then, seeing only the half-laughing face of a boy, he simply smiled at the presumption, and deliberately emptied the entire contents of the *kuja* all over him.

"You wretch!" gasped Scott; and for an instant he was on the point of flying at the Bramhan, holy as he was, with his clinched fists. But his eye caught the piece of silver he had laid on the platform; and, thinking his own coin the best to pay him in, he picked it up, and, with a shout, ran away.

The Bramhan only laughed over the joke; and, dripping with water, Scott crawled back into the carriage again, where he found Richard also convulsed with laughter.

"I came within an inch of breaking his neck," he said defiantly. "And I almost wish I had."

"It was a little better not to, under the circumstances," replied Richard; "for the person of a Bramhan is very sacred, and I fear your wanderings in India would have come to a speedy close."

"Is a Bramhan so much better than any one else?" asked Scott.

"Decidedly," said Richard without hesitation. "Any one who strikes a Bramhan is sure to become a hog as soon as he dies."

"Sooner be a hog than a Bramhan, any day," muttered Scott sullenly; for his wet clothes were very uncomfortable. "I suppose those fellows are so very holy, that they never do any thing wrong themselves," he added, as the horses started again.

"That is precisely the case," said Richard. "They are so holy, that they do about as they please. Sin runs off from them like water from a duck's back. What would defile any other caste in India will really do them no harm at all. At any rate, the people believe so; and that is all that is wanted."

"They're a good-for-nothing set anyway," Scott grumbled.

"You're mistaken there, Scott," said Richard; "for, really, they have been the sharpest and most profound scholars in the world. If they were not held back by their bigotry, we should see wonderful things in science accomplished by them. It is to these Bramhans that India is indebted for all her profound knowledge ages ago. They are very sharp and shrewd, many of them; and a missionary almost dreads seeing them come in to his meetings."

"Do they attend Christian churches?" exclaimed Scott, again becoming interested.

"Certainly they do, and some of them are very constant attendants."

"I should think they would be afraid of being converted."

"On the contrary, many of them enjoy it; and there are

some Bramhans who know almost as much about the Bible as a good many Christians. They are very fond of getting into arguments, too, after the services are ended. I was once at a mission sermon, where the text was "Faith." The missionary had been very earnest; and a fine-faced Bramhan, who had listened intently through it all, rose as soon as the benediction was pronounced, and, in the politest way, asked if he might say a word upon the sermon. I saw the missionary looked very sober; but as every one stopped, and appeared in no hurry to go out, he could find no excuse, and had to give the permission.

"'Faith is very good,' said the Bramhan; 'but no faith is better. See how the monkey carries her young. She does not trouble herself to touch them. They cling about her neck with a death grip. She could not even shake them off if she tried. She can go where she will with them. That is faith. You are the little monkey. But see how the cat carries her little ones. She takes them tenderly in her mouth. She does not hurt them, or drop them. They are perfectly safe, and have nothing to do but let her carry them. That is no faith. That is better. I am the kitten.'"

"That was a sticker, sure," said Scott, somewhat downcast to see any thing that in any way belonged to him trodden on. "What could the parson say to that?"

"He got out of it better than I thought. He grew red in the face, as the audience applauded the Bramhan, and he saw all his earnestness worse than lost; but suddenly a happy thought struck him, and very quietly he said, 'O Bramhan, you are very wise. You should not defame yourself in that way. There are idiots and helpless fellows that have no strength, and must be carried; and, thank God, there are cats to carry them! But there are also strong, brave, and able men, who do not need to be pushed through the world, but can cling for themselves. You, my friend, are brave enough and strong enough to be something more than a helpless kitten.' "

"Good one!" cried Scott. "I can see that old Bramhan going out with his tail between his legs."

"And so can I," returned Richard, laughing.

"And so there are monkeys here too, are there? I had not seen any, and had forgotten my geography. I meant to ask you."

"There are a few," replied Richard very gravely.

"Only a few?" repeated Scott with a sigh. "I was in hopes we should see them as thick as they are in story-books."

"A few million, I mean, or probably a few hundred million would be nearer right," replied Richard. "They are very sacred animals here, and run about the cities even, and do as they please everywhere, and even have temples erected for their especial benefit, where they are boarded free of charge. You will see one if we go to Benares."

"It must be fun," said Scott.

"It is fun for a time, but you will soon have too much of it. They are as troublesome as the squirrels in Beverly. A friend of mine, a European physician, was particularly well patronized by the wretches. They would come into his windows every time they were left open. They would eat up every thing that was eatable, and spoil what was not."

"Why didn't he kill them?" asked Scott.

"He had too many native servants, who would have reported it, and won him the ill will of the natives. But he took a better way. There was one big monkey in particular, who was the most familiar. He would sit on the limb of a huge tree, just outside the doctor's office-window. He would

THE DOCTOR'S PATIENT.

contentedly scratch himself, and watch all that was going on; and if any thing was left on a plate, and the room was vacated for a moment, it was sure to be gone. One morning the doctor saw the monkey watching, and quietly emptied a large bottle of Brandeth's liver-pills on to the plate. He pretended to eat some of them, and then went out. The monkey watched him drive away as usual; and a half-hour later, when the doctor came back, the plate was entirely empty. He lived there for three years after that, and told me that he never again knew of a monkey coming into the house."

"Good enough!" exclaimed Scott, laughing. "But I don't suppose there is really any danger from them, is there? They would never hurt any one."

"That depends," replied Richard. "When there are a lot of them together, or when they are offended at something, they will sometimes attack a man. When I was seventeen years old, I was employed on one of the surveys for a railroad in India. It was a very rough life that we led, with a guard of English soldiers to protect us; and we had to go well armed ourselves, for there were many attacks from wild beasts, as well as offended natives. We did not mind much about dress, and were rather ragged before we had finished our work. All we cared for was to protect our heads from the sun. After the day's work was done, the youngest of us used to make raids, contrary to the officers' orders, in search of cocoanuts and other fruit. I was out on an expedition once, with a large mastiff belonging to one of the officers. He was an ugly fellow, but was very fond of me. I saw three elegant cocoanuts lying on the ground, just in the edge of a jungle. The dog would have made a fuss if there had been a tiger round, so I felt safe enough in making a dive for them; but I had no sooner made the leap, than all of a sudden it seemed as though a dozen packs of fire-crackers were all set off at once, all about me, and I found myself literally surrounded by a host of monkeys. I don't imagine they would have hurt me, but that 'Spit,' the dog, was mad that he was taken off his guard, and snapped at the tail of one of them. He gave a howl, and instantly the whole lot were upon us. I had my clearing-axe in my hand, but it was absolutely all I could do to keep it swinging right and left among them; for they even caught my arm, and held my feet so that I could not move, and clung about my waist, where I could not touch them; and they could very easily have got the best of me, but that Spit used his teeth with a vengeance; and the cries of pain from the wounded frightened the rest, and they began to draw back a little into the trees."

ALL FOR THREE COCOANUTS.

"Did you get your cocoanuts?" asked Scott.

"Yes, I got my cocoanuts. I thought I had earned them, and I would not go back without them. But you may be sure that when I had them safe in my arms, I made good time out of the jungle."

Just then the carriage whirled into a grove, through two high gate-posts; and the rattle of wheels was lost on the soft, yielding roadway.

"Here we are at last!" exclaimed Richard, as they drew up before a massive veranda of heavy stone pillars and stucco arches, and a smooth, stone floor, with a broad, curtained door at the back, and two deep windows.

There were a dozen servants standing by the veranda to welcome Mr. Raymond, and two colored lanterns were hung in the porch.

"This is a grand old spot!" Scott exclaimed enthusiastically, as he alighted.

"It was the home of a wealthy Mussulman once," replied Richard, in a voice that caused Scott to look up suddenly; and he thought he detected tears in Mr. Raymond's eyes as he welcomed his home and his old servants again: so he at once turned away, and walked slowly down the veranda.

Early in the morning, after the *chotà hazri* that Richard had spoken of, the two went out for a walk through the grove and garden. A more gorgeous spot Scott was sure he had never seen.

"I don't wonder you love it!" he cried. "But why have you never told me how beautiful your home was?"

"I am very glad if you like it," Richard replied, without answering the question.

Just behind the house they came out upon a superb little lake.

Scott gave one cry of joy, and stood enraptured.

All about the border drooped beautiful flowering shrubs. Just behind them rose trees with dense green foliage, filled with fruit such as Scott had never seen before, but often read of; and again behind them towered the long, slender trunks and bushy heads of the palm-trees. All this was reflected in the water; but, as if that were not sufficient, the whole surface was dotted with brilliant aquatic leaves and blossoms, where, predominant, was the sacred *tala*, growing up from the coolest, deepest depths of the lake, a tiny green stem, till it reached the surface, then shooting heavenward its bright leaves, tinting the whole surface of the water. At one end of this lake was a flight of rough marble steps, all ivy-grown, leading down into the water.

"Here is a fishing-pond, where you may drop your line as often as you like," said Richard, smiling at Scott's enthusiasm.

"A fishing-pond!" said Scott reprovingly. "Don't call a beautiful spot like that an old mud fishing-pond. What is it, Mr. Raymond?"

"It is the marble-bedded tank that supplies the house and the servants' huts with water. It is the salvation of crowded India, that all the natives but the vilest of the breed of fakirs, and a few in the mountains, are forever bathing. They will never even eat in the morning till they have bathed certain parts of their bodies. If I were a native, now, I should call this a sacred *tulao;* but, being only a Christian (as they say), I can only call it my water-tank."

"It's pretty enough either way," said Scott. "But I should say the natives have the best of you there. A tank makes a fellow think of an old attic and musty water."

THE BEAUTIFUL TANK.

Extending back from the house, on either side of this tank, were the huts of the servants; for none of them ever sleep in the house of the master. They have families of their own; and, except as they may steal more or less from the mansion, they support themselves and their families, both in food and clothes, out of their earnings.

"It must be rather expensive, running a house with so many servants," Scott remarked, as they walked past the line of low huts, where the front wall was only a bamboo matting, that through the day was drawn back, letting the sunlight literally stream through the whole house, in front of which extended a platform of smooth stone, on which a dozen naked little children were playing, and their mothers were cooking the breakfast or working.

THE WATER-CARRIERS.

"It would be expensive in America," replied Richard; "but here the servant costs almost nothing. Do you see that fellow on the bullock yonder, and the one beside him? They are my *bhistis*, or water-carriers. The place is very large, so I have to have two; and those clumsy things on the animal's back are goat-skins, in which they are going to draw water at the tank. They carry all the water for the gardeners, and all the water for the baths and the table and the cook. You noticed, perhaps, that the legs of all the tables and chairs in the house stood in little metal cups?"

"I did, indeed," said Scott. "And it was only reading my letters from home that put it out of my head to ask what the matter was. You may think me pretty inquisitive."

"That is one way to learn," replied Richard, smiling. "Another is, to go to college. But those cups the *bhisti* has to fill with water every morning. It keeps the white ants from getting into the furniture. If they once get in, they are as much worse than American moths as can be. They will literally eat up every thing, — the wood, the upholstering, the stuffing. They will grind it all to powder. Then the *bhisti* has to sprinkle the Kus-Kus mats before the doors and windows, through the dry weather, to keep the air in the house damp and cool. And all the poor fellows get for it is a dollar a week, to feed and clothe themselves and their families."

"It doesn't cost him much to clothe the children," said Scott, looking at the ragged little *dhuti* that was twisted about the loins of the oldest child in sight, — a boy of about nine years, — while the rest of the entirely naked little fellows were playing in the sun. "But what's the use of having so many servants anyway?" he added.

"That is a matter of necessity," replied Richard. "From their mode of life, the Hindus have not the strength and endurance that we have, as a rule. Nationally they are a slow and lazy set: so it has come about that they have taken to doing just one thing, whatever that is; and their children have grown up to do just that, and nothing else, till it is an actual division of religious caste with them; and those who are born *bhistis* will die *bhistis*, and the boys that wait on us will do no other work. The cook will not wait on the table; the little brooms, as we call the fellow that sweeps, will not wash our clothes; and the *dhobi*, or washerman, will not cook, or do any thing else. He washes by beating the clothes unmercifully between two stones, in cold water; and he tears them so every time, that we have to keep a tailor in our list of house servants."

"Why doesn't he use a tub and scrubbing-board?" asked Scott.

"Oh! his father and grandfather never did, and he says what was right for them is right for him."

"But I would make him, if I wanted him to," said Scott.

"You would have harder work than you think for. By a long struggle I have succeeded in introducing some of our notions, but it was almost more than they were worth."

"Why was that?"

"Why, because, the moment I suggested some new style, the servant would always object to it. He would think there was some evil in it, or would fear being defiled in some way. If I insisted, or brought it about in any way, by hiding his old implements, he would sometimes consent; but if he hurt himself with the new thing, or if any thing happened to him or his family, — if one of his children fell sick, — he would instantly declare that it was because he had used it, and would leave my service."

"I'd say 'Good riddance,' and get another," remarked Scott spitefully.

"That's easier said than done, my boy. For he would instantly spread it among his friends and caste, charging all his sorrow to the infernal machine and to me; and several times I have had to give it up, or send to Goa for Portuguese Christians to come down and do the work."

"What is that fellow doing?" Scott asked, as they passed one of the little huts, at some distance from the house, where

HE IS SACRIFICING TO HIS TOOLS.

a native, with a plate of rice in his hands, was bowing before a low bench, upon which was a collection of curious tools and a wreath of flowers.

"That is my carpenter," replied Mr. Raymond. "He is going to begin an addition to the stable to-day; and, as it is a large undertaking, he is sacrificing to his tools, with an idea that they will do the work better for it."

"What a fool!" muttered Scott. "I guess he'd find a little elbow-grease would go a good deal farther."

THE COBRA AND MONGOOSE.

"I don't know," replied Richard. "There are hosts of Christians who believe that the great efficacy of prayer is not so much in persuading God to do one way or another, when he has already decreed the end from the beginning, as it is in putting the one who is praying both in sympathy with God, and in sympathy with what he is praying for."

"Where are the stables?" asked Scott, who had a New-England boy's admiration for the horse and every thing pertaining to him.

"Just around yonder corner," replied Mr. Raymond. "I

was on the way there; for, thinking you might like a horseback ride before it was too warm, I ordered the horses saddled."

"Thank you! thank you! That'll be just the boss!" exclaimed Scott, starting eagerly toward the stable.

"SHE RECOGNIZES ME."

On the way their attention was attracted by the Portuguese butler, who was leaning through the dense growth at one side of the path leading to the house.

Creeping slowly up to him, they saw a little animal no larger than a cat, and with a much more slender body, just in the act of killing a large snake.

"Gracious! I should have bet on the snake every time!" exclaimed Scott. "How in the world did that little fellow ever do it?"

"It is a little *mongoose*," replied Richard. "That is the

way he makes his living; and, if it were not for him, these jungles would be uninhabitable, they would be so overrun with poisonous snakes."

In the stable they found the *scyce*, or groom, just oiling the last hoof of a sleek, black mare. She looked eagerly forward, and neighed as Mr. Raymond entered.

"She knows me," he said, going up to her, and patting her, and taking up one foot after another, while the *scyce* stood back, grinning, and happy to see his work examined and commended.

"What was that place before each stall?" Scott asked, as they started.

"It was where the *scyce* sleep. They never leave the horses while they are in the stall; and, when the owner drives without the coachman, the *scyce* always runs beside the horse,—to hold him, or be on hand in case of accident."

"But there was a place in front of *each* stall."

"Yes. We have to have a different *scyce* for each horse, for their custom laws will allow them to take care of but one horse at a time."

They did not ride far beyond Mr. Raymond's grounds, but they were extensive enough to have given them more than one morning's enjoyment. Just before them, through the entire drive, ran an ugly little spotted dog.

"He doesn't belong to you, does he?" Scott asked, seeing that Mr. Raymond noticed him watching the dog.

Richard laughed. "He does, indeed! and I am very proud of him. Don't you think him beautiful?"

"It might be something like Esofali's curry and cardimom-seed sauce. I might get used to him in time," replied Scott doubtfully.

"He has saved my life more than once, and he may save yours this very day," said Richard solemnly.

"That makes him look better right away. But how did it happen?" asked Scott. "And am I in any particular danger?"

"None just now," returned Richard. "And the way that I know it, is that that ugly little dog is trotting along contentedly before us. He is cross, he is dirty, he is an incorrigible thief, he is a native dog; and I call him 'Pariah,' because he possesses all the worst qualities of that lowest and worst class of Hindus. But all the beauty that he lacks everywhere else has centred in his nose. He can smell a tiger as far as I could hit him with my rifle. It was right in this very spot."

Scott cringed a little, and fixed his eyes on the spotted dog, that suddenly became an object of decided interest to him, and a little ugly lump of flesh upon whose judgment he was resting an immense importance.

"I was riding along here, thinking of a sugar-factory that I was building, and paying no attention to any thing about me, when that little cur began to whine, and slink back beside the horse. Then, with his tail between his legs, he began to shiver, and stood right still in the middle of the road. I thought it was probably a snake in the grass; for I didn't know the dog well then, and was about to drive on, when, as I turned, my eyes fell upon the handsomest tiger I ever saw, right in that tall grass over there. He was surely a man-eater, and very hungry, or he would never have come so near the house. I have never seen one about here before or since, and was not expecting it."

"Didn't it frighten you?" asked Scott.

"It certainly would if I had had time," replied Richard; "but he had evidently been creeping nearer and nearer the huts, driven by hunger, waiting for the first thing that should come in his way; and now he stood erect. His head was thrown back, and he was just in the act of settling on his haunches to spring at me. He looked even larger than he was, in comparison with that little cur; and the worst of it was, that my horse caught sight of him, and began to rear and lunge, and try to turn."

"Why didn't you let him go?" asked Scott. "I should have bet on his heels, I think."

"You would have lost your bet, then," said Richard; "for, as sure as he had turned, the fellow would have sprung: but seeing the commotion, and that we were in no hurry to get away, the tiger stood up again, and began to watch us, as though he rather enjoyed the fun. I had a large forty-four-caliber pistol with me, but that was all."

Scott still kept his eyes on the little dog, saying, —

"I thought that looking at a wild beast would frighten him away."

"That will do very well for a story-book," replied Richard; "and, indeed, it is a fact, if every thing else is in order. If you come upon a creature suddenly, when he does not expect you, or when he is not driven by hunger, and if you keep perfectly still, with your eyes fixed on him, the chances are that he will either turn away, or that you will never live to tell of having tried the experiment, and failed. But when the beast has the best of you by being ready to spring when you see him, when you are sitting on a horse that is frightened out of his wits, and dancing to the best of his ability, and when hunger has already made the creature mad enough to come right into your own lawn, why, the thing is changed. I had on a broad-brimmed, soft hat, with a long white puggery on it; and, just to keep the horse quiet, I threw it over his

"HE SEEMED TO ENJOY THE SHOW."

ears and eyes, and with one hand tucked it under his bridle to hold it fast. The tiger pricked up his ears, and seemed to enjoy the show hugely. He even stood up straighter, and I could see his muscles relax. I had not thought of it before, but this gave me an idea. He was off his guard then, and the horse would obey me. Very quietly I drew my pistol, and cocked it. Then I sent the spurs deep into the horse's side, and, with a leap and a groan, he sprang right at the tiger."

"Glory!" ejaculated Scott.

"I said so a little later, but not just then," observed Richard, wiping the perspiration from his forehead, as the thought of that exciting moment sent the blood rushing through his veins. "The tiger was not twenty-five feet away. He actually started up onto his hind-feet, he was so surprised at the sight of a horse with a felt hat on, and a huge white puggery, bearing down upon him. Then I fired, and struck him in the breast. With a frightful yelp he rolled over on his back. He was not dead, by any means, but had only lost his balance. I tried to stop the horse; but he was wild, and in an instant had planted a fore-foot directly on the tiger's furry side. He sprang and lunged; and had not the tiger held him fast, fixing his savage teeth in the horse's fore-leg, he would have unseated me. But it gave me a magnificent shot; and, without waiting to see how long I was going to stick to the saddle, I leaned forward, and fired with my pistol not five inches from the tiger's ear. And that finished him."

Scott drew a long, quivering breath. "I'd rather be excused from tiger-hunting," he said decidedly.

"But tiger-hunting is quite another thing; for there you are prepared, and nine times out of ten the tiger is wholly unprepared, and it is he who would rather be excused. The butler was telling me this morning that there is a tiger giving them a deal of trouble in a little village not far away, where I have a farm and a factory, and that they are very anxious to have me get up a hunt, and rid them of it. They call it their great-uncle, they are so afraid to offend it, lest it should have some divinity about it, and revenge itself. Wouldn't you like to go upon a hunt?"

It was altogether too tempting; and, forgetting his fears, Scott exclaimed, "Indeed I should! When can we go?"

"In three days, if nothing happens," replied Mr. Raymond. "But we must hold ourselves open to having our plans changed the moment our agents discover any clew that we can work upon."

"Yes, indeed, sir!" responded Scott eagerly; for, beyond every thing else, he did not for a moment forget the mission upon which he had come, or lose an atom of the eagerness he had at first felt, to carry out the end for which they were in India, no matter where it might take them, or what it might cost.

"Had you ever any other tussles with tigers?" he asked, as they rode toward home again.

"Nothing so close as that," replied Richard. "It's a great mistake that our friends in America make, to think that terrible tigers and poisonous snakes and frightful reptiles grow on every bush in India. But long ago, when I was only a boy, working on the railroad, I saw a man-eater take a feast. The work was done for the day, and most of the men were lying round the flag-centre, enjoying the sunset. The soldiers who were not so tired were strolling at a little distance. There was a young Irishman in the guard, who had thrown himself carelessly on the ground, with his gun beside him, when suddenly the natives about him gave a cry, and started away; for, from a high bank almost over his head, a tiger sprang upon him. Before any one could move, it had seized him by the throat, and dragged him back into the jungle.

where they dared not follow without torches, it was so late. The officer was standing very near when the attack was made, and he was a brave fellow too; but he was not quick enough to save the soldier's life. He had a struggle with the tigers once himself. His bungalow, or house, had to be some-

A FATAL LEAP.

thing movable, of course; but as he was going to occupy it for a year or more, while we were at work, he had it made as comfortable as possible. We were right in the heart of the tiger districts: but it was so hot, that he had to have his bungalow as open as possible; and, to prevent an unexpected visitor, he had the front made of light but strong bars, and open, like a prison-window."

"I should think he would have felt like a bird in a cage," said Scott.

"It proved very effective, however: for one day, while he was reading, he was suddenly aroused by a crash on the bars; and, looking up, there were two enormous tigers sprawled out against the grating, panting, and reaching their great paws within ten feet of his head."

SURPRISED BY UNINVITED GUESTS.

"That was a menagerie turned inside out. He had a chance to see how the animals must like it to have the boys poke them with sticks at the circus," remarked Scott.

"That may all be; but there was no certainty that those bars would not break. He had not estimated the strength of two tigers at once. But he had several rifles at hand; and, picking up one of them, he fired a ball right into the open mouth of one tiger. The other turned to retreat; but, with the other rifle, the officer gave him a parting shot, that caused him to leave his track in blood for nearly a mile, to a jungle, where the men found him dead the next morning."

Another mail was waiting, with more letters from America, when they reached home for breakfast.

AN OLD-TIME MAIL-TRAIN.

"Only the twenty-ninth day from Beverly!" Scott exclaimed, as he read the date. "That's what I call on time in two motions."

"It took the mail three months to reach us from America, even in Bombay, when I first came out."

"Well, how on earth did they ever succeed in sending letters so far into the forests and hills as this, before there were railways?" asked Scott.

"They had a native mail-train that was wonderfully rapid, when one considered what it was made of. They put the letters into two little bags (there were never many of them), and the bags they tied on to the ends of poles. Two Hindus took these poles over their shoulders, and two more, carrying torches, went with them, — one in front, and one behind. These men were trained from birth to run very rapidly, and for a long distance. They bound their girdles close about them, and started with the mail."

"Why didn't they send horsemen?" asked Scott.

"Simply because the men could go faster and farther than the best horses, and would not wear out under it. When they came to the jungles, the men with the torches lit them, and, shouting as they went, threw them about their heads, to make them smoke, and frighten the wild beasts."

Scott had forgotten his letters for a moment, in hearing of the old postmen and their long routes; but now he turned again to the welcome sheets. He read and re-read; and at last, folding them with a happy sigh, he said to Mr. Raymond, who was waiting the result, —

"It's all good news. Father is better, and can already begin to speak again."

"I have also a pleasant letter from the famous native king of Baroda, who has always been very friendly to me, and invites us to one of his great elephant-fights. He says, that, if we will come, he will have two young rhinoceroses fight too."

"Cracky!" exclaimed Scott. "Isn't that quite like the Spanish bull-fights that Christians sit down on in America?"

"Not at all," replied Richard, laughing. "There is no killing done here. It is only a test of strength, in the case of the elephants at least; and, the moment that there is any danger of the rhinoceroses hurting each other, they are separated."

"Doesn't that clean out the fun?" questioned Scott.

"It would to the Spaniard; and that is precisely what we object to, I suppose. Perhaps I am heathenized; but it is a right interesting sight to me to see two huge elephants struggling against each other in the arena, till one or the other is pushed back against the wall."

"Well, of course, I want to go," Scott replied.

"Then, I shall write that as soon as our tiger-hunt is over we will start at once for Baroda."

"And now for the tiger-hunt!" said Scott, his cheeks aglow with excitement, and his eyes brilliant with unseen sights. "What a whirl there is ahead of me! I don't wonder you like India."

"But that is far from the most beautiful part of this beautiful land, my boy," Richard replied earnestly.

CHAPTER XVI.

TIGERS.

THE weather was warm again. Even Puna felt it. But it was the morning to start for the tiger-hunt; and, in spite of the heat, no one was ready so soon as Scott. They rode on horseback out of the Hindu town just as the sun, round, red, and fiery, was coming up over the hills. They were accompanied by their boys, Moro and Sayad, and three or four servants, all well mounted; for Mr. Raymond's stables seemed inexhaustible. Scott was very proud of the rifle that hung upon his saddle, and over and over again he thanked fortune that he had learned to shoot a gun. His father had been a little timid about it; but he had learned, and now he was going on a tiger-hunt.

A short, brisk canter took them away from the native huts that cluster about every centre of civilization in India, and they were in the wild, free country.

"If I were an Englishman," said Scott, "I suppose that I should say, 'This is jam!' But I think it is better than any jam I ever tasted."

"Not better than currant and crab-apple jelly, is it?" asked Richard.

"Yes, and better than pumpkin-pie," returned the boy.

They left the immediate jungle, and rode for some time along a ridge of one of the low hills overlooking a broad plain, where a small river ran at the base of the mountains opposite, along whose banks the mists still lay, shut off from the sunlight by the line of higher hills.

Pointing in that direction, Scott exclaimed,—

"Why, Mr. Raymond! I did not know that there was another large city so near to Puna."

THAT WONDERFUL CITY.

Richard looked in the direction indicated.

"That is a very remarkable city," said he. "It is famous all over the world. People at the North Pole know of it. Schoolboys read of it. Pilgrims often hail it with delight. They hurry toward it; and every one who enters its gates is presented with a bag of gold so heavy, that he has to hire ten bullocks to carry the treasure away."

"Cæsar! let's go over," said Scott, turning his horse's head that way, and looking back at Richard, sure that he was cracking some joke upon him, but hardly knowing what.

"You may go," replied Richard, "and I will wait here for you. You will not be the first American who has run after that city."

"Run after it? Why? Will it run away from me?"

"It certainly will not be there when you reach it, to borrow an Irish bull."

"What! is it a mirage?" said Scott in wonder.

"Yes, it is a mirage, and a very good one," returned Richard.

Scott allowed his horse to stand still while he watched. But he had not much time; for, as the sun came over the hills, the mists crept into the river, and there was nothing but the green plain, and the flashing silver line that marked the river and the darker mountains.

"Well, if any thing in this world ever looked exactly like any thing, and wasn't any thing after all, that city was the thing," he observed, as they started once more.

At eleven o'clock they reached the village, and began to organize the hunt.

First, all the particulars had to be known,—where the beast had been seen last, and where he most frequently spent the day. Three Englishmen, friends from Puna, whom Mr. Raymond had invited, were already on the spot. The very night before, the tiger had carried off a man and a calf. He had doubtless gorged himself, and would be found in his lair, wherever that was, sound asleep.

The natives knew well which jungle they had to fear, for bodies had more than once been traced there. It was not far; and they started as soon as a force of natives had been marshalled, whose duty it was to surround the jungle, and, beating into it from all sides, discover the particular den in which the animal was lying, start him out, and send him from the jungle.

The mounted hunters were arranged in a semi-circle about that side of the jungle where the tiger was to be driven out. Richard took pains that Scott should be next to him. The hunters were placed some distance apart, so that each had an imaginary triangle, from halfway between himself and his neighbor on either side to the jungle, which he held as his individual possession.

There is a deal of glory, a deal of pride, and a deal of pleasure, to the hunter in India, in bringing down a tiger; so that, to avoid confusion, the hunter upon whose triangle the tiger appears has the first shot at him. If his shot does not tell, the one next him, upon the quarter which the tiger takes, has the next shot; then the man on the other side. By that time there is usually a necessity for every man to look out for himself, if the tiger is not dead; and the man whose shot kills the animal is the one who takes the glory and the hide.

Scott was in a state of "tremendous excitement," as he expressed it, when the beaters, with howls and yells, began their work. It was all in vain that Richard warned him to be calm, that every thing depended on a steady hand and sure aim at instant sight, as it is harder to hit and kill a tiger leaping over the ground than it is to shoot a bird on the wing. But he was doomed to have time enough to recover. The men beat the jungle through and through, and all in vain. Not a sign of tiger or lair could they find.

"I should think they would be afraid of being killed themselves," said Scott, when they had waited so long that all began to sit more easily in their saddles, and to believe that the bird had flown.

"They do get killed sometimes," replied Mr. Raymond. "But when they go in a crowd, they are something like the monkeys, — they forget about being afraid. Then, if they are careful, they are not in much danger; for their racket frightens the animal, and he is more anxious to get away from them than he is to stop and kill one out of so many. It is only when he is maddened, that a tiger will fight against odds."

Now the coolies came out thoroughly exhausted, and declared that there was no tiger there.

"But there is," insisted Mr. Raymond. "No tiger would eat a man and a calf in one night, and then go off on a pilgrimage. Hold my horse, some of you: I am going in to look for myself."

There were remonstrances from several: but all were anxious to have a shot; and knowing that Mr. Raymond was a prudent man, and well acquainted with tigers and their ways, they yielded the point, and even followed him.

He had hardly entered the jungle, when there was a cry from some of the natives about him. He started forward. His friends rushed toward him; but all were too far away to have helped him, as a huge serpent rose at least three feet from the grass, and darted toward him. At that instant, however, a native with unusual courage, instead of running, as all the rest had done, sprang forward, at one leap clearing at least twelve feet; and, even before his feet had touched the earth, he had dealt the snake a terrible blow with his beating staff, that severed his head from his body; and the open mouth fell within three feet of Mr. Raymond.

Richard turned about quietly, and said to the Hindu,—

"You have saved my life, Balaya, at a risk of your own. I shall not forget it."

The Hindu touched his closed hands to his forehead, and, bending very low, said in a voice that was hardly audible,—

"When the last drop of my blood has been given for you, Raymond Maharajah, I shall still be in your debt. You have done much more for me and mine."

As soon as the excitement of the incident had subsided, they began again to beat the jungle in earnest. A half-hour elapsed, and it was growing dark, when Richard's keen and educated eye discovered a dark shadow under a clump of undergrowth, that even in the gathering twilight looked suspicious.

"Throw a stone in there," he commanded one of the coolies.

The coolie obeyed; and, sure enough, the stone did not strike the ground, but disappeared.

"There you have it!" exclaimed one of the Englishmen.

"It is a den, at least," replied Richard. "The next thing is to know if there is any thing in it."

They remained perfectly silent for a moment, and listened. There was not a sound.

"Throw a larger stone in, and throw it hard," commanded Richard.

Another stone was thrown, and again all listened. Suddenly the air began to tremble, as with the low, half-audible notes of an organ. It seemed to Scott like the purring of a giant cat. Every one started.

"He is there," said Mr. Raymond calmly.

They all drew back a pace; for, after all, they were not

so anxious to be the first to face the beast in the dark jungle as they had been outside.

Mr. Raymond crept a little nearer alone.

"THROW A STONE IN THERE."

"Come back! Come back, Sahib! Back Maharajah!" shouted several of the Hindus.

"He will not leave that place so easily," replied Richard, as he bent forward, and threw another stone into the cave.

The rumbling was increased a little, but that was all.

"He is securely stowed away," Mr. Raymond continued,

turning away. "He will not budge an inch for all the stones about here."

"What must we do?" questioned one of the Englishmen.

"Burn him out," suggested another.

"Right you are. Give him fire!" exclaimed a third.

"It is the only way we can start him," said Richard. "But, if we burn him out at this time of night, we shall have to stand about the mouth, and take him on the first leap; and, if we miss, it is death to some one, for he will not stand on ceremony after that."

Richard was evidently reluctant, and it made Scott decidedly fearful. But the majority were for burning him out, and the coolies began to gather the fuel.

"I'm afraid you'll have to lose your chance at a shot, after all, Scott," said Richard, sitting down upon a log, but keeping one ear turned toward the cave, and both eyes all about him. "You are not quite used to this business, and had better get up in a tree."

"I'm not a coward. I will stay where I am; and if he comes at me, and I am not smart enough to look out for myself, why, I ought to be eaten up: that's all," he replied indignantly.

"That's all first-rate, Scott," said Richard approvingly. "But you must remember, this time, that you did not come to India to go on a tiger-hunt. The time may come when you will have to look out for yourself sharp; but just now it will be no cowardice, but justice to Paul, that you keep out of danger, and get up this tree behind me, at least fifteen feet. From that limb there you can see it all, and be all right."

On second thought Scott obeyed.

In a few minutes the wood was gathered, and the fire started. It lit up the jungle with a frightful glare and weird, black shadows. Strange noises sounded from all around, as animals which were hidden there became frightened, and crept away. The Hindus carefully disposed themselves behind the cave, with the exception of a few of the bravest of them. One or two of them followed Scott's example, and he was surprised to see two of the Englishmen do the same.

The leader of the beaters crept up to the fire, threw on some fresh wood, and poked the whole as far as he could toward the cave. Still all was silent; and a moment later he crept up again, and, catching some lighted embers, threw them into the very mouth.

"Take care," muttered Richard sharply, whose quick ear had caught an ominous sound. The fellow sprang backward, tripped on the rocks, and fell. He was none too soon. Mr. Raymond stepped backward to a more secure position behind the trunk of a tree, which Scott and a native had climbed, holding his rifle aimed at the mouth of the cave, and ready for instant use. There was no one to dispute his claim to taking the shot.

The fire-brands had done the work. Almost at that instant the earth seemed to shiver, as a terrific shriek sounded, and the next, with a terrible roar and a wild bound, the tiger flew through the air. His eyes were shut, and his savage mouth wide open. He swept like a dark cloud through the flames, and over the glowing embers, and almost under Scott.

A piercing cry of fear rose from the natives. A report sounded from Mr. Raymond's rifle. Over and over, in a huge mass upon the ground, the tiger rolled, stone dead. The ball had passed from ear to ear.

The cry of the natives was changed to one of triumph. They gathered about the great creature, stretched him at full length, struck him with their feet, pretended to spit upon

A SUDDEN APPEARANCE.

him, and expended all manner of devotional symptoms toward Mr. Raymond.

"It was only a very lucky hit," replied Richard. "I could get no aim."

"Aha!" replied the leader of the beaters, in tolerable English, "I know the Barra-Sahib when, little one boy, he work on the railroad. I know him every day till now. I see Barra-Sahib cut you candle-light far, far off. I see Barra-Sahib kill you pheasant on wing, no hurt you pheasant. I see Barra-Sahib shoot one you rebel just here." He put his fore-finger between his eyes. "I see Barra-Sahib hit big one elephant in little his eye. Now I see Barra-Sahib bring my great-uncle right in you ear. Often I see Barra-Sahib shoot; but never, never, I see my Barra-Sahib shoot, and not hit. No, never!"

Then the applause began again; and one of the Englishmen, coming up, and slapping him on the shoulder, said to Mr. Raymond, —

"Look here, old fellow, what's the use of being so modest? It's that confounded Yankee blood, that you can't get out of you. But it doesn't set here any better than fresh pheasant. Balaya has told the truth. You're the best shot in the country. Now own up to it. How many does this make you?"

"You're honorable as an Englishman," replied Richard, laughing. "This is my fifty-second. But come! It is time we were getting out of this."

The tiger was left for the natives to skin; and, after one of the most exciting days of his life, Scott reached home at about nine o'clock, nervously on the alert, but thoroughly tired out.

As they rode through Puna, the new moon was creeping above the roofs, and all along the street the people were pausing, stopping each other, and making the motion of reverence with their closed hands.

"What is the matter?" asked Scott.

"They are only saying a welcome to the new moon, for luck," replied Richard. "I hope that their prayers will be answered, and that we shall all have it. We must hurry to bed to-night, for to-morrow we shall start early for Baroda."

"I don't feel like going to bed," said Scott. "It comes over me, over and over again, that this is the last I shall see of your beautiful home. I am not at all sleepy. Can't you sit up a little while?"

"We'll sit up as long as you like; but a long horseback ride and a tiger-hunt is tiresome to one who is not used to it. You must not be overdone, and get ill."

"No, indeed, I will not! But I want to know all about tiger-hunting, now that I have begun. Tell me about that, to begin with. Do they ever hunt in any other way?"

"Oh! I might talk till morning, and then not tell you half the ways," replied Mr. Raymond. "The natives usually hunt upon elephants when they can. They feel safer there. Here is an old Hindu painting of a native tiger-hunt," he added, calling Scott to one side of the room, where a curious device in a unique frame was hanging on the wall. "It is not very high art, but the natives devote little time to this branch. I only bought it to help on a young Christian convert who seemed to have some talent; but I keep it because I rather like it. The tiger has tackled the elephant, you see: and they will quite frequently do it when they are hard pressed; for they often deal with them wild, and know their weak points."

"That is a beautiful painting above it," said Scott, looking at a large oil painting in a heavy frame. "It is a Hindu scene, but not by a Hindu artist, I fancy."

"No, it is not by a Hindu artist, and it is not a Hindu scene. But I don't wonder you are mistaken. It is certainly no other kind of a scene. It is a magnificent painting. I brought it with me from England. It was painted by one of the leading British artists; but unfortunately, like many literary

THE CONVERT'S WORK

works upon India that are ably written, and attract attention of people who really want to learn something, it is the work of a man who knew nothing at all of what he was painting.

It is supposed to be the meeting of Rebecca and Isaac, when Abraham's servant came back from his pilgrimage with a wife for his master's son. Every thing is absurd about the picture, except the execution; but that was so fine that I bought it."

"Well, that's not precisely tiger-hunting. Is there no way of killing the creature that is safe as well as exciting?"

"The danger is what makes tiger-hunting exciting, I suppose," replied Richard, shrugging his shoulders. "If there's no danger, it is not much more than shooting at a mark. I was invited once upon a tiger-hunt with a *maharajah*, one of the native princes, that was certainly the safest thing I ever undertook. Down on the river-bank, where the animals had to come to drink, he had constructed a tower out of a ruin, and on the summit was a broad platform. Here he had an elaborate lunch served for us, while we sat and chatted together in the moonlight, and ate till the natives on watch reported that a tiger was in sight, coming down to drink. He could not help coming within range; and he could not touch us, no matter how little we hurt him, or how mad we made him. I shot just once, and killed. But it seemed like a cowardly thing to do; and I gave it up, and spent the evening enjoying the *maharajah's* lunch and the magnificent scenery."

The noise of the servants shutting the great door and the windows for the night sounded from down below. The butler came in to receive his orders for Mr. Raymond's absence; and finding that, after all, he was tired, Scott said good-night, and was soon dreaming.

The noise and bustle outside aroused him early the next morning; and, finding himself alone in the great house, he wandered out into the court formed by the servants' huts.

TIGER-HUNTING.

In the veranda behind the house the bootblack was busy upon the shoes, and the tailor sat at work. There was to be a substantial breakfast, instead of *chota hazri*, that morning; and from the cooking-hut issued a savory smell. Scott remembered what Mr. Raymond had told him about avoiding the kitchen if he wanted to keep his appetite; but he

THE SCENT OF THE KITCHEN.

said to himself, "This is the last meal, for some time at least; and I am sure I have seen worse things." And slowly he walked toward the open door.

It was not so bad as his imagination had pictured it, after all. And his appetite was sharpened, instead of injured, by comparison with his previous fancy.

On a smooth and polished composition floor sat the head

cook and an assistant. The cook sat like a dog on his haunches. It is a very common way of sitting in India, when one is so occupied that he cannot sit cross-legged on the ground. The fellow was peeling potatoes, there was no doubt of that; but he was certainly holding the knife in his toes. He had a curious little stove, with a charcoal fire burning before him. There was only a chance for one pot at a time on the stove; but all around were curious pots, all the same size, all made to cover up hermetically, and fit the little opening above the little fire. There were several fixed-fire-places, too, about the room.

The cook looked up, and smiled.

"Dis you Hindu stove. Berry good stove," he said emphatically. "English stove he no good. Big one fire no cook. Dis you stove little one fire big cook. Berry good stove."

As Scott turned away he found Mr. Raymond directly behind him.

"That was said for my benefit," he said with a cheerful good-morning. "I have been trying to make the fellow use an English range that I have; but he is quite correct about the fuel. A little handful of charcoal will do a deal of work there."

CHAPTER XVII.

A HAREM.

TWO stalwart coolies placed their luggage upon a native dray, and then, acting as horses, started off for the station. They were strong, and straight as arrows. They wore but a single garment, except that one of them had on an English shirt, that he seemed to feel very proud of. The single garment was a long piece of cloth, twisted about them in different directions, but so as to cover, with more or less completeness, nearly the whole body, except the lower parts of the legs and arms.

"There are not many seams there to be ripping, or buttons to come off," Scott remarked with a significant smile, as they watched the coolies away before starting themselves; for he remembered with what zeal Mr. Raymond's native tailor had been kept at work upon his own wardrobe ever since they reached Puna.

"But what do you suppose that that stuff is, that they are dressed up in?" asked Richard.

"Coarse canvas, or sacking of some sort," replied Scott.

"That, my boy, is because you have not looked into it."

"Bah!" exclaimed Scott with a smile and a shudder. "I looked as far into it as possible, and could see nothing but dirt."

"That may all be," responded Richard; "but the groundwork of that dirt, figuratively speaking, is fine camel's hair."

"Camel's hair!" exclaimed Scott incredulously, as he thought of the value of his mother's camel's-hair shawl, and of the way he was punished for pinning it about the neck of his big Bernard dog.

"Those fellows have come down here from Cashmere. They do the lowest and dirtiest and hardest of my work, and do it for four or five cents a day, swelling about in real camel's-hair shawls."

COOLIES IN CAMEL'S HAIR.

"But how in the world can they afford them?" asked Scott.

"They can't afford them, or any others either; and that is just why they wear these. Their great-great-grandfathers wore that identical piece of cloth before them, and their great-grandchildren will put it on by and by, and think it just as good as new, without even having it pressed over."

"But what do they do when there is one great-grandchild too many?" asked Scott.

"Scott, you're too much for me," replied Richard, laughing, as he jumped into the carriage. "They either kill him, or kill his great-grandfather, or split one of the largest shawls in two."

Baroda was over two hundred miles to the northward; but the carriages were so comfortably fitted up with cooling apparatus and soft couches, that Scott slept that night almost as soundly as though in his quiet room in Beverly: and, before he woke in the morning, Sayad had brushed his boots, cleaned his clothes, laid out fresh linen, packed away the old, drawn water for his bath, and hung the towels where he could most easily lay his hands on them; the compartments of the cars being supplied with all conveniences.

Sayad was touching him lightly on the shoulder, when Scott opened his eyes, and, pointing out of the window, said, —

"Baroda! Juldi! kick, Sahib!"

"Who's that he wants me to kick?" Scott asked Mr. Raymond, who had already dressed himself, and lain down again on his divan.

"He's trying to tell you that Baroda will be here quick," replied Richard. "And, if he keeps on as he has begun, he will soon know so much English, that I shall have to discharge him. But you'd better get up, all the same."

When the train reached the station, one of the king's carriages was waiting for them; but, aside from the beauty of the carriage, Scott's first impressions of Baroda were not more favorable than the first of Bombay had been. But he was learning that the very worst of every thing Hindu is that which the stranger sees on the outside.

The street was almost empty at this early hour; and the long rows of low roofs, with their heavy thatches, that were often more than a foot thick, looked almost like avenues of haystacks. Then they turned down more narrow streets, where the houses seemed to strike against the sky, and the pavements were damp and slippery, for the sun never touched them. The few who were in the streets knelt, and touched their foreheads to the ground when the coach passed them, recognizing the king's carriage.

"It makes a fellow feel kind of tony, doesn't it?" remarked Scott, as they passed three or four kneeling figures.

"Until you reflect that it is the carriage and horses to which they are kneeling," replied Richard. "They probably knelt just the same when it went down to the station empty."

NATIVE STREET.

"What are those girls doing?" Scott asked, as the carriage passed two young women in front of one of the low doorways, clad in a costume he had not seen before, and each with a long pole, pounding something on the hollow of a dug-out stump. "Are they churning out some of that white-livered butter?"

"Not exactly," replied his friend. "Have you never read, in a very old book, about two women grinding at a mill?"

"Of course I have. But that's no kind of a mill."

"It does the work for these people as well as the upper and nether stones did for the Hebrews. They are beating rice there, to take the hulls off."

"Well, how came they to have such ugly clothes and pretty faces?" asked Scott, who could not help noticing that the faces were really much handsomer than many of the faces he had seen.

BEATING RICE.

"Both are the fault of the place where those women were born," replied Richard. "They are evidently women of Cashmere. Goodness knows why they are down here; but we find them all over India. Have you never read of 'the beautiful eyes of Cashmere'?"

"Tom Moore wrote about them, didn't he?"

"That he did, and some beautiful poetry too," replied Richard. "And there is any amount of native poetry celebrating their beauty. It is a fact, I think, that the Cashmere women are the handsomest in India."

"Well, I think their husbands are brutes to let them stand there, in those old clothes, pounding rice," said Scott indignantly.

"As for their clothes, Scott, they are rather proud of them.

It is a sort of trademark to say that they came from Cashmere; and it is custom for the women to pound the rice, and do a great many things that are not customary in America. Our people make a great many mistakes, and expend their pity in a very wrong direction often, in regard to the women of India. They forget that fashion rules these people, just as it does others, and that their positions and occupations are not what they are because their husbands are tyrants, always, but because they themselves uphold the customs."

"Well, perhaps it is the higher women that are down-trodden," suggested Scott: for his mother was the president of a large society, in Boston, For the Introduction of Enlightenment into the Hindustani Zenanas, and Instruction of the Women of India; and he had often heard her talking of the terrible state of the women in this benighted land.

"Well, we will not argue the point," replied Richard. "I am going to find some means to show you the inside life of the high-caste women of India, if I can, and let you judge for yourself."

They drove along a border-road now, and were passing a low building at the left, guarded by a line of graceful cocoa-nut-trees. Mr. Raymond had been there before, and recognized their royal quarters.

They were cordially received by the secretary of the king, who announced the entertainments for the next day, and informed them that in the stable of the house they occupied there were five elephants at their disposal while they were the guests of the king.

"What in the world are we to do with five elephants?" questioned Scott, almost breathless with excitement, as soon as the secretary had gone.

"Why, we shall have to cut ourselves up into five pieces, and put part into each *howdah*, I suppose," replied Richard solemnly.

"Or turn three of them out to pasture," suggested Scott.

"That would never do," said his friend; "for the generosity of the king is quite as much for his subjects as for us. We shall have to let the entire troupe go round with us everywhere, to show the people here what magnificent guests the king has, and how magnificently he treats them."

"It'll just be a regular circus, I vow!" said Scott. "I believe I shall feel half ashamed of myself, and as though I belonged to some wandering menagerie. Can't we go out to the stable, and look at the beasts?"

While breakfast was preparing, and the "boys," as Moro and Sayad were always called, were arranging the rooms that their masters were to occupy (for there were to be other guests in the house), Mr. Raymond and Scott went out, and found the elephants already prepared for immediate use. They were standing and lying in a half-circle before the stable.

"Those cages on their backs," said Scott, pointing to the *howdahs*, "may be all the go here, but they haven't half the style to them that they had in Barnum's last show. His were all fixed up like the State-house dome in Boston."

"You may enjoy riding in them just as much," said Richard.

"They make them lie down, and we get up by those ladders, I suppose," said Scott gravely.

"That is the very way," replied Mr. Raymond with mock enthusiasm.

"But I was thinking," continued Scott, "what if we should

go off for a ride, and forget the ladders, and drop something, and have to get down, and pick it up?"

"Have to shin up a palm-tree, and get the elephant to back up to it," replied Richard gravely.

"Can't speak his language," returned Scott.

"Well, when you go to ride," replied Richard, "there

THE KING'S COURTESY.

will be a man sitting on that elephant's head, with a little iron crowbar in his hand,—a *mahoot*, they call him; and you will find that that little crowbar can translate all you wish to say to the elephant."

The breakfast was even an exaggeration of Esofali's; but Scott was beginning to have an appetite for the highly spiced food, that is always engendered by life in the Orient.

After breakfast one of the wealthy nobles of the court called upon Mr. Raymond, inviting him — "by the permission of the king," he said — to a feast that he had announced in his honor for that evening.

"He is a jolly fellow. He beats Esofali all to pieces, name and all. Can you pronounce it?"

"Gulamhusin Khan Kajulala Kabeerkhanbhoy," repeated Richard very rapidly, and then added, smiling, "When he is in state, at his dinner, or at the king's court to-morrow, there are about a hundred and fifty or two hundred titles that we shall have to add every time that we address him."

Scott groaned. "You can bet I sha'n't bore him to death, with conversation at least," he added, after a moment of reflection.

"No, you will not do that; but I shouldn't wonder if you chatted with him like a magpie, for he is one of the most go-ahead men in India. You will like him."

Scott shook his head.

"Not only that," continued Richard, "but I am thoroughly in luck here. I had not thought of him, but I am going to get him to take you through his harem. He'll do it, I'm sure."

"Great Cæsar's ghost!" cried Scott (that was an oath that he always reserved for the most terrific hours of life). "Don't send me a rod alone with him. Suppose I should want to speak to him."

"He speaks as good English as the Prince of Wales."

"Say his name to me once more, will you, please?" asked Scott humbly.

A little later they paid their respects to the king. Scott followed Mr. Raymond with fear and trembling, which was much abated, however, when he found the great man seated in an English easy-chair on a beautiful veranda, quietly smoking a *hookah*, dressed in white linen, cut after the fashion of a loose English business suit, and wearing a little cap of the same material. By his subjects he is called the "Gaiakwar."

The conversation was wholly in English. He even spoke to his servants in English, and spoke to them himself, without any intervention of a secretary, though the one who had met them sat on a rug beside him.

Before they went away the king ordered a lunch for them, and called after the servant who went to prepare it, "No wine and no *hookahs* (or cigars)." Then turning to Mr. Raymond, with a laugh, he added, "That's an abominable trick of yours. But England would stand a hundred per cent higher in India if half the Englishmen followed your example."

"He's just a perfect brick!" exclaimed Scott, as they were on their way to the nobleman's dinner. "He knows a deal more about America than I know about India. But what an every-day sort of fellow he is!"

"It's not the most of a brag that's the most of a man. He is one of the few native rulers who have succeeded in nominally holding rank and people, in spite of English accession," replied Richard.

The native feast was, as Mr. Raymond warned Scott in advance, the most tedious kind of a bore. At one end of the magnificent hall sat the host, Mr. Raymond, Scott, and a few of the most illustrious guests, while at the other, in a half-circle, sat a hundred native friends of the host.

These friends were all seated on the floor; and Scott found much more pleasure in watching them than in any thing else. The food was brought to them in curious flat dishes, and they all ate with their fingers. Above them, at the end of the dining-hall, was a balcony with graceful marble arches; but the space between the arches was filled with a fine gauze, in heavy folds, so that only dim shadows could be seen behind it.

"Is that what you call the harem, up there?" Scott asked Mr. Raymond when he found an opportunity.

"Not exactly," he replied. "But those are the inmates, so to speak."

"Do you suppose all of his wives are up there, or is that only one squad?" Scott asked a few moments later.

Mr. Raymond laughed. "You must not take it for granted that every man in India has a hundred wives. Gulamhusin Khan"—

"Never mind the rest of it," Scott interrupted, laughing.

"Very well, then: the aforesaid gentleman has only one wife. He has often told me that, and he is very proud of her. He says he has no children, for he has only one girl."

"And girls don't count," interrupted Scott again, who recalled so much from his mother's society talk.

"They count in the father's heart, as you will find upon conversing with him. After the dinner there is always a dance. Half a dozen *nautch* girls, such as you saw at the temple in Bombay, will come in with their musicians; and, for two hours and more, they will sit down and sing, and stand up and dance, and sit down and sing again. It is intolerably stupid. Most of the guests go to sleep under it; and, when it is half through, I am going to ask my friend to take you through the zenana. It will be a frightful innovation; but he rather likes to do shocking things, and I think he will do it."

"But what sort of a zenana can a man get up, with only one wife?" Scott asked rather disappointedly.

"Why, he has a wife, a daughter, a mother, and a widowed sister; and there will be several friends, probably, to see the feast; and there will be several important servants, like companions in America, and a small army of less important servants, that are always called slaves when we hear them spoken of in America."

The "Society" pictures of harems at once rose before Scott's eyes; and he almost shuddered, as he thought of the horrible prison of worthless, senseless butterflies into which it might be his lot to penetrate.

When the time came, and the proposition was made, their host even astonished Mr. Raymond with the readiness with which he assented, and, motioning to Scott, said rather quietly, —

"My very good friend tells me that in America you have a horrible idea of the private corners of our little homes. He calls you a boy. In this country you would have been married years ago. My daughter is not half so old as you, but she has been married two years. She is still living at home with her mother, to learn to be a good wife. But as you are still a boy in America, and as boys are not forbidden the zenana, and as I would do any thing in the world for my very good friend Mr. Raymond, I am going to frighten my little women out of their wits."

"Don't scare them on my account, Mr. — Mr. — Mr." —

"You are not the first one who has stopped when he got so far," said their host, laughing. "But never mind scaring them. They will get over it. They call me crazy and an infidel now, because I make them eat with knife and fork, and sit in chairs, and sleep on beds, and a host of such things. It will only make them sure of it. Come on." And, turning, he led the way, only stopping for a moment to beckon Mr. Raymond, and add, "Don't whisper this at court, and don't let the boy turn out a man as soon as he has solved the terrible secrets, and boast about it; for you know I am a Mussulman at a Hindu court."

THE HOST'S MOTHER.

Scott hesitated. He did not quite like that way of doing things; but the host took his hand, and, laughing, led him out, saying cordially, —

"You must not mind my way, young gentleman. You know this is an old, gray-bearded nation, that has been tying up knots of fashion for centuries and centuries. We cannot undo them in a day, no matter how much we dislike them. We will outgrow them by and by, and we will all be Englishmen, or something better," he added with a twinkle in his eye.

They had reached the lower end of the hall, by a corridor leading outside. He stopped at the stairs leading up to the balcony.

"Ayah!" he called; and, as a woman appeared, he explained to Scott, "This is my daughter's nurse. She will take you round, and introduce you."

"But I cannot speak Hindustani, or any other Indian language, sir," said Scott, much alarmed, and forgetting old Joe's caution not to "go sirrin' round."

"They all speak English," the host replied; "and the worst of it is, that my wife and daughter read it too. It is very expensive procuring books for them, and answering their questions when they kidnap my newspapers." Then he turned to the ayah, and asked, "Are there any visitors?"

"They all went, Sahib, when the dance began," she replied.

"That is good," he said, half to himself, and half to Scott. "Women are great talkers. They are worse than English papers for spreading the news; for the paper has to tell it the same to every one who reads it, but our women have a way of making a good thing a little better every fresh time they go over it. And they will go over it every time they find any one who has not heard it. If there were one single stranger here, I should hear, by daylight to-morrow, that I had brought all the Englishmen in India to Baroda for the express purpose of marching them through the zenana."

"I am afraid I had better not go," said Scott.

"Tut, tut! Go as a favor to me," exclaimed the host. "My own people will never lisp a word. It would be like putting on a wrong *sari*, or wearing colors that clashed, — a little out of fashion. It is quite safe, quite safe." Then turning to the ayah, who was waiting at a respectful distance, he said, "This is a very great prince, from a country twice as far away as England, and ten thousand times larger. He has heard that mine is a model house, and will see it.

Say to all, that it is my command that they remain as they are. They shall not put on veils, and shall speak with the prince when he speaks to them. — Go on now, Sahib," he said to Scott in a loud voice.

"Shall I not wait till she has given your word?" Scott asked timidly, and in the low tone.

"Oh, no! there is no need," replied the host in the same low tone. "They have all heard it already. Our women have a way of listening from somewhere or other, whenever there is any thing interesting going on, and then spreading the news like a fire in the jungle."

He turned abruptly, and went back into the hall; and Scott approached the ayah, who was evidently even more frightened than he, and who bowed very low, touching her forehead with her closed hands. Then she turned, and, without a word, led the way.

First, they passed through the balcony above the dining-hall. The carving and tapestry was much finer there than below. Scott thought it a pity that it should be hidden by the thick folds of gauze, but was surprised to find how easily those behind could see and hear all that went on in the hall. He hesitated for an instant, for his eyes fell upon three ladies who were sitting on the floor at one end. There were cups of tea before them, and a silver pot of curious construction, in which tea was evidently kept hot for further draughts. There was a *hookah*, too, in which the tobacco was still smoking; but the long, curving stem was lying idly over the bowl. He wondered who could have been smoking it, and curiosity drove his fears away. He bowed as politely as possible, and said, —

"I hope I am not disturbing you."

They only smiled.

"If you were smoking, I hope you will not stop for me," he added.

They looked at each other; and one of them took up the stem, and, putting the mouthpiece to her mouth, began to puff away with a genteel delight, that reminded Scott of the way some of his school-girl friends smiled, and ate chocolate caramels, when he tried to talk to them.

IN THE HAREM.

He began to feel braver himself, and to enjoy the adventure.

They passed through several very pretty chambers, that Scott vainly endeavored to recollect exactly afterward, where there were hanging-lamps and delicate odors and fine carvings in marble walls and bright-colored tapestries. One of these was a sort of conservatory, where there were several swinging-gardens, and flowers in curious pots. Among the flowers Scott caught sight of a little girl, or a grown woman, — he could hardly tell which, — who was demurely smoking a *hookah*. She started, and gave a little cry, and drew her *sari* over her face as they passed. She had evidently not heard the command. Scott feared she might go into hysterics, or something of the sort, from the cry she gave. He had heard of such cases, and involuntarily looked round after they had passed the door. It was an incredibly short time; but there was the little creature's head thrust beyond the curtain, looking at him with wondering eyes. It dodged back again in an instant.

Still the ayah led on. Scott was on the point of asking her if her object was to begin at the farther end, and work backward, when she stopped at a curtained door, coughed slightly, said a few words softly in her own language, to which a faint reply sounded; and, drawing the curtain, she bowed, and announced the mother of the host.

Scott found himself before a woman young enough to be the man's wife, he thought, but with a very stately grace, and not a very homely face.

"She'd not be an over-agreeable mother-in-law," he said to himself, as he looked at the erect head and firm mouth; but there was so much real common sense there, and such a ladylike bearing, that it was a shock even to the boy, when the sight of the immense collection of jewels drew him back to the fact that she was one of the useless inmates of a real harem.

"She's got some vim, if she is a slave and a butterfly," he said to himself. He had almost forgotten to bow; but he did it at once, remarking, "I have had a very plea — interesting evening," remembering his party etiquette. He was on the point of saying "pleasant," but it stuck on his tongue; for he had been taught that there was both a letter and spirit to what is called truth.

"My son is insane," said the lady decidedly, without moving a muscle in recognition of his bow. She was evidently not at all afraid; and, in even ratio, Scott began to feel somewhat timid.

He hastened to remark, " But he seems to be a very fine gentleman."

" You may be great, but Allah and his prophet are greater," she added sternly.

" But I am very young yet," Scott urged timidly, without thinking precisely who it was that he was peering at.

" My son will be older than his God before he has half the brains of his father," she returned.

Seeing that he was making but little progress here, Scott ventured to say, " I wish you good-evening, ma'am," and withdrew.

"The good mother is old," said the ayah, when they had entered another room that was empty. "The Barra-Sahib must not remember what she has said, for she has learned only a few sentences in English. She cannot understand a word."

" She is not old!" exclaimed Scott.

" She is forty-one," replied the ayah.

" Bah! that's only a young girl," said Scott. "I thought her son was thirty, at least."

" He is twenty-seven."

"Cæsar's ghost! his mother only fourteen years older than he is!" Scott muttered.

" He had a brother a year older, but he is dead," the ayah replied apologetically. " His widow was smoking in the flower-room."

"Why, I thought the widows had a horrible time of it," said Scott, recalling the merry little face among the flowers.

" I am a widow too," replied the ayah. " It is very sad."

" So it is," returned Scott consolingly. " But did you say the mother did not understand what I said?"

"Not a word, Sahib. She was old when her son said

that we all should speak English, and had a teacher come. She could not learn: she only committed a few sentences, to say to her daughter-in-law, when she was particularly pleased or displeased with her son."

"But she spoke very correctly."

"We had a good teacher, and she has said those sentences a great many times."

"Then she is often displeased with her son," suggested Scott.

"It is a mother's position to reprove," the ayah answered humbly.

"Did you learn English here?" asked Scott.

"I went to the mission-school in Bombay when I was a girl, and I was an ayah in England for five years after my husband died."

"How old were you when your husband died?"

"I was about thirteen: I do not know exactly. I was very poor, and a good missionary lady took me home with her."

"Did she make a Christian of you?" Scott asked, intent upon sifting the whole matter.

The ayah turned abruptly, and said solemnly,—

"God is God, and Mohammed is the prophet of God." That is the great Mussulman creed. Then she added, "Jesus also was his prophet, Sahib. He came to teach you the way of life. Follow your prophet: let me follow mine. One heaven, one God, waits to receive all the faithful."

Scott felt that he had been rebuked by that poor ayah; and he followed her silently into the next room, where she again tapped and coughed by a curtained door, and said something in Hindustani. Again there was a soft reply, and Scott entered.

Upon an ordinary ottoman sat the wife and daughter of the host. Scott said to Mr. Raymond afterward, that he could "hardly tell one from the other, they looked so near the same age, especially the mother."

They did not wear so many jewels as he expected, though each had heavy gold bands, beautifully twisted, about their ankles. They were dressed in the most elegant clothes Scott had ever seen. It was delicate silk, wonderfully worked with gold and silver thread embroidery. They were not what Scott thought pretty, but they were far from bad looking.

"I hope I am not intruding," Scott said, feeling his ground, in the first place, to find out whether the wife could really understand English, and then to see if such a reception waited for him as he had received from the mother. What was his surprise, when, with a clear, bell-like voice and a pleasant smile, the lady replied,—

"No, indeed, sir! I should like to receive all of my husband's foreign friends just as the English ladies do, and he would like to have me. I think that we shall bring it about by and by." She motioned the ayah to bring a chair; and Scott seated himself, glad of something to do for a moment to collect his thoughts.

Seeing that he was a little embarrassed, the lady continued, "You are not an Englishman, I think?"

"No, ma'am, I am an American," replied Scott.

"Oh, how pretty every thing must be there!" she exclaimed, giving her daughter a little squeeze, and laughing merrily. "I have several lady friends who are Americans. They have told me so much about it! and I have read some very beautiful stories too. I cannot understand them very well; but I think that song by Henry Longfellow, about

Hiawatha and Minnehaha, is one of the sweetest things I ever read, except our own beautiful songs."

Just then a little girl, all bespangled with ornaments, came timidly in, and presented a tray with tea and rose-water to the wife, who held it toward Scott, asking him to take the refreshment. The little girl sat down by her mistress to wait till he had finished.

THE PRETTY WAITER.

"Thank you, Mrs.— Mrs." — Scott hesitated. He began to tremble before that terrible name, and wish he had not undertaken it.

The lady laughed heartily.

"Zyna is my name," she said at last.

"Mrs. Zyna, that is lovely!" exclaimed Scott.

"No, Zyna all alone," she cried with another peal of laughter, in which all in the room joined more moderately. "We are not like English ladies. We would rather our husbands would have all the titles. They are not nice."

"I suppose you have nothing to do but read and sing," said Scott, thinking of the "Society" for the Enlightenment of the Zenanas.

"Oh, yes, indeed!" replied Zyna. "My daughter and I make all our own clothes, and"—

"What! not embroider them?" exclaimed Scott, looking again at that exquisite needlework.

"Oh, yes, indeed!" she replied. "We weave the silk sometimes, and always embroider it. Isn't it pretty?" she asked, tossing out a fold of the *sari* that was covered with delicate flowers in silver and gold.

"It is the finest thing I ever saw," said Scott enthusiastically. "Why, I thought you never did any work at all."

Zyna laughed again. "That's what the American ladies say; but last year, Reyhamut (my daughter) and I sold four thousand rupees' worth of embroidery in the bazaar. We had woven and embroidered it all ourselves."

"Sold it!" cried Scott aghast. "What for?"

"Oh! joined to do all that we could for the poor that were suffering in the famine. But that was not much. Our great India Sultana, the Banoo Begum, gave a million rupees to the poor of Delhi, that she had earned all herself. Oh, we are very proud of our women! Some of them have been great poets; and women have ruled India, too, more than once. But that is not our place, and we do not like that. There is something comes up every day to do. To-day Kashee — where is Kashee?" she asked, looking round. "Ayah, go and bid Kashee bring in the little boy." Then, turning again to Scott, she continued, "To-day Kashee found a poor little boy in the street, who was almost dead with hunger. She brought him home till we can find out who he belongs to. We have worked a little girdle and a little cap for him, and it makes him feel like a rajah."

Then Kashee entered timidly, with her eyes turned away from Scott. But the little boy picked up in the street had no such diffidence, and looked him right in the eye, and laughed, though he had absolutely nothing on but the little girdle and the little cap.

Scott now began to notice the heavy and very handsome

KASHEE AND THE BOY.

rugs upon the floor, and the embroidered screens and carved marble walls.

"Every thing is very beautiful here," he said to himself; and, without half thinking, he added aloud, "But why don't you have pictures on the walls too?"

"It is too much like idols," Zyna replied with a shudder. "The Hindus have pictures, and pray to them."

"But we have pictures, and we don't pray to them," said Scott.

"Why, I have always heard that you kneel down to pictures of Jesus and his mother, and pray to them," said Zyna.

"Oh! that's the Catholics," said Scott scornfully.

"Well, every thing is so mixed up over there, that all I read only confuses me. I shall never be able to understand it all, I think. It is all so simple here in India."

Scott looked up in astonishment. He had thought, that, of all that was mixed up and unintelligible, it was the state of society in India.

The little girl who had brought his tea took it away again, and returned with a silver plate, and some green leaves carefully folded up on it like little horns of plenty. She offered them to Scott, but he looked at them doubtfully. Zyna laughed.

"Perhaps you don't chew betel?" she said. "Never mind. I think the Americans never do. But we do," she added; and, taking one, she put it in her mouth, and all the rest did the same. In a moment all their lips began to have a little red line about them, and their teeth were red; for no one in the zenana had stained teeth, though all their finger-nails and toe-nails were dyed red.

"Some of your customs I like very much, and some I don't like at all," Zyna continued. But another maid came in, and spoke to her softly; and, laughing, she said to Scott,—

"My husband's mother is old. She does not see with his eyes. She says that she thinks it very wrong for you to have come, and that I must tell you it is time to go."

"That's so," said Scott, springing to his feet. He had quite forgotten himself.

"If you please," Zyna continued, "it is customary for us to make our guests a little present; and, as we have been talking of Mussulmani women, I should like to give you this little painting on ivory. It is very old. It was painted nearly three hundred years ago. It is a portrait of the great sultana, who discovered that perfume could be made from flowers, and who made the first attar of roses. She was preparing a drink to tempt the appetite of a wounded soldier."

THE GREAT SULTANA.

"Thank you, thank you, ma'am!" exclaimed Scott, as he took the precious treasure; for he had heard that it was never wise to refuse what was offered, and he was sure she wished him to keep it. "But I am very sorry I have nothing with me that can return your kindness."

"Never mind," she said carelessly. "You can send me a pretty American story-book some time."

"I'll send you a whole library full!" said Scott enthusiastically, as he rose, and was conducted back again to the hall, where the dancing and singing were still going on; and, as Richard had said, all who were not smoking and chewing betel were sound asleep at the lower end of the hall. Mr. Raymond and the host were playing a game of chess.

CHAPTER XVIII.

AN ELEPHANT FIGHT AND A MOUNTAIN RIDE.

WHEN they reached their bungalow again, which was not till two o'clock in the morning, Scott showed the ivory portrait to Mr. Raymond.

"There is a souvenir indeed!" he exclaimed. "It could not be bought for five hundred dollars. In fact, it could not be bought at all. It is one of the relics of India's palmy days, under the glorious reign of the great Moguls."

"She's an odd stick, according to this picture," said Scott; "but what in the world is that that she has got beside her? Is it a snake?"

"It's only a *hookah*," said Richard.

"A *hookah!* To smoke? Great Cæsar's ghost! Why, it's a regular hose-pipe. I don't wonder she got a jaw like that, puffing away on such a thing. What awful bellows she must have had to work it!

"By the way," he continued a moment later, "what were those things they had to hold their tea in?"

"I do not know," replied Richard. "I was never in a harem."

"Never?" asked Scott in surprise. Had it been a few years later, Richard would doubtless have replied, "Well, hardly ever;" but, as it was, he stuck to his first proposition.

"No, never! nor has any other European man, or native either, as for that, except in his own. You have done a wonderful thing; and you will not find one in a hundred, who knows any thing about India, who will believe you when you tell him. However, I would be very careful, and not speak of it till after you are out of India, as it might bring reproach on the kindness of our friend."

The next thing was the arena; and, preparing themselves for the day as soon as breakfast was over, they started for the palace, where a large throng was already collected. The nobles were gathered upon a balcony, where mats were laid for those who wished them, and arm-chairs for the Europeans, of whom there were nearly a score. Opposite them there was a raised platform, where those of the populace who could gain admission were permitted to sit; and the roofs and windows and trees in every direction were crowded.

Horsemen of the royal body-guard were about the gate as they entered, proudly displaying their horsemanship, which was, indeed, something well worth seeing.

In the arena, which was an enormous square, two large male elephants were fastened by heavy chains, far apart from each other; and outside, on a low hill, three female elephants were standing, where they could overlook the entertainment.

"Elephants are something like men," the king said to Scott, as they seated themselves. "They always show off their best prowess when the ladies are looking on."

Indeed, the male elephants seemed fully to appreciate the occasion, and were furiously dashing about in their chains, eager to test their strength.

"What makes them so much more excited than other elephants?" asked Scott.

"They have been fed on butter and sugar and rice and spices for the last three months," replied the king, "to make them what we call 'musti,' or vicious."

All around the high stone wall that fenced in the enclosure, there were little doors about as high as a man, and as broad as a man. Mr. Raymond explained that these were for the natives to dodge into, and escape the furious elephants when they went into the arena, and were chased by them.

"I could do that myself," said Scott. But when he saw the struggle begin, and the lightning rapidity with which those huge animals would turn about, face any one who annoyed them, and charge across the field, he made up his mind that he would rather be excused.

The time came at last, and two men approached the two angry elephants.

Scott started to his feet. They were going very near. He thought they must surely be killed.

"There is no harm," said the king, who had taken a seat beside Scott. "They are the keepers. The elephants know them, and are never so angry that they will injure them."

It was a fact; for the fellows went deliberately up to the animals, and even made them take them on their trunks, and lift them to their heads.

"They're going to have the front seats in this show," Scott observed to Mr. Raymond, as other natives came in, and loosed the irons and chains about their legs; but, a moment after, he forgot about talking altogether.

The two animals started for each other the moment they found they were free. There was only a shrieking whistle from each as a signal, and they came together. The two great heads struck with a fearful blow; and the tusks, that were cut short that they might not injure each other, clattered and rang with the rapid strokes that only lasted for an instant, and then all was still.

The keepers had been obliged to cling for life to prevent themselves from being thrown off in the first blow; and the enormous bodies of the elephants had been lifted till their fore-feet were swinging in the air, as, with all their mighty strength, they pushed against each other with their hind-feet.

The moment they were still they began twisting their great trunks round each other; but that was the only motion, as each keeper urged his elephant on, and each animal laid every jot of power that he possessed into the muscles of those hind-legs.

Scott was trembling with excitement. The king even became so interested in the struggle, that he got up, and leaned against a pillar of the balcony.

"Look!" said Richard. "That fellow at the left is giving way."

"Why, he is pushing the other backward!" replied Scott excitedly.

"Yes; but he'll turn. See!" And sure enough, having made that desperate effort, and thrown the other from his balance, he turned suddenly, and ran toward the stable-door.

"What made him do that, when he was getting the best of it? He's a regular blockhead," said Scott scornfully.

"That was the last jump," replied Richard. "He saw that his strength was giving way. He did not stop to think that his opponent had been weakened by modern improvements, and had lost the sharp points to his tusks; but instinct told him, that, if he turned and ran, the other fellow would stab him in the side, and that, if he stood there much longer, he would be doubled over backward. So, when he found that he had got to go, he gave the other fellow a push that made him lose his balance; and, while he was settling on his feet again, he escaped."

Irons were put on to the vanquished elephant's feet, and he was led away. He did not make much objection. He seemed to feel ashamed of himself. The other fellow swelled up his sides with pride, swung his trunk in the air, looked up at the female elephants on the hill, and then looked around him for new worlds to conquer.

He did not have to wait long; for a dozen natives, naked to the waist, with shaven heads and very small turbans and the most meagre of breeches, ran into the arena. They were stalwart, finely-formed fellows.

"They are dressed rather thin: I envy them," said Scott, as he wiped the perspiration of excitement from his forehead.

"That is so that the elephants will have nothing to take hold of," replied the king.

"Why, what are they going to do?" asked Scott.

"Those fellows with lances are going to have a sham fight with him; and the men with poles have fuses in the end, which they set off in the elephant's face, in case of accident, to frighten him, and prevent him from doing any hurt."

"Is no one ever killed?" asked Scott.

"I never saw one killed," replied the king; "though my English friends tell me it is reported in their country that deaths are very frequent."

Now the fellows with the lances began a tirade upon the elephant; and, as the sharp points stuck into him, he would whirl one way, and then another, after the men, who would fly from him, while others on the other side attacked him. But at last he seemed to hit upon one who had either worried him more than the rest, or who had something peculiar about him by which he could identify him. Then he made for him; and the poor fellow had to use his legs with might and main to escape him. Sometimes the shave was so close, that the elephant could not stop himself, and would bang his head into the wall over one of the doors, that was too small for him to go through.

This seemed to be the thing that was sought for by the men in the arena; for the crowd considered it the very best of jokes, and applauded vehemently.

Then a horseman came in. His horse was a very graceful creature, until he turned round; but his tail was not only cut off very short, but clipped beside, so that the elephant could not take hold of it.

Scott thought this performance the most interesting part of all; and the least interesting, that part upon which most stress was laid as the great occasion of the day, — the rhinoceros-fight, when two of those clumsy animals were driven into the arena from opposite sides.

They no sooner saw each other (or heard each other, for they can only see a very short distance) than they began a lumbering trot, intent upon meeting. This trot grew faster, till in the centre they were going almost as fast as the elephants. But they had not aimed exactly right, and were too clumsy to turn. The result was, that they shot past each other, and brought up at opposite sides of the arena.

A shout went up from the spectators. The king and his guests roared with laughter; and the animals roared with passion, as they turned and again charged, only to miss as before.

This time they were not going so fast, however, and the third time brought them together. Then they fought furiously with their horns, almost as though educated fencers, till one made a lucky stroke, and fixed his horn under the other's throat, — their only vulnerable point, — that instinct told him was the place to make the attack. The other, by instinct, parried this blow by twisting his head suddenly, so as to bring

RHINOCEROS FIGHT.

the horn against his jaw, instead of his throat, where it could do no harm.

"That last elephant out was the Executioner," said the king to Mr. Raymond a little later, while they were eating an elaborate lunch upon the balcony. "Did you recognize him?"

"I did, your highness," replied Richard; "and, with your

permission, I would like to take my friend to the stable to see him before we go."

"I will go with you," replied the king; and, in a few minutes, he rose and led the way. He walked about the great stables, talking with the men he met there exactly as though he were one of them. He would take Scott by the arm, and lead him here and there to obtain the best views of the fettered animals. He had a menagerie that would have excelled all the circus combinations of America; and many times, as they were talking and laughing, Scott stopped suddenly, and looked up into his face. Could it be that he was one of those horrible heathen kings that were painted in "Arabian Nights" tales, even in some very modern and professedly very accurate literature!

"Why do you call him the Executioner?" he asked, as they passed the cages, and approached the enormous elephant.

"Why, because, years and years ago, when our good friend Mr. Raymond and I were little fellows, they used to have a way of executing prisoners that was so severe, that, as soon as we began to pick up bright ideas from the foreigners, we abolished it. They made this old elephant the executioner, and he enjoyed his work hugely."

"How in the world did you make him executioner?" asked Scott.

"Mr. Raymond saw one of the last executions that took place," replied the king. "It was then that I met him for the first time. He is more than half responsible for its being abolished, and for my being here to-day. He will tell you about it."

"Why is he called the Executioner, Mr. Raymond?" Scott

asked abruptly, coming up to Mr. Raymond when the king left him. Mr. Raymond started. He was evidently thinking deeply of something past. But in a moment he replied, —

"When a man was convicted, they used to tie him to this elephant's heels, and let him be dragged through the public streets; and, if that did not kill him, after a certain time they laid his head upon a block, and the elephant went deliberately up, and put his fore-foot on it, resting all his weight possible on that foot."

Scott looked up at that towering beast, so much larger than any he had ever seen, and shuddered, as he thought of what those huge feet had done.

But the thought of the other questions that he had to ask drew Scott from the fearful sight; and he said, —

"Will you please tell me, Mr. Raymond, — the king told me to ask you, and said you would, — how it was that you put a stop to that style of punishment, and are responsible for his being the king to-day?"

Richard turned clear about, and looked him in the eye for a moment. Then, with a light laugh, he muttered, "Stuff! You must not believe, Scott, all that these complimentary Orientals have to say."

They remained but a day longer at Baroda.

"I am in haste to be off," said Mr. Raymond, "for we must have important news at Allahabad soon. It will hardly take us longer to go by *garri* to Burhampur; and by that means you can have a taste of very different travel, and see the first of the famous marble banks of the Narbada River. We cut off two long sides of a triangle in not going back again to Bombay, as we should have to, to go by rail."

Scott did not see the *garri* till all was ready for the

start. It came the night before, and was made ready before he was up in the morning.

"What a wagon!" was his first exclamation.

"It is the regular *dak garri*, or post-chaise," replied Richard, laughing. "I intended hiring one of our own; but,

THE DAK GARRI.

finding that the regular weekly post left this morning, which would secure us a much surer lot of fresh horses and a certain progress, I thought we would take it."

"So we are going to carry the mail, are we? And what's that bed in there for?"

"To sleep on at night," replied Richard.

"At night? What will the hotel-keepers say?"

"In two hours we shall be beyond where they know so much as the name. You'll see no more comforts, my boy, till you strike the railroad again."

"Jew-pe-ter!" said Scott. "That's not so bad. But I

suppose we stop ten minutes now and then for refreshments."

Comfortably seated on camp-chairs, with the mattress disposed of in one end, and Moro and Sayad rolled up in one corner, they started off. Scott, as ever, was on the alert for every thing new; and "What is this?" and "What is that?" seeming to live upon the tip of his tongue.

"Look at that," Richard said, as they were entering the first village. "That is a Mohammedan slaughter-house."

"Hope they've stuck it outside the village far enough,"

THE SLAUGHTER-HOUSE.

said Scott. "They must have the monopoly there, or they'd put it in where rents might be a little higher; but the patronage would be enough better to pay."

"It wouldn't do here," replied Mr. Raymond. "This is a Marathi country, where every thing is Hindu. The Hindus don't believe in killing any thing, you know, and, most of all, a cow. So, if the Mussulmans want meat to eat, they have to come out here and get it, where it will not shock the nerves of the Hindus."

"Why don't they import it from somewhere, and done with it?" asked Scott.

"Because they are so particular about the way it is killed. To make a piece of meat set well on a Mussulman's stomach, it must come from an animal that has had a prayer said over it while it was alive, and then been killed at a single blow, in the name of God."

"I should hate to be a butcher," muttered Scott.

They had nothing to complain of as to the speed of their conveyance. They had two horses, and sometimes three, harnessed one before the other, and native drivers, who, every one in turn, would boast that he could drive faster than any other man on the line, and then proceed to prove it.

While they were changing horses, however, Scott obtained many an interesting view of native life. Once a curious individual was coming down the street, dressed in limitless rags, and shouting at the top of his lungs.

"A *fakir?*" Scott said, turning to Mr. Raymond.

"Not this time, but next to it,—a doctor on his way to visit some sick person."

"Heaven have mercy on the sick man's soul!" groaned Scott.

"You would say so, indeed, if you could follow that doctor," replied Richard. "He will go to the house; and unless some simple little thing is the matter, that he understands instantly, requiring some simple cure, he will begin and beat the poor patient, to make him confess that he has offended some god. Ten to one, the sick person has done something wrong within a short time, and will confess it. The doctor will advise the family to pay some some sort of a sacrifice; tell them, that, if the god that is offended is satisfied with their worship, the sick man will get well, and, if not, he will die. Then he will collect his fee, and go away."

"I shouldn't think his practice would increase much at that rate," said Scott.

"On the contrary, the more people who die under his care, the greater man he is thought to be. They say the doctor can only advise them, and that life and death are in the hands of God. Once, when I was going through one of these villages, I saw a poor fellow bitten by a snake; and, having the antidote with me, I applied it instantly, and saved his life, to the astonishment of every one. But, as soon as it was sure that he was going to live, the family said, 'The wicked snake made a mistake that time: he must have bitten the wrong man.'"

"That's interesting," said Scott. "You must have felt rewarded for your trouble. Is that the way they do business all over India?"

"That is the old style; but they are losing faith in it, thanks to modern civilization. In the large modern medical college of Madras they even admit women, and have several ladies there, who are actually taking the laurels away from the men."

"Why, they won't let an American lady take a medical diploma in Harvard College," said Scott in surprise.

"That's a fact, Scott," returned his friend; "but it would astonish these benighted heathen to tell them so."

"That is a pottery, that we are passing now," he added a moment later. "See that fellow moulding with one hand and one foot, and that woman turning a reel with her hand, and moulding with both feet."

"That's doing business on all fours, — or three of them, at least," said Scott. "Is that where they make the stuff that our girls paint, and stick up on the shelf, and think so precious?" he added.

"That is one of the very places; and it may be that you'll have one of those very jars some day, all covered with

A NATIVE POTTERY.

daisies, standing in the hall, pretending to hold umbrellas, when one wet one would spoil it."

"How much do they cost?" Scott asked, with an eye to business.

"Four or five cents apiece," replied Richard; and they drove on.

They reached the last station that they were to pass in

the *garri;* and sending Moro on with the baggage to wait for them at the next, — where they would meet him, and take another mode of conveyance over the mountains to the railway station, — Mr. Raymond and Scott, accompanied by Sayad, left the carriage, to make the next stage by the river. It was a little village, where the Narbada lay before them, stretching over a broad and beautiful plain.

NARBADA RIVER.

White-marble rocks glistened in every direction, emphasized by the dense green of the foliage and the profusion of flowers. A little boat lay against the bank: there was no wharf. In this boat they disposed themselves. It was late in the afternoon when the boatmen began to pull them up the river.

The scene was inexpressibly beautiful. Long shadows crept across the water, and the boat was perfectly mirrored in that absolutely rippleless surface. There was not a motion of leaf or twig. Not a bird flew, or a bee hummed, in the still air; and even the splash of the oars seemed to die on the water before it had gone far from the source. Up, up, up the river, slowly they went; and down, down, down into the west, the sun sank.

Scott thought he could almost see the sun dropping, as he saw the boat move; but suddenly it appeared to him that it was dropping over a broad plain that they were leaving; while, to rise again, it must come up beyond a high bluff that rose almost perpendicularly, over two hundred feet high, out of the water. He had understood that they had a long row before them; as the boatmen pulled very slowly, and that there was a strong current against them. He saw no current, and looked in astonishment at that impregnable abutment of marble that effectually cut off any farther progress.

"What's the matter, Mr. Raymond?" he asked.

"Are you tired of this scene?" his friend responded. "If so, it will be changed in a moment, and you will have quite another. Keep your eyes aft. Don't look forward, or it will hurt the surprise."

Scott obeyed, and in a few minutes realized that the water was bubbling and boiling about the boat; and, by the way the boatmen grunted and half exploded in their eternal song, he knew that they must be having hard work.

Still he kept his eyes aft, and watched the glow growing redder and redder on the water, that had been of the clearest azure when they started.

He thought of the "Arabian Nights," and of some of those wonderful transformations,—of water-babies, with Mother Be-done-by-as-you-did putting a bandage on little Tom's eyes with one hand, while she took it off with the other; and how Tom found, that, in that twinkling, he had been taken up those wonderful and mysterious back-stairs, and was in a new world.

And yet Scott was wholly unprepared for the remarkable transformation, when Mr. Raymond said to him, —

"Now, Scott, shut your eyes, turn round, and then open them."

Scott obeyed; and, when he had opened his eyes, he started back in astonishment, and even forgot to say any thing about great Cæsar's ghost.

Instead of that broad mirror of silent, rose-red water, they were in the midst of a dashing, gurgling torrent, black as night. Instead of the sparkling white and green and blue, and the forests in the distance, there rose upon either side of him high walls, — high as the spires of the churches of Boston, — flashing and white as hoar-frost; one solid, unbroken bank on either side, and only sixty feet apart. Instead of the absolute quiet that had reigned over all, there was a bedlam of chattering everywhere, for those marble walls were literally lined with monkeys; and, the moment the boat entered the gorge, they began to chatter, while, far up against the blue sky, the tiny forms of peacocks could plainly be discerned, spreading their gorgeous tails in the sunlight, as it flashed along the upper cliffs.

"What a shot!" Scott exclaimed when his admiration had cooled sufficiently for him to appreciate the fact that an enormous monkey was hanging, head down, over the water, clearly outlined against the marble, and only a hundred feet ahead of them. He went forward to get his rifle, that he had laid in the prow.

"Better not shoot at him, Scott; for you might possibly miss," suggested Richard.

"What of it?" asked Scott, still preparing to shoot. "Then, again, I might hit; and, if I did, I should have a stuffed monkey to carry home."

"Do you see those little brown balls all over everywhere?" asked Richard, pointing up the ragged sides of the cliffs.

"What are they?" asked Scott.

"Bees' nests," returned Richard solemnly.

"Bother the bees' nests!" said Scott. "I've seen them before in Massachusetts."

"But you might glance your ball, and shake one of them," added Richard demurely.

"What are they, — hornets?" asked Scott.

"Honey-bees," returned Mr. Raymond.

"Humph!" replied Scott, as he shouldered his rifle. "Honey-bees can't see but thirty-eight feet anyway."

"That may be; but they always manage to get within thirty-seven feet of any thing they want to sting," suggested Richard, so gravely that Scott lost his balance, and let his rifle fall, while he stopped to laugh.

"We might get some honey by it; and I'll risk the stinging if you will," he said a moment later, as the monkey, who had moved a few feet farther up the river, came into another position quite as good as the first.

"There'll not be much honey," replied Richard. "Those bees are neither used to working for the market, nor laying up a stock for a long winter. They only make for home consumption on rainy days, and it gives them a deal of time to spend in keeping their stings in working order. I'm inclined to think you'd find more sting than honey."

Scott hesitated again.

"Did you ever hear of any one getting badly stung here?" he asked.

"I was floating down this gorge years ago, prospecting with an English engineer. We were all alone in the boat; for we were going down stream, and the boat was very small.

THE MARBLE GORGE.

Halfway down he fired at a big monkey, and brought down a bees' nest. I saw it fall, but thought nothing of it, till, in a moment, the very air seemed full of insects. They were as large as New-England black hornets. They sighted the boat. They settled down on us like hail. I had on only a thin shirt and linen breeches. Three or four of them stung me, and that was quite enough. There were as many as fifty upon me, looking out for a good place to begin. 'Jump for your life!' cried the Englishman; and, as he was my superior in the engineering party, I obeyed without waiting an instant, supposing that he followed me. I swam under water with the swift current; but the fellows followed me, and every time I put my head above water to breathe, for over a mile, they were right upon me. At last I was beyond them and out of the gorge. I crawled up on to the bank down there; and, while I waited for the boat, I picked off thirty-two of those bees, that had clung to me till they drowned. A little later the boat came down the stream. I swam out to it; and there, in the bottom, lay the poor English engineer dead."

"Stung to death by these bees," said Scott with a shudder.

"Stung to death," repeated Mr. Raymond.

Scott laid down his rifle, and looked on in silence, as the sun set, and the moon rose white and clear over that sparkling gorge.

The crying of the peacocks, the chattering of the monkeys, the buzzing of the bees, — all was still. Now and then a fish rose; and once they passed a lumbering crocodile lazily pushing himself up against the current. Where a moonbeam by chance reached the water, they could follow the shivering shaft far down into the black depths, and even see the white sides of the fish flashing in the light.

"It must be good fishing here," Scott said a little later.

"The fishing is good enough, but the fish are poor: they are soft."

"There are not many caught, I should think, by the number left," said Scott.

"Only the very poor people live on them," replied Mr. Raymond. "It is a curious thing: almost everywhere we are told that fish are good for brain-food; but here, — in this region at least,—if a man is an idiot, or if one man or woman wants to call another a fool, they simply say 'fish-eater,' and that covers the whole ground."

They slept in the boat that night, and in the morning found themselves made fast to a little landing, where an ox-*garri*, that Moro had sent for them, waited.

It was not a two-days' trip over the hills: but, as it would take more than one daylight, Mr. Raymond thought it best to make two days of it, especially as they were a day earlier than they expected to be; and he did not wish to have Scott overtax his strength.

The passes through the hills were not bad. They were to go all the way in ox-*garris;* but there were no springs, and only two wheels; and, as the bullocks started off at a trot, with a relentless driver seated on the pole between them, Scott was bounced up and down till he eagerly welcomed the rising ground that should force them to walk. The servants and baggage came on in another *garri*. There were four extra coolies hired to push and pull if a wheel got into a rut, or in going up a hill so steep that the bullocks quietly refused to undertake it, which several times occurred. There was also a head servant to conduct the affairs; making a retinue of nine servants, four bullocks, and two wagons, to do the work that one hack, two horses, and a hackman would have done in America.

"It must be rather expensive travelling in this way," said Scott; "but it makes a fellow feel like a nabob."

Richard replied, "This fellow contracts to take us for the two days, and guarantees to land us safely or but half pay, for just four cents a mile. Then, our food by the way will cost perhaps a dollar more. The most expensive thing we have done so far was to visit the king."

"What! didn't he pay the bills while we were his guests? That's a pretty kind of hospitality!" said Scott.

"Oh, yes! he paid all the bills," replied Mr. Raymond; "but that was not the worst of it. He furnished us over twenty servants, including the elephant mahuts; and every night, and the morning we left, the whole troop of them came

LIKE THE CEDARS OF LEBANON.

for *backsheesh*, or presents. It is their custom. It cost about ten dollars a day just to keep them going.

At the foot of the hills they plunged into the forest, and began the gradual climb. Pointing to the scraggy branches of gnarled trees growing on the opposite hillside, Mr. Raymond said, "Look at those, Scott. They are the famous *deodas*. They are the same as the cedars of Lebanon. These are not remarkable specimens; but if we get up as far as the Himalaya Mountains, which for your sake I hope we shall not, you'll see forests, miles in extent, where these trees average over two hundred feet in height."

Every hour the jungle became more dense.

"See that tree covered with snow!" Scott cried, as they rounded a hill, and approached another valley.

"It is not snow, Scott," said Mr. Raymond: "it is only one of the moss-oaks that has wandered out of Scind, where they are very plenty. In some of those valleys you would certainly think there had been a heavy fall of snow. The leaves are such a black-green that the sparkling moss looks even whiter than it really is."

Moro ran past them while they were talking, and disappeared in the jungle.

"There's a village down there," Richard explained, — "one of the aboriginal towns. Moro came through here once before with me, and I fancy he made a friend there that he wants to see."

A little later they had turned the hill themselves; and Scott, who was looking eagerly forward, seeing only a few low mounds, with the road running past them, and Moro sitting on one side of the road, and two almost naked fellows on the other, exclaimed in disgust, —

"A village! I should call it a graveyard. I can see a few tombs, but where in the world is the village?"

"You can't see much of the village, for it is all under ground," replied his friend. "The aboriginal tribes do not pay much more attention to architecture than their fathers did, which was none at all. Those are the roofs of the houses that you see. The houses are all one hole scooped out of earth underneath."

"Cool place to board in the summer-time," said Scott, who began to feel the oppressive heat of the enclosed valley.

"When Moro and I came through here, we were obliged to stop for two nights and a day in this town," replied Richard. "There was as severe a storm as I ever saw in these hills. We were glad enough to reach here, I assure you; and, as

THE MOUNTAIN VILLAGE.

there was no hotel in the place, we put up at the largest private residence."

"Hotel!" exclaimed Scott. "Why, there are only five of those things you call houses in the whole valley."

"Certainly," replied Mr. Raymond. "Three of them form the centre, don't you see, and they have the flag there for voting-day; and then there are two more in the suburbs."

"But the hotel!" said Scott again.

"I said there was none," responded Richard.

"Of course there was none!" exclaimed Scott.

"Certainly: you are quite right," returned Richard; and Scott began to realize that he was unnecessarily interrupting a story.

"Well, we put up at that largest private residence: you'll see it in a minute. There it is down under the rocks there, to the right of the flag. When we got into the cellar, — that is all there is to it, — we found that it was a two-tenement house. There was no partition-wall; but, by common consent, the goats lived in one half and the human beings lived in the other; and the weather was so bad that the whole of both families were at home. There were a little over a dozen of the goats, but there were more than two dozen of the human beings. The goats were the cleaner by far; for they were out-doors more, and had some of the dirt brushed off: so, for both comfort and elbow-room, we put up with the goats. Do you see that hole in the top?"

"That square hole? Yes," said Scott. "What is it, — a window?"

"We thought so," replied Mr. Raymond; "for it is the only opening they had; and, as that roof is two feet thick, it lets in only a little light at the best. But right under it, there is a hole in the floor like a washbowl, in which they have their fire. I spoke of the hole as a window. The old fellow corrected me. He said it was a chimney; but that chimney was the only place in the whole house where that smoke did not go. It hung about the house till it died for want of exercise. The old fellow had a lot of eggs in a basket in one corner. He said he was waiting till some of his people went on a pilgrimage, to take them, and sell them in the crowd. The old fellow sold them very cheap. I took two dozen, and he urged me to take more. He even gave me a dozen; for he said they were of no value to him, as he had set them so many times that his people did not like them, and he could not make one of them hatch."

"Did you like the eggs?" Scott asked, as the *gharri* drew up at a little brook to give the bullocks water.

"It didn't matter much," replied Richard; "for all I gave the man to cover my entire indebtedness was an old felt hat, an old coat, and a white umbrella. The fellow rigged himself out in them, and, with his seven wives arranged in a circle about his door, gave me a most honorable farewell."

THE OLD MAN AND HIS WIVES.

The next village they entered was of greater importance and more modern. A Hindu driving a bullock-load of straw down the street stopped to look at them.

"That's the first time I have seen any one pay us so much attention since we landed," said Scott. "Why, if you should set one of these fellows down in America, the whole country would be at his heels every time he showed his head out-of-doors."

A HINDU DRIVING BULLOCKS.

"That is partly because they see more of us over here, but chiefly because they are very different people, and thoroughly believe that whatever is, is right. They take things as they are, and care very little about what happens so that they are let alone. That is one of the worst features of the Hindu character. In Bengal," he added, "they call that fellow a *raiyat;* and the straw he has on his wagon is rice, or *padi* as they say. It just turns American notions of civil disturbances upside down."

"That's a fact," said Scott, laughing; "for it makes the *raiyat* raise the *padi*, while with us it is the Paddy that raises the riot. Good enough!"

They stopped for the night at the Dak Bungalow, — something that takes the place of the old caravan-sarai, which still exists in many parts of the country.

The Dak Bungalow was at the extreme end of the village. It was a picturesque little place, just on the border of a mountain lake, that reflected the hills opposite and the dense foliage like a mirror. Little native boats were slowly moving over the lake. The two travellers hired one for an *anna* (less than three cents) for as long as they wished it, and pushed out.

"What a beautiful spot!" Scott exclaimed, looking up the steep hillsides, seeming to rise almost perpendicularly from the water on one side, while, on the other, rhododendrons grew more luxuriantly than he had ever seen them in America, to the very water's edge; and white and red roses, in wild forests, filled the air with perfúme.

In the morning they were up early, for they had ordered the men to be ready at five o'clock for the start. They ate their breakfast, and waited. Nothing was to be seen of any one.

"Where are they?" asked Scott.

"Lounging about somewhere," replied Richard carelessly.

They waited an hour. No one appeared.

"You paid that fellow in advance, didn't you?" asked Scott.

"I paid him half: that is the custom. No native will do any thing unless he obtain something in advance. For the rest, it was safe delivery or no pay."

"I'll bet he's gone off," said Scott.

"You'll lose your money if you do," replied Richard, laughing. "He's only lying round here somewhere, waiting for us to grow anxious, and offer him extra pay to go on."

"Let's hire some one else," said Scott indignantly.

"We can't do it, and he knows it," replied Richard. "There's not a vehicle in town that would take us."

"Then we are at his mercy," growled Scott.

"To some extent we are."

Just then one of the coolies came up.

"Where is your master?" asked Richard.

"Don't know, Sahib," replied the fellow.

Richard lay down carelessly upon the bed; and, calling to the keeper of the bungalow, he said, —

"Have dinner ready for us at noon."

The coolie did not seem inclined to move on; and at length Richard said to him, —

"Is your master still in the village?"

"Yes, Sahib: he is down on the lake, fishing," he replied.

"Go, and tell him that he may take his team, and drive back; and I will send on one of my servants for another *garri*. I did not like the way he drove yesterday."

"I am not hired to do errands: I must be paid for it," replied the coolie solemnly.

Richard threw him a copper, and he went away.

"Will he tell him that?" Scott asked, when the conversation had been explained to him.

"Not by any means," replied Richard, laughing. "He will go no farther than the village drinking-shop; and there he will stop, and drink and smoke till the money is gone. Then he will come back for more. In the mean time the rest of the servants will appear, one by one."

He was quite correct. One after another they came, in quick succession; and each easily obtained his copper, and went off upon his errand.

"What are you doing that for?" asked Scott indignantly.

"It's less than eight cents," replied Richard; "and now I am sure of them all. They are all at the coffee-house. Pretty soon the head man will turn up; and we will go down there with him, and start the whole lot of them together. Before we could not have found more than one at a time."

While he was speaking, the first coolie came back again.

"Aha!" said Richard with a smile. "This is a new game. The leader has sent this fellow for his copper, instead of coming himself. It would be about as well to give it to him, and then go down, and take the whole; but, instead, we'll have a little fun out of it." Then, turning to the coolie, he said quietly, —

"Did you find him?"

"Yes, Sahib," he replied; "and he said he would come at once."

"Is he here?"

"No, Sahib: I do not see him."

"Then he did not come."

"No, Sahib. He had gone down the lake."

"But you said that you found him."

"How could I, Sahib? He was not there."

"Do you know where he is now?"

"Yes, Sahib. I saw the boat coming back over the lake, and I came here at once to tell you."

"Very well," said Richard, half rising. "We will go down to the lake, and meet him, and tell him ourselves."

"But before this, Sahib, he will have landed and gone away," said the coolie, not at all disconcerted.

"I can find him," replied Richard.

"I will find him for you, Sahib, and bring him here for a half *anna*."

"Very well. Bring him here, and I will give you two *annas*. I want to thrash him."

"When the Sahib pays me half in advance, I will go," replied the coolie.

"Get out!" said Richard, starting to his feet. "I want to go down on the lake to sail now, and I don't want to be bothered."

The coolie started off; and, in less than two minutes, the leader came hurrying up to the bungalow.

"O Sahib!" he cried, falling on his knees, "I am in terrible misery. I have been hunting all the time for a lost ox. He strayed away during the night. I'm a poor man: the loss will kill me and all my dear family. Help me, Maharajah; help a poor dying man."

"But one of your *garri* wallahs told me you were down on the lake, fishing," said Richard.

"The fellow is a liar and a dog!" exclaimed the leader fiercely. "May he eat dirt, and be defiled! May the wind be in his bones! If I lie, master, may the sin be upon my head!"

"Then, we will start with one team, and hire some coolies here to drag the luggage," said Richard.

"But, master, two of the other oxen are sick: they cannot move. Oh, I am undone! I am undone!"

"We will wait till to-morrow, and let them get well."

"They will not get well: they are dying, Sahib. And, beside, there is a party coming from the South to-day—a very large party—who will require the bungalow. The Sahib has no tents: what can he do?"

"Do? Why, I will start on, and walk. I'll pay enough to induce the whole village to come out, and carry me on their backs. Don't fear. There are a hundred things I can do. If you are not here with the two teams in just half an hour, I shall do something, but I shall not go with you."

"If the Sahib would give a little present to a poor man"—

"But I shall not give you a present, and in a half-hour I shall not be here."

"An hour, Sahib! an hour!" pleaded the prostrate man. "My servants are all off looking for the ox."

"No, they're not: they are all down at the drinking-house," replied Richard.

"Just a little present, Sahib."

"Not the smallest in the world. No: if you are good, when we reach the end you shall have a present, but not before."

"I will be here in ten minutes, Sahib," replied the fellow; and in three-quarters of an hour he was on hand.

"He will do that same thing again when we get out into the woods," said Richard as they started. "And if he is wise, and strikes where it is bad walking, he will get the best of me; but, if it is good going, we will get Moro and Sayad to throw off the luggage from his cart, and we will start on. That will bring him to terms."

"Why don't you pound him?" asked Scott. "I'll try it, if you will back me if he gets the best of me."

"That is one point, Scott, where the British government has not only done enough for the Hindu, but too much. There are times when a thrashing is a good thing for a man; but the Hindus are weak and vexing, and the Englishmen are strong and quick-tempered. A few years ago there were several cases where native servants were actually brutally beaten. The government took it in hand, and has made it a grave offence to strike a native. The natives know it, and have grown decidedly worse under it. See that tea-house that we are passing, up on the hill there," he added, pointing to a low, long building, where was a crowd of natives busily engaged. "They are raising tea all over North India now, and making a good thing of it on the high land."

"But do you mean that they will really punish an Englishman for striking a native if he has cause?" asked Scott.

"Certainly they will."

"That's a healthy way of doing things!" said Scott scornfully. "Do you know, Mr. Raymond, it strikes me that India is the greatest muddle imaginable. One minute I think it the perfect heaven of earth. I think I would always live here. I make up my mind, that, as soon as I am a man, I will come back. Then I think it is a horrid place. I hate every thing about it, and I wish I had not to stay a day here."

"That's because it is a rough ploughed field now, between the old style of doing things and the new. Where you see either one alone, it is good; but where they come together, look out. It will all be smooth again by and by."

They reached the railway-station without another demand for *backsheesh*: in return for which Richard doubled the present he had intended to give the leader and his servants, and sent them off the happiest and most devoted set of fellows in the world.

"They are grateful vagabonds, after all," said Scott, feeling his heart grow warm toward the rude natives, and forgetting the struggle to get them started that morning.

"They seem so now," replied Richard. "But we have a half-hour more before the train starts; and, if I am not mistaken, the most of them will be back again, complaining about something, and asking for more, before we get away." He was quite correct.

"What's all that fancy-work around that collection of broken-down shanties over there?" Scott asked, as they started for a short walk, and approached several very large and low native buildings in miserable dilapidation. The ground about them was covered with something of the most brilliant coloring.

"That is a goolie-shop," replied Mr. Raymond. "That is where they dye cloths and mats in those magnificent shades that our people have tried so long — and all in vain — to imitate."

"Can't we come up to an establishment like that?" asked Scott, looking scornfully at the dilapidated goolie-shop.

The first train to leave was "a local," or accommodation.

"I am glad of it," Mr. Raymond remarked: "for, though a local is the most disagreeable thing in India to travel on, it will give us a few hours in Jabalpur to wait for the night-express from Bombay to Allahabad; and I have a permit that will admit us to the great Thuggi prison there."

"The what?" asked Scott.

"The prison where the condemned Thugs are confined. I want you to see them."

"And what in the world are they?"

"They are the very worst side of India," replied Mr. Raymond. "If we go north from Allahabad, as I expect we shall, you will see much of the magnificent side of one of the grandest empires the sun ever shone upon. But ancient India had bad features too, and the system of Thuggi was one of the worst."

While they were on the way to Jabalpur, Mr. Raymond

THE DYE-HOUSE.

and Scott talked over that terrible system that England has finally succeeded in crushing.

Mr. Raymond explained that it was a great secret society, with watchwords and passwords, and signals as elaborate as those of Freemasonry. Even the wives and relatives of the greatest Thugs in the land often did not know by what occupation they made their fabulous fortunes. Literally they were murderers and robbers. They professed to be humble devotees of the terrible goddess Bhawani, — the wife of Siva, the Destroyer in the Hindu triad. She is the same as the Kali, whose idol Paul saw on the banks of the Jumna, while seated on the broad shoulder of Dhondaram.

She is believed to exist upon the blood of the dead, and the Thugs committed their murders to supply her with victims. Then they robbed the dead to supply themselves with wealth. To prevent noise and blood-stains and occasional failures, they did their murdering with a *rumal*, or knotted handkerchief, which they threw over the head of the victim from behind, and, by a peculiar twist, strangled the man before he could utter a cry.

They went in organized companies, over systematically laid-out routes. They went as other travellers, professedly upon some business. Before the railways were laid out, all the merchandise of India had to be transported by travellers, and all the gold going from place to place had to be carried in the same way; so that their opportunities were almost unlimited.

Their operations were hard to detect: for the travellers were often obliged to take long journeys, and, as the mode of travelling was very slow, they were often gone from home for months; and, even if they were murdered by the way, there was rarely any reason to find it out till long after the robbery was committed. The Thugs were careful, too, to leave no track behind them, and to leave no one to tell the story; and they generally succeeded.

The pickaxe, with which they dug the graves, was the sacred emblem of the society. They held a religious service over it before they started on the pilgrimages. They were

THUGS.

very superstitious fellows: they believed that the goddess directed them by all sorts of signs.

All this, and a host of anecdotes from his own experience, Mr. Raymond related to Scott,—making the local seem like a flying express, so short was the time before they reached the beautiful town of Jabalpur, lying in a protecting valley open to the sun and the bracing mountain air (for they had reached a high elevation); while in the distance the Narbada River, that Scott looked upon as an old friend almost, was circling its way through the sand, like a silver thread in the sunlight. The first of the marble gorges is ten miles below.

Scott shuddered as they were led down into the solid-walled stone vaults where the Thugs were confined.

There were seven of them, crouching like caged panthers in the corner of one cell.

"Ugh!" said Scott. "I should not like to tackle those fellows in a free fight in the dark, even if they had forgotten their *rumals*."

"They're not at all savage-looking fellows," replied Mr. Raymond. "See that one standing in the corner at the left: he's as gentle as a kitten."

"Maybe, but I'd rather be excused," said Scott. "But what a stylish twist that fellow's got on his mustache!—the one that is sitting down in front of him. And what awful side-whiskers that next one in the middle has got!"

"That used to be all the style in India," said Richard. "Have you not noticed men going about the street with their faces all done up in cloth?"

"Yes, indeed! and I thought they had the toothache from smoking too much of a *hookah*."

"They had been shampooing their beards with a preparation that would harden a little in time, and had bound them back in that way to make them stay in the fashionable position."

"What fools!" muttered Scott.

Richard laughed. "American ladies do precisely that same thing; and they use a preparation that they call bandoline, that is copied from this very material the Hindus use."

"I've seen a bottle of that on my mother's bureau; and I've seen her go about, while she was dressing, with a white cloth over her forehead. Guess she'll stop it double-quick when I tell her about that gent sitting down there."

"Do you think she will if it is the fashion in America to use it?" asked Mr. Raymond.

"Never thought of that," replied Scott. "But she's president of the Society, you know; and she's an awful reformer."

"But reformers stick closer to fashion than any other class of people in the world. It's only an odd fashion, that's all."

But the time was up; and they had to leave for the station, and establish themselves on the express for Allahabad,—a city almost in the centre of India as far as the great railway and river systems are concerned, with a name that, Mr. Raymond explained to Scott, meant "the City of God."

CHAPTER XIX.

THUGS AND TRAITORS.

THE first view that Scott obtained of the City of God was the immense railroad-bridge crossing the river.

"What river is this?" he asked; and, looking more closely, he exclaimed again, "Why, what is the matter with it? One side is white, and the other is black."

"This is the confluence of the Ganges and the Jumna Rivers," replied Mr. Raymond. "The Ganges is supposed to flow from the mouth of Bramha: it is the most sacred water in the world. Then the Jumna is very sacred; and, to make a collection here that cannot be equalled, they have arranged a plan by which the Sirasvati, — the Divine River coming directly from the throne of Bramha by an invisible passage — joins the two here."

"That's not so bad," said Scott; "but what is it makes the water all black one side, and white the other?"

"Because the Ganges and Jumna, though they rise very near together, flow through such different soil that one is muddy and the other clear. That is all, and they hate to mingle."

The hotel was in an open square opposite the old fort and palace compound, near the river. The fort rose up perpendicularly out of the water.

The letters which Mr. Raymond received were important, but not explicit.

"We must go to Benares to-night, instead of to the North as I expected. I struck the right track the first time, but it remains to be seen what will come out of it. Do you

THE OLD FORT.

remember the man who rode with us part of the way from Liverpool to London? He gave me the name of an intimate friend of Dennett's, in many a rascally game here, — an infamous half-caste, who has such a peculiar knack in handling native laborers that he keeps himself in employment as an overseer or foreman. I found that he was finishing some embankments on the road to Mogul Sarai, opposite Benares, and sent to him right away."

"I should have thought that would be dangerous," said Scott.

"So it might have been," replied Richard, "but that I have had occasion to bother him a little already, and he knows that it is in my power to give him as much trouble as I like: so, when he found out that I had my eye on him in this matter, he owned up to it instantly."

"To knowing about Paul?" exclaimed Scott, white with excitement.

"Yes, to knowing about Paul."

Scott sprang to his feet; and, throwing his arms round Richard's neck, he gave him a resounding kiss before he remembered that he was no longer a boy.

"But you must be patient, Scott. It may be very hard work to learn much, and harder still to do much. We can only go to Benares, and see what we can do."

"Can't we start before to-night?" asked Scott anxiously.

"Patience, patience, my boy!" said Richard gently. "I know exactly how you feel; but, if we hurry, we shall do much more harm than good. We shall have to go so slowly, and act so indifferently, that I fear you will be angry with me a hundred times."

"No, never!" exclaimed Scott.

"Don't promise, Scott. If you are angry, speak it out, and perhaps I can explain it; and, whenever we have a chance to, be sure that I shall go as fast as steam or animals can carry us. But remember this: that, if you move slowly after a tiger carrying away a lamb, the chances are, he will run from you, dropping the sheep; if you rush upon him, he will make a stand, and strike to keep his prey; and, if you press him too hard, he will be very apt to tear his prey in pieces, even though he give you an opportunity to kill him while he is doing it."

"I will remember," said Scott bravely; "but I wish that there were something we could be doing now."

"We will take a walk," replied Richard, "and after dinner we will sleep for a few hours; for we shall reach Benares at about two in the morning, which will break our rest."

"Sleep!" exclaimed Scott; but Mr. Raymond looked at him. He knew what it meant, and replied, "Of course I will try."

They walked through the lower native quarter by the river, and on to the banks of a little stream. There they sat down in the shadow of some overhanging branches.

"Are there any Thugs now free?" asked Scott, thinking of Paul.

"Oh, yes!" replied Richard. "Not as a band, and not as murderers, for that is entirely broken up; but some of the most notorious are still at large, escaping every endeavor to capture them."

"Did you ever see one out of the prisons?" asked Scott.

"Yes: I once saw a very notorious fellow,—Dhondaram," replied Mr. Raymond.

"I thought you told me he was a muni," said Scott.

"He is a muni, and a Thug too; and in the mutiny he was one of the most influential leaders. Since then he has been the terror of every native, great and small, who fought with the English in that struggle for the freedom of India."

"What has he done to them?"

"He has murdered over fifty of those men that he calls traitors, already, to the knowledge of the government, and"—

"Can't any one find him?" asked Scott impatiently.

"They can find him. They hear of him very often. Several times officers have almost laid their hands on him. The government offers a reward of ten thousand dollars for his head, and yet he lives."

"What would they do with him if they should find him?" asked Scott.

"Hang him; starve him to death; cut him up,—any thing, I fancy," replied Mr. Raymond, with a cold, metallic, vindictive ring in his voice, that made Scott shudder and suddenly look up, to see a frown darker and sterner than he had imagined could ever have shadowed the face of the invariably calm and gentle Richard Raymond.

"The British government would not do that, Mr. Raymond!" he exclaimed.

"The British government, Scott! Is the British government responsible for what her officers may chance to fancy wise in an emergency? If so, Scott, then the British government was actually outrageous and horrible and barbaric in its dealings during the mutiny with the Hindus. At the very outbreak fifty rebelling sepoys in Col. Nicholson's command were tied to the mouths of British cannon, and blown to pieces. A young sepoy twenty years old, whose turn it was next to be executed, came up to the officer, and smiling in his face, and tenderly stroking the ugly gun, said, 'There's no need to bind me, captain: I am not going to run away.' On the 30th of July, 1857, over a thousand prisoners were bound and shot by the English, really to get rid of them; and fifty who escaped were recaptured, and put in prison, where they starved to death. On the 28th of August nearly seven hundred helpless fellows were put to death. On the 23d of September, after the British took Delhi, two

"THERE'S NO NEED TO BIND ME, CAPTAIN."

of the king's sons, who had fled to the sixty-four-pillared hall out in the plain, were found there, lying unarmed on the altar; and, though they pleaded for mercy, they were shot in cold blood by a British officer who had a squad of soldiers behind him. Three other men of the royal family surrendered themselves to the officer in command, who had them taken in their coach to the large square; and there, before his soldiers, he got into the coach, made them strip their breasts, and shot them, each one, in cold blood. At Cawnpore nearly two thousand sepoy prisoners were shot at command of the British officer; and, before they died, many were condemned to lick with their tongues the spots of blood

SCENE OF THE MASSACRE OF TWO THOUSAND HINDUS BY THE BRITISH.

in the palace, where they had been commanded by Nana Sahib to kill his English prisoners, to prevent them from being retaken by the British. At Jhansi the harem was sacked, and many captive Hindus were either hung or shot; till the moat of the palace of the Rani Bai, the queen, was filled with the bodies of the dead."

"Why did they take a queen's palace?" asked Scott with a shudder.

"Because she was one of the most zealous in the struggle for the freedom of her country," replied Mr. Raymond; "because Sir Hugh Rose, of the British army, reported to Parliament that the most dangerous and the fiercest *man* opposing England was the Rani Bai, the queen."

"I have read of terrible atrocities perpetrated by the Hindus, but nothing of this," replied Scott.

"Of course not," said Richard. "And can you not see why not?"

"I read a terrible story the other day in the hotel, about a massacre by the Hindus at Cawnpore."

"Every one reads of that," replied Richard with a frown.

"I thought the Hindus were all to blame."

"Every one thinks so," replied Richard. "Yes, that was a terrible massacre. Nana Sahib was at the head of the rebels in that quarter. He was as much of a fiend as some of the English officers. He ordered his soldiers to go into ambush on the steps of a low temple leading down into the water, and, as soon as the barges with the English prisoners came past the temple, to open fire upon them till all were dead. This many of his soldiers refused to do; though they were fighting for their very lives and homes and families, and were only ignorant Hindus at the best. He could not drive them or persuade them. He was forced to gather a promiscuous crowd, and, by wine and bribery, forced them to do the bloody work. The British army came still nearer; and Nana Sahib heard from every side of the fearful deaths his people were dying at their hands, and of their merciless marches. In his fury he ordered the women who were his captives to be killed at the last moment, when it was certain that the British were upon him."

THE SCENE OF NANA SAHIB'S MASSACRE OF THE BRITISH.

"Their bodies were thrown into a well, were they not?" asked Scott.

"Yes: into the well that is now the famous Scar of Cawnpore, kept fresh in British memory by a chapel that has been built over it, and a marble angel that stands directly over the well."

"What started the mutiny?" asked Scott.

"Too much of a complication for us to discuss just now," replied Richard.

"And you said that that Dhondaram was one of the leaders?" said Scott a moment later, for there seemed to be some strange fascination that was drawing him continually toward that name.

"Yes: he was the right hand of Nana Sahib," replied Richard.

"Is he really a very bad man?"

"I do not know, Scott," replied Richard with a sigh. "These Hindus are not of our world. What seems very wrong to us seems right to them. God may have some different way of judging them than by our codes of laws."

"Was he as bad as Nana Sahib?" asked Scott.

"I think not," replied Richard. "He was a very different man. He was a religious teacher, in the first place. He was a frantic fanatic. He is certainly a brave man. When the rebellion sprang up, he entered into it heart and hand. I saw him myself once on the porch of a temple, sword in hand, in a crowd of Bramhans, crying to the people to rise and free themselves. Roderick Dennett and I were together that day. We had a narrow chance of it in escaping, and the report that we took to the British authorities gave us our first fair start in India."

Mr. Raymond was silent. The old times were coming back too fast to be lived again with indifference.

"How did that help you?" Scott asked.

"It did not help me so much as it did Dennett at the time," Richard replied. "It brought me into notice afterward; but Roderick was older than I, and took the lead in those days. He received an appointment at once to keep track of Dhondaram; but, instead of doing it, he really turned the muni's friend, and sold much information to Dhondaram, for which he received a good price. But, to wind up, Dennett at last offered to find Dhondaram for the government, for a thousand pounds and pardon for several crimes for which he was imprisoned. Dhondaram found it out just in time to save himself. Then Dennett left India for England. He was followed there, and nearly caught; but at last he escaped, and went to America. When we ran away from Beverly, we went under false names; and when Dennett reached America again, no one ever knew what sort of a character he had been,

PREACHING THE INSURRECTION.

until he showed them in Boston, a little while ago, the kind of a man he really was."

"I should have thought he would have been afraid to come back here to India," said Scott.

"To any other country he would have been afraid," replied Richard; "but here the European population is continually changing. I know very few indeed now who were here when I was a boy. People forget, too, in a land like this. Any thing that is out of sight for a little while is out of mind forever. Only his old associates would remember him, and to them he could go in safety. That is why I was so sure of hitting him soon, and why I succeeded at once."

"Wouldn't Dhondaram remember him?" asked Scott.

"If he is alive, he will remember him: there is no doubt of that," replied Richard. "But it is time we were taking our nap. Let us go to the hotel."

CHAPTER XX.

PILGRIMS, PRIESTS, AND PEOPLE EVERYWHERE.

"SCOTT! Scott! this is Mogul Sarai. We have reached Benares," said Richard Raymond, gently stroking Scott's forehead as the boy lay asleep in the night-express.

Scott started up with a cry.

"Excuse me," he said an instant later, rubbing his eyes. "I had a dream. I thought that Dhondaram was carrying Paul away.

"I thought Benares was a large city," added Scott wonderingly, as he stood on the platform.

"So it is a large city, Scott, but on the other side of the river. They could not put the station on the other side; for the Hindus consider Benares as holy ground, resting on the back of a divine mud-turtle, and they fought so hard against a railway that they had to put the station on this side the river."

"What was it that coolie just said to you?" asked Scott.

"He has a lantern, and I suppose he wants us to follow him to a boat. I could not understand him."

"I thought you understood all their languages," said Scott.

"There are over seventy entirely different languages spoken in India, beside a host of dialects," he replied. "It would take a lifetime to learn them all."

There were three boats waiting on the bank. They were

miserably weak affairs, even as seen in the dim lantern-light; but the man who had led them down proved to be the post-office employee with the mail-bag; and, thinking that the mail-boat would probably be as safe as any, they followed him, much to the disgust of the other boatmen, who, as soon as they were under way in the muddy, rushing river, attempted to show them what a mistake they had made in point of speed. This excited the oarsmen of the mail-boat,

BENARES.

and the three boats creaked and bent as they were pushed through the water.

The yellow water splashed in their faces, and the little waves made the boats rock. Scott began to fear they might have a shipwreck there in the Ganges, but Richard only laughed.

"This is the first time in my life," said he, "that I have needed to urge a native to go slower, instead of giving him *backsheesh* to hurry."

By dint of utmost exertion they avoided striking a clod

of some sort that was floating in the river. The next boat, not so fortunate, hit it fairly, and sent two of the three boatmen overboard, much to the amusement of those in the other boats, who did not stop pulling for an instant, but left them in the water.

"What in the world was that?" asked Scott.

"A cow going to glory," replied Richard solemnly.

"What!" exclaimed Scott, seeing that there was a joke somewhere, but being quite too sleepy to take it in.

"Why, the Ganges is very sacred, you know; and when an animal dies whose master hopes to own it again in the sweet by and by, he just throws it into the river, instead of burying it. When men die, they burn them, and throw their bones in too; for they believe, that, in some way, this river flows back again into the mouth of Bramha, from whence it comes."

"Must be as nourishing as Cochituate water in Boston in midsummer by the time it gets back again to the spot that it starts from. I wonder if Bramha has a filter in his throat," said Scott.

Had it been daylight, they would have obtained a view of the holy city, lying on the opposite bank, that would have occupied Scott's entire thoughts; but, as it was, they landed as much in the dark as they embarked. Still, there was no appearance of the city anywhere.

"Now we must take a *garri*, and ride for nearly two miles," said Richard, as they walked up the bank.

"What in the world did they stick the city off in such an awkward spot for?" muttered Scott, whose drowsiness made mountains out of mole-hills.

"It was a great mistake," replied Richard seriously; "but

you see, three or four thousand years ago, when they laid the foundations of Benares, they did not figure, as they should, on the probability of its growing to sufficient size to require a railway."

They easily made a bargain, as there were several drivers on hand, and they were the only passengers, and were soon rattling down an ill-paved street in a poor imitation of an English cab.

Here and there dim shadows of huts could be distinguished along the way; and now and then a low fire was smouldering in the middle of the street, and around it sat a few nearly naked natives, either sleeping, or shivering like pet hounds in the winter. But, awake or asleep, they did not move when the *garri* rolled by. It had to turn out for fire and men together.

"If I were driving, I would run over one of those fellows now and then, to teach them better than to build their bonfires in the street," said Scott, after they had turned out for a dozen or more.

"But they are the great guardians of the peace," replied Mr. Raymond. "They are the native police of Benares."

"What do they want those fires for? It is hot enough to roast."

"So it is, but that is only custom. The fellows would sit on those fires and roast in reality if it were custom, and their fathers had roasted there before them."

"But what do they go to sleep for if they are policemen? Is that custom too?"

"It is just that exactly. They have nothing to do but be on hand, where they can be called if there is trouble; then to look on carefully, see the whole with unprejudiced eyes, report it to the *jemadas* in the morning: and the soldiers will then arrest the offenders. These fellows would not know how to make an arrest, even if they dared to, in the night."

Where the huts by the roadside were near enough, it often happened that they saw a row of heads lying over the door-sill. At last, however, they reached the Dak Bungalow, where Richard preferred stopping, that they might remain in seclusion.

"It is a very pretty spot," Scott said, as he looked out of the broad door that stood open to admit the breeze, when he woke in the morning. There was a little lawn about the bungalow, with several tropical trees growing upon it. "But what are those natives there for? Is it to see some Americans?" he asked, pointing to a dozen or more Hindus who were seated on the green lawn.

"They want to see us on business," replied Richard.

"Business?" exclaimed Scott, thinking of Paul.

"Nothing of importance," Richard hastened to add. "Only that, as soon as they see we have finished breakfast, they will all come in with all sorts of native merchandise to sell."

"I don't want any of their stuff," said Scott impatiently.

"Every one says so," replied Richard; "but they are good salesmen. We have not much time to spare; but this is one of the sights of India, and we will wait a few minutes for it. I warrant, that, before you know they have even tried to sell you any thing, you'll be wishing you could purchase the lot." He was quite correct.

They scarcely spoke a word, only now and then making some slight remark about the place that some treasure came from, as they undid their bundles, and spread upon the floor about them a tempting array of every thing imaginable that

India furnished. Mr. Raymond occupied the time in writing and sending a note to the foreman, instructing him to meet him at the bungalow at one o'clock. When he had finished, he looked up, and asked,—

"Well, how do you find it, Scott?"

"You did not tell me they had such jolly things," said Scott.

"No: I left you to find that out for yourself. What do you want?"

"I should like that little Cashmere cap, or perhaps two or three of them, to carry home; and I should like some of those sandal-wood cases so beautifully carved; and those peacock-feather fans are beautiful, and—well, I don't know; that ivory box would be a splendid present for mother, and those embroidered silk handkerchiefs are wonderful. How Bess would like them! She must have them. And I should like one of the *hookahs*, too, just to show the boys what fire-engines they smoke through, you know."

"But I thought you didn't want any of their stuff," said Richard, smiling. Scott had forgotten his remark.

"There are over one thousand temples in this city," said Richard, as they started for a drive. "It is almost entirely a Hindu city, but there is one Mohammedan mosque. First I am going to take you out on the river, and then to the top of the observatory, that you may see the whole. Most of the temples crowd upon the river, and from them marble steps extend down into the water for the bathers. Then we will see all we can of the best of the temples near the river before dinner, and afterward drive to the distant ones."

They reached the river in the carriage, and dismissed it. Seating themselves in a curious boat with a fancy canopy to protect them from the sun, a half-dozen oarsmen pushed them past the miles of marble *ghats* (or steps) leading into the water. They were dark with bathers. All sorts and sizes of people, crowded their way into the water, dressed just as they had come from the street, and just as they were going back again into the street as soon as their clothes were dry. There were broad, flat umbrellas, — a forest of them, — under which

TEMPLES BY THE RIVER.

bathers were sitting on the steps, waiting for an opportunity to go into the water. Those already there would take the dirty water, and pour it over their heads, repeating a prayer, and touch it to their lips and breasts, still praying. Sometimes a carcass would float down, and become entangled in the bathers; but they would only push it out of their way, and go on praying.

"Are there no crocodiles here?" asked Scott.

"Lots of them," replied his friend; "but they are fed so well up the river and down that they rarely venture into the crowd. There was a sensation here a while ago, however, when a crocodile was several times seen and often felt. He would grasp by the legs the women that were bathing, and often succeed in pulling off their gold and silver ornaments that they wear about their ankles. They dared do nothing to disturb him, for he is one of the most sacred animals of India. But his depredations were suddenly stopped one day, when a crocodile's head rose out of the water with a fearful cry. There was another crocodile close behind. Suddenly the one behind gave a bound, opened his mouth, grasped something just beneath the water, gave it a shake. The head flew off, and all saw the body of a native beneath it for an instant, as it went down in the jaws of a genuine article."

"What was it?" asked Scott.

"Why, a fellow who put on the head to deceive the bathers, and then, swimming under water, robbed the women of their jewels."

"Good enough for him," replied Scott. "But what is that pile of wood there for?"

"That is at the top of the burning *ghats*. There are no bathers there; but at night there are fires all along the *ghats*, where they are burning the dead. We shall round yonder corner in a moment, and you will see them better. Before we are out of sight, look at those two tall towers. They are the minarets of the mosque."

The boat rounded the corner, shutting out the distant minarets, but bringing into better view the temples and the burning *ghats*.

"The most beautiful bathing *ghats* in the world are not far from here. I wish we could have stopped there, and have seen them as we came through Mirzapur on the way to Benares. They are of pure white marble, with magnificent ornamental work, and a little temple at the top, and a wonderful balcony of carved marble. It is enough to make one want to go in bathing just to see it."

BURNING THE DEAD.

"Unless the water is cleaner than it is here, I think I should rather be excused," said Scott, shaking his head.

"If you once saw the place, especially by moonlight, you'd change your mind, I fancy," replied Mr. Raymond. "It's almost enough to make one wish he were a heathen, just for half an hour. Only long enough to wash his sins away, you know."

They left the boat just below the *ghats*, and turned into one of the narrow streets, — so narrow, and with houses so high, that the opposite eaves seemed almost to touch. All along the street there were little booths, where all sorts and sizes of idols were for sale; and the streets were filled with pilgrims in rags and dirt, and princes and rajahs in magnificent costumes, all seeking the holy water; and priests without number, with scanty clothing or flowing robes, and long silken beards that they never cut. Munis were everywhere, and there were monkeys in every alley and on every roof. In the most crowded parts of every street, there were cows contentedly feeding on offerings that those who passed were

THE BEAUTIFUL MARBLE GHATS.

continually making to them. Some of the cows had garlands of flowers about the horns or necks.

"I should think it was Decoration Day," said Scott. "And what in the world is the matter there?" he added, pointing to two men and a woman who were flat on their faces before one of the cows, right in the thick of the throng threading the narrow alley.

"The cow is sacred. They are only saying a prayer before her: that is all," replied Richard.

"Great Cæsar's ghost!" muttered Scott, as he carefully stepped over the extended legs of one of the devotees.

They climbed by a long, winding staircase, through dust and dirt, to a broad, flat roof, raised high above the surrounding buildings.

THE OBSERVATORY.

"This is one of those observatories I was telling you about," said Richard. "Look at these dials for the sun and moon, and this complex affair to regulate the Luna dials to the different months, and this block of marble, with a little groove in it pointing up to the North Star. Then there are a host of other things that I know nothing about, that you will understand when you study astronomy. This is one of the most modern observatories in India, and most of these things were copies from others much older; but even these were here when we were ready to hang Galileo for the first and simplest discoveries that he made with his little telescope.

"We!" said Scott. "They never asked me what I thought about it, or I should have told them to leave it to these heathen to settle the matter. And wouldn't the old Pope have been mad! What a bull he would have sent to doze me!"

The view from the summit of the observatory gave Scott still another idea of the densely crowded holy city.

On their way out of the forest of temples, they passed through an alley even gloomier and narrower than any they had seen before.

"Look through that little hole in the wall, Scott, and see how you like the view," Richard said, pointing to a hole so small that Scott almost lost it in trying to stand on tiptoe to reach it; but at last, with a cry of surprise, he attained the position.

He seemed to be looking into a vast chamber of dazzling sunlight and polished marble and burnished gold. The draught that was drawn through that little hole was laden with the sweetest fragrance of rose-oil and sandal-wood.

"It is the Temple of Siva, — the great Golden Temple to the especial deity of the city," Mr. Raymond explained.

"Will you have a drink?" asked Richard, as they stopped beside the Well of Knowledge a moment later.

Scott stepped upon the platform, and looked down into the well. A vile mass of decaying flowers and sprouting rice was floating there; and he replied that he would rather be excused.

"It is very efficacious water," continued Mr. Raymond. "The god Ganesh, in the shape of a serpent, representing Wisdom, jumped into this well. As the result of it, the well became at once imbued with wisdom."

"And with serpents too!" exclaimed Scott. "I saw a dozen of them, at least, sticking their heads above the water. And do people really drink it?"

"Look at them," replied Richard, as two pilgrims came up, deposited their coins, and took a drink. "They imbibe the wisdom."

"And the serpents, too, I'll bet! But the thing must pay like a soda-water fountain on a hot day. Look there! There go three more ignoramuses. What a set of people these Hindus are! One minute you think they're smarter than chain-lightening, knowing all about astronomy before the stars were created; and the next you find them paying half a cent or so a drink for dead rose-leaf and snake tea, thinking they are going to grow wise on it."

As it was not far, they walked back to the bungalow; and on the way, just at the gate of a rajah's palace, they passed a funeral procession, where three of the male relatives were carrying the body of the dead in a sort of palanquin, supported by poles, on their shoulders. They were wailing a song as they went, or something intended for a song.

"If they were rich, they might have two or three fellows going with them, with tomtoms and drums and a fife or two, to keep up their spirits, and keep them in time," said Richard as they approached.

"What are they singing?" asked Scott.

"Moro understands them. Where is the boy?" returned Richard, looking about him. But Sayad was following alone.

"Oh, I remember!" he added. "I told Moro he might bathe; and I suppose he will take a month for it, he has such an accumulation of sins. But never mind. They are singing the praises of the dead man, and a long list of good things that he did when living: that is what they always sing."

A FUNERAL PROCESSION.

"Poets and musicians must be plenty," observed Scott; "for there seem to be a plenty of deaths."

"But this is the same old song, both words and music, that they have used at every funeral for centuries. They don't want to say any thing but the best of a dead man; and when they have the very best that can be said, all written down and set to music and learned by heart, what is the use of any thing new?"

"And a fellow knows, that way, what is going to be said of him. That's comfortable," added Scott.

The foreman came to the bungalow. He admitted that Roderick had left Paul with him for a few days; and said that he had turned him over, according to orders, to some pilgrims who were going up the Ganges and Jumna, to Delhi, to the feast of the Pungas, for he had been directed to send Paul's clothing there. Further than that he refused to speak. Richard asked him of the whereabouts of Roderick Dennett; but he replied indignantly, —

"I'm not that sort o' man, Mr. Raymond; and you know it, that you do. Roddy Dennett's not my kind; no, he ain't. He can go back on his friends; but I, no! He's my friend, — Roddy is. God knows he'd go back on me for a rupee any day: but I'll not go back on him; no, I won't. You told me, if I'd let out all I knew o' the little kid, you'd let up on me; and I've done it. And you'll do it; for you're a man o' your word, yesterday and to-morrow and every day, you are: and I'm not afraid to tell you to your face, top o' that, that not a word'll I breathe o' Roddy Dennett, so help me God! no, I won't. No more you won't touch me, neither, till you find out I've held something back about the kid. I know you, Raymond Sahib, and there's no use your talking more; for I have your word, and I'd's soon have that as a sealed pardon from the viceroy. I'll send you the kid's clothes that's left behind before two hours, and that's all I will do. Good-day, Mr. Raymond."

"That's not quite all," said Richard. "I told you you must help me find the child."

"Right you are there, Raymond Sahib; and I'm your man. I'll go with you if you say it, or I'll go alone, or I'll stay where I am; and, be it one or all, tell me where to find you, and I'll give you my word — for what it's worth — that, the first thing and every thing I learn o' the whereabouts o' the kid, you shall know it by telegraph.

"Course you'll pay expenses and a little beside," he added as he went out.

"All that is left us, then," said Richard when he and Scott were alone, "is to go up to Delhi, and watch there for the pilgrims coming in from the river. Let me see: this is sixteen days since we landed."

"It seems like a year, at least," said Scott incredulously, as he began to count the days again.

"They started two days after we landed," Richard continued, "and could not possibly reach Delhi in less than a month. We have time to go slowly, see a good deal by the way, and still be well established before the feast of Pungas."

"Why not strike the river, and search the pilgrims?" suggested Scott.

"Because it would be impossible. The very ones that had Paul in charge would look the most innocent. There will be hundreds of boats going up to the feast, and we have only the word of this vagabond to go upon. While we were searching the wrong ones, the right one would hear of it, and escape us. The best way is to say nothing. There is no fear but that Paul will be well cared for. The Hindus love children, in the first place; and, beside that, whoever has him will be well paid for care, and well threatened if any thing happens. I know Dennett. He has not taken all this pains, to lose his prize now."

Scott had no choice but to wait, and let matters take their course; and, as soon as dinner was eaten, they sent for a carriage, and drove out ten miles to Sarnath, the site of the first Buddhist city in the world, stopping by the way at a famous temple.

Richard had said nothing of what sort of a temple it was, wishing to surprise his friend; but Scott noticed that he took off his cork helmet just as he was entering the gate, and was in the act of following the example, and of asking why he did it, when his own helmet was lifted from his head.

There was no one near him; and Scott looked up in surprise, to see at least fifty little black hands with long wiry fingers, with the nails bitten off very short, in a squirming wreath about his head, and half as many dark woolly faces turned disconsolately upward, while their tiny black eyes followed the successful monkey. He leaped from the wall to a tree, from the tree to the porch of a little temple, from the porch to the ornamental tower, and from one ornament to another, till he perched upon the very highest attainable point; and, with the huge helmet in his little hand, he turned round, and made a face at Scott.

Scott picked up a stone to throw at the intruder; when at least a hundred and fifty monkeys all about him began to howl, and two priests in hideous robes, with cowls over their heads, sprang forward, and caught his uplifted hand. He pushed them angrily away; when Richard, coming to the rescue, said, —

"Be careful, Scott. Those monkeys are terribly sacred, and so are the priests. This is the great monkey-temple. It wouldn't do to insult the gods."

"But he's got my hat," cried Scott angrily, and looked up the tapering tower, — all jutting ornaments, to give the monkeys a good chance to climb. When he saw the old monkey at the top, however, he could not himself refrain from smiling: for the fellow had forced the hat down between two ornamental projections, and, seating himself in it as though it were an easy-chair, he had crossed his legs, and thrown his head back against the marble tower; and there he sat, quietly scratching himself, and looking down on the bareheaded boy.

"That's one way they take to make a living out of tourists," Richard explained. "Perhaps you cannot see the joke, but they want you to give them some money to pay them for trying to get the hat back again."

"Will they guarantee to do it?" asked Scott, who had inherited a financial turn of mind from his father.

"I don't believe they'd sign a contract," replied Richard; "and, unless you gave them nearly what they can get for the hat if they sell it in the bazaar, I hardly think they will succeed."

"They won't have a chance to try," returned Scott, quietly taking from his pocket a little cashmere cap that he had bought of the pedlers after breakfast that morning. "If they can't furnish their gods with rocking-chairs, I will. And I'll wear this till I can get me another."

Even the priests smiled at the business-like way in which Scott turned to examine the temple and monkeys, without so much as looking up again. He even bought some of the pop-corn and candies that they keep always on hand to sell to travellers who wish to feed the monkeys.

But when Scott came to the real idol, the great monkey-god, in the centre of the little temple, in fact filling the temple completely with his innumerable heads and legs and arms, he turned away in disgust.

"I'd give more for one sick monkey than a dozen like him," he exclaimed. "Why, Paul's got a jumping-jack at home that'll beat him all to Goshen!"

They did not remain long, but taking the carriage again drove out to Sarnath.

"You'll hardly think it worth seeing," remarked Richard. "It's only what they call a tope, or solid tower, an enormous thing, and quite dilapidated; but it was built upon the spot where Gautama, the Hindu prince who renounced his throne, pitched his tent when he went into hermitage."

THE OLD TOPE AT SARNATH.

"What did he do that for?" asked Scott.

"Because he believed he was divinely appointed to preach a reformation to the Hindus."

"That was a pretty way to preach a reformation. Why didn't he stay a prince? it would have had much more weight," said Scott.

Richard did not reply directly: he only said, "Jesus of Nazereth was a carpenter's son. He had not where to lay his head when he preached a reformation to the Jews."

"How long has this tope been standing?" Scott asked as they were examining it.

"Over two thousand five hundred years," replied Richard. "Gautama — who is now called Buddha, or wisdom — began to preach to five disciples who gathered about him out here, four hundred years before Christ was born."

"How did he succeed?" asked Scott again, with the financial tendency uppermost.

"When he died, after only forty-five years of preaching, and never to any but those who would come out to hear him, he had over eight million followers."

Scott whistled.

"And to-day," Richard continued, "over two hundred and ninety millions of people, or over a quarter of the whole world, are Buddhists."

"But where are they all? We have not seen them, have we?"

"There are very few in India," Richard replied.

"That's bad," said Scott. "It don't look well for a thing to be driven away from its home that way."

"How many native Christians do you think there are in Syria, Scott?" asked Richard.

"Never thought of that," said Scott; "but is Buddhism really good for any thing?"

"Of course it is. There are a great many good things in it; but they are all to be found in Christianity, and a deal more that is not in Buddhism or all other religions combined," Mr. Raymond replied earnestly.

"There is a little crowd over there," said Scott: "are they pilgrims?"

"We will go and see," replied Richard, directing the driver to go over to where the fifty or more people were gathered.

"Barnum!" cried Scott as he reached the little company, and found many of them prostrate before three of the most peculiar beings he had ever seen, two of whom were sitting on raised chairs, and one standing behind.

"We are in luck," whispered Richard eagerly. "They are pilgrims. They are three of a family of eight,—the hairy people of Mandelbar."

"You don't mean to say that that long black hair all over them is natural?" said Scott.

"Indeed I do," replied Richard; "and, more than that, that person standing—the one behind—is a woman."

"A woman!" exclaimed Scott, "a woman, with all that beard, and hair all over her forehead and arms and hands?"

"Yes, a woman, and one very proud of her personal appearance."

"Great Cæsar's ghost!" muttered Scott. "But what are they praying to them for?"

"They are not really praying to them as to God: they are only receiving their blessing. They suppose, from their peculiarity, that they are in some way under the especial care of Providence; and so they make them presents of money and any thing they have, and take their blessing in return."

"Why, that beats going with Barnum, by a large majority," said Scott as they turned away. "I thought America would surely be ahead in circus-show facilities."

CHAPTER XXI.

AMONG THE PALACES.

FROM Benares they went direct to Agra.

"I believe we'll drive right to the house of a friend of mine here, a right good fellow. His name is Royal Cliffton. He came from America with his family, a few years ago, and has settled here. He has two of the prettiest little girls I ever saw."

"But I am hardly in a state to make a call," said Scott, looking at the dust on his clothes, and general disorder that Sayad had tried in vain to right, in the disagreeable carriage on the branch road.

"I don't mean, to make a call: I mean, to stop there while we are in Agra," replied Richard.

"Won't it be taking your friend too much by surprise, especially if I go?" suggested Scott, who, after all, was overjoyed with the prospect of seeing an American family again.

"It's a way we have in India," replied Richard. "We are always glad enough to see any one, to forget about ceremony."

Mr. Cliffton's house was a little out of the city, and they found it a most delightful home. In the afternoon they all drove over to the fort, built upon the banks of the Jumma River, a branch of the Ganges.

They entered through the famous Delhi Gate, of red sandstone. It was not particularly beautiful, but was exceedingly strong, rising seventy-five feet high. Over the wall, that is two miles long, they could see the domes and minarets of the mosque and palace as they approached.

There was a bazaar or market-place outside the gate, where the booths were covered with kus-kus mats, like the awnings over the windows of the private houses. A multi-

THE FAMOUS DELHI GATE.

tude of beggars crowded around them as they made their approach. They were a ghastly set. Some of them had a leg swollen from the hip till the foot was entirely hidden. Some had horrible deformities. All of their faces were full of misery; and many had their arms full of babies, and most of the babies were full of a variety of afflictions. They clung about them with the utmost persistency, in spite of all Mr. Cliffton's endeavors to drive them off.

"I don't see what makes the beasts hang on so to-day," he said impatiently.

"I threw them all the small pieces I had in my pocket, when they first came up. I thought it would stop them, but it didn't work worth a cent," said Scott.

"It has worked like a charm, and it always will," replied Royal Cliffton, laughing. "If you want to draw a crowd of beggars in India, just give something to the first one that comes.—That's the way; is it not, Raymond?"

"I never knew it to fail," said Richard.

British soldiers were guarding the gate; and without a word they roughly pushed Moro and Sayad back, with the butts of their guns, when they attempted to follow their masters.

Mr. Cliffton came up and explained, that, a year before, one of the magazines in the fort had been fired through some mistake; and, as no one could discover just whose mistake it was, they declared with one voice that it must have been the work of a native, and forthwith issued an order that no native could safely be allowed to enter this palace of his fathers; and all were consequently forbidden.

An enormous court surrounded them, paved with marble except where beds of gorgeous flowers bloomed; and here and there were dark-green arbors. All around them were marble buildings so beautiful that Scott sought in vain for words to express himself. Even "great Cæsar's ghost" was inadequate for the occasion. He simply stood in rapt admiration.

"Come this way first, and we will go into the mosque," said Mr. Cliffton. "They call it the Moti Musjid, or Pearl Mosque. What do you think of it, Scott?"

"It's an odd place for a church," replied Scott; "but it is certainly the finest thing I ever saw, whatever it is."

"Ah! we've something better yet to show you. Wait till we take you to the Taj Mahal," said Mr. Cliffton.

"Has any one lived here lately?" asked Scott.

"It was about three hundred years ago that the royal family went to Delhi," said Mr. Cliffton.

"Three hundred years since they moved away!" Scott drew a long breath. "Why, pray, how old is this place any-way? It is as fresh as though it were built yesterday."

"That is true; for it was well built in the first place, and the air does not discolor and injure the marble here as it does in America."

They passed through the magnificent audience-hall where the Mogul emperor, Shah Jehan, once sat in judgment; and where, twice every week, the meanest and lowest in his realm were allowed to come into his presence, and say what they chose to him, complaining about any wrongs or injuries they had received, without any third person to misrepresent their words. They were just going through a low arch to the left, on the way to the zenana, when Mr. Cliffton added, "Look over the river there, Scott. Do you see that white bubble coming up out of the water and the jungle?"

"I see it," said Scott in a low tone, for the beauty was something that seemed to rebuke any thing boisterous.

"That is the great Taj Mahal, the finest architectural work in the world, the most elaborately and expensively ornamented of any building on earth, the most beautiful mausoleum ever erected; and yet it is only the tomb of a Mohammedan woman."

"You can't surprise me that way, a bit," said Scott, as

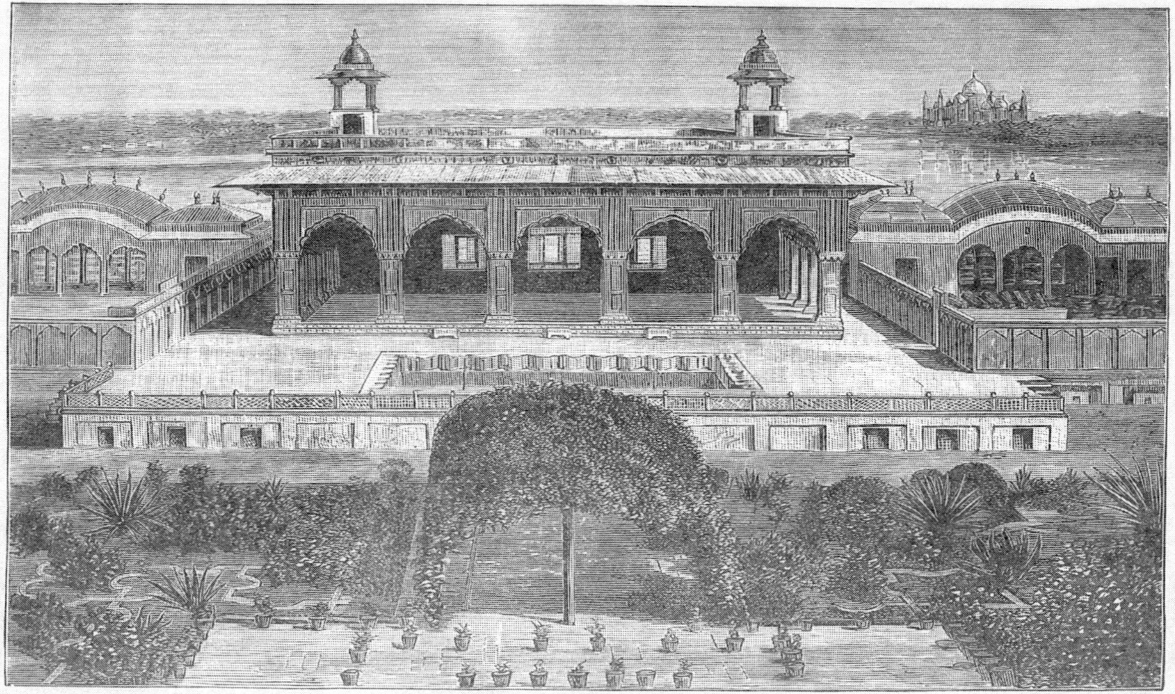

PALACE COURT, AND TAJ MAHAL IN THE DISTANCE.

they went on; "for I have had my notions about these heathen women changed a deal within the last few days. I've found out that they are some pumpkins, and pretty big ones too."

"Well, here we are where they lived when in the palace," said Mr. Cliffton, as they entered a room, or rather a long series of rooms that were separated by marble walls, but walls that were carved through and through with beautiful open-work designs right in the marble, and magnificent pillars that were carved from top to bottom, and inlaid with gold and precious stones in exquisite designs. And there was a marble aqueduct in the floor, carrying water through the middle of every room.

"This water is brought from mountains miles away," said Mr. Cliffton.

"They'd have had hard work to keep out the mosquitoes," remarked Scott, looking through the open-tracery walls, as he followed Richard out upon the balcony surrounding the zenana that overlooked the fort-wall from seventy-five feet above the river.

This balcony was surrounded by a balustrade of marble, carved in open-work geometric patterns, and was shaded by an awning of thin marble.

"Guess if our Society folks saw this, they would not mind being harem women themselves on hot afternoons," said Scott triumphantly.

They went through the royal bath-rooms, where mirrors were inlaid in the marble instead of gold and precious stones, and where a hundred little fountains played when the emperor was in Agra. As they passed a low marble building on the way out, Royal Cliffton remarked,—

"The famous sandalwood gates are kept in there. The Afghans took them about eight hundred and seventy-five years ago, and carried them home. The English prized them so much that they obliged them to bring them all the way

THE BALCONY.

back again. I should like to show you the gates; but every one who sees them must have a special permit, and that permit is only to be obtained by making personal applications upon a man who, I believe, is never at home."

Taking the carriage again at the door, they drove for two

miles down the strand road, to the Taj Mahal of which Mr. Cliffton had spoken. The gateway was so beautiful in itself that Scott thought it impossible for the Taj within it to be more so. He stopped for a moment on the marble platform, looking up at the great red-sandstone tower decorated with

THE BEAUTIFUL GATE.

white marble: then he followed Mr. Cliffton and Mr. Raymond under the arch.

"Moonlight is the time to see the outside of the Taj," said Royal Cliffton; "but then one has to sacrifice the inside, which is yet more beautiful. We'll come again, and see it by moonlight."

Within the gate there was a tropical garden extending away over broad acres in every direction, and one mass of luxuriant vegetation, — tall palms and twining vines, flowering shrubs in tropical confusion, with long avenues leading through it in various directions, bordered with fountains.

"There are eleven hundred of those fountains in this garden," said Mr. Cliffton.

From the gate they walked down a long avenue of

THE TAJ FROM THE GARDEN.

cypress-trees, that were trained in an arch above their heads. Though it was broad day, they seemed to be in twilight. Here and there a pauper or pilgrim sat in rags and holy contemplation, or sadly puffing away upon a hubble-bubble, or primitive and simple clay *hookah*, by the side of the walk. When they reached the end of the avenue, they suddenly found themselves at the brow of a gentle hill, that gradually fell away, densely covered with a magnificent floral display;

and over the valley, on the brow of a hill opposite, seeming to rest on the green forest like an ivory dream, was the wonderful Taj.

It was of pure white marble, octangular in form. Four alternate sides were formed of one immense arch each, and the other four of four smaller arches each. Above the whole, rose a great heart-shaped dome; and around it were four smaller domes, as near like it as a little drop of water and a larger one; and every dome was tipped with gold.

"That golden ball on the top of the central dome is two hundred and eighty-four feet above the platform," said Mr. Cliffton.

Scott held his breath for a moment, then hardly above a whisper said,—

"Fifty feet higher than our big church-steeples! Whew!"

This beautiful building stands upon a very large platform of polished marble, raised sixteen feet above the garden; and at the four corners of the platform are four slender minarets. At a little distance from the Taj, upon each side of it, are two smaller buildings with graceful Saracenic arches facing it.

"It took twenty thousand men twenty-three years to build that Taj," added Mr. Cliffton after a moment's pause. There was a great deal sent in tribute; and the labor was nearly all of it the work of prisoners or tributary force, that cost nothing. But the material alone cost the emperor Shah Jehan what to-day would be worth more than fifty million dollars."

Again Scott looked in breathless astonishment.

As he followed Mr. Cliffton down into the garden, he asked,—

"What is the use of the minarets that all Mussulman mosques seem to have?"

"It is from them that the call to prayer is given. Sometimes four Mussulman criers go up to the little nest in the top; and, joining their hands behind their backs, they throw their heads back, and all together shout the call. They become by practice so strong that they send the cry for miles often; and every devout Mussulman who hears it should fall on his knees, and touch his forehead to the ground, at least. It is a pretty call: '*La-illa-il-ulla-Mahamad rusol-il-ulla.*'"

As they went down into the garden, the Taj still appeared. It was so arranged as always to appear; but the surroundings so continually and completely changed, that it ever seemed as though one were looking at something new, that, if possible, was more beautiful than the last view.

Then they entered, and all the beauty without was only intensified. As they passed under one of the great arches, they found themselves in an immense circle, in a square of a hundred and eighty-six feet.

"The entire Koran, the Mussulman Bible, is inlaid in black marble over the outside of the Taj," said Mr. Cliffton; "and, do you see, over this immense interior there is not a place where you could lay your hand without touching a precious stone."

"Oh! but what beautiful designs!" Scott exclaimed. "There are entire vines and leaves and flowers; and all are inlaid in their own proper size and shape, and even color, in these jewels! And there, see! there are little pearls for drops of dew. It would be worth a journey to India, if one had to walk all the way, and could only see this one wonderful Taj."

And now, for the first time, he noticed that there were no windows in the Taj; and, looking about him, he discovered that the soft reflection that filled the room was stealing through the very marble walls, where vines of light seemed trailing from the dome, carved through and through the marble.

About the centre of the interior, there was a marble balustrade, where all the skill that had been expended elsewhere seemed to have been redoubled. In the centre of this, were two large marble slabs. One stood in the exact centre, and the other at one side.

"Are there two people buried here?" asked Scott.

"This is not where the bodies are laid," replied Mr. Cliffton; "but in a vault below, that we will go down into presently. There are two more slabs directly under these, that have only fresh flowers from the garden on them, and nothing inlaid. Yes, there are two bodies lying here. The sultana Murmtza-i-Mahal, the wife of the emperor, for whom the tomb was built, lies in the centre. Then the Shah Jehan ordered the architect to build him a tomb for himself, across the river, even larger and more beautiful. The architect began, and the foundations yet remain; but when they were raised he died, and no one could be found capable of carrying on the work: so there it stands; and, when the emperor died, he directed that his body be laid here too."

The Taj stands directly upon the river, and the most beautiful view of all was obtained as they were rowed away toward the city.

"You are sober, Scott. Don't India please you?" asked Richard, as they had almost reached the landing below the fort-wall.

"I hardly know, Mr. Raymond," he returned: "there are such extremes, such terrible extremes. India makes you mad with her, then makes you feel like dying for her if it could assist her. She makes you sad, she makes you laugh; she makes you crawl all over with horror and disgust: yet I feel as if I had seen enough to-day to make me happy and humble for a lifetime. She makes me pity her, and the next moment I think that every civilized mortal should get down on his knees before her. I do not know."

A RAJAH OF THE GOOD OLD DAYS.

In the bazaar Scott bought an ivory medallion of one of the noblemen who used to inhabit the palace.

"We will drive out to Futtehpur Sakri to-morrow, and drive back the next day: I want to show you some more extremes," said Royal Cliffton, laughing.

"I am sure I can see nothing equal to this," said Scott.

"You're right," said Mr. Cliffton. "Search the world, and there is nothing to compare with it. But Futtehpur Sakri is worth seeing. It was the summer city of the grandfather of the Shah Jehan."

They started very early, for it was a long day's drive; and at four in the afternoon were approaching the summer city. Nothing could yet be seen of it but a jumble of glistening walls in the distance, and the high tower of Elephanta.

"This is a very popular road for pilgrims and caravans," said Mr. Cliffton as they rode along. "See how the enlightened native dealers have taken up the American notion of sticking advertisements in stencil-painting on the rocks? They are nearly all of them advertisements of some kind of American inventions. Do you see that large stone there, with a Hindustani sentence in large letters upon it?"

"Yes: 'Use Perry Davis's Pain-Killer,'" repeated Richard, translating the prominent sign.

ADVERTISING ROCKS.

"Well," added Mr. Cliffton, "they have scratched it out now, but a while ago the missionary society sent out a Hindu convert to paint a lot of Scripture-texts in the best places he could find. He could not read a word, either of what was already written or of what he had; but he thought that a splendid place, and he picked out his largest plate to put right under that. What do you think it was? 'Thou shalt have no other gods before me.' And every one who could read, at once decided that Perry Davis's Pain-Killer was a new god that was setting up decidedly grand pretensions."

"We must go into the court of the mosque to see the tomb of the sheik Selim Christi, before it is too dark," said Mr. Cliffton as they began their walk through the beautiful marble city. "He is the man, Scott, who was going through the Indian desert when he found a little girl only a few hours old, and a baby boy, her brother, where their mother and father had left them to the mercy of God, while they went on a little way to die alone; for they were out of food and water, and a long way from help. He took them to the court of the emperor Akbar, and there they grew up. The

THE TOMB OF SELIM CHRISTI.

little girl, some say, was the 'Light of the Harem,' that Tom Moore wrote about in his famous 'Lalla Rookh;' and that the boy married a daughter of the sheik, and *their* daughter was the sultana for whom the Shah Jehan built the Taj."

"Isn't that rather mixed?" asked Scott. "I can't see through it, at any rate."

"Well, it only amounts to this: that the man who lies

here rescued from death and gave the world the heroine of 'Lalla Rookh,' and the heroine of the Taj Mahal, — one of the most beautiful poems, and the most beautiful mausoleum, in the world."

"He got a good tomb to pay for it," said Scott; "but it strikes me that these tombs are the biggest things in India. If I had been one of these old fellows, I would have lived in my tomb, and been buried outside."

"So they did live there until they died," replied Richard, laughing. "These tombs they made their great reception-halls, and gave immense dinner-parties, etc., here, and tried to make their friends as happy as possible; that when they were dead and buried, and the places closed up, they might be remembered and missed."

"That was a jolly good dodge. But don't any one live in this city now?"

"Not a soul but these beggars. You might if you wished: no one would stop you, or ask for rent."

"Too lonesome! too much fancy-work for me: I'd rather be excused," replied Scott. "But I should think that these Hindus, who are used to it as you might say, would come up here for the summer at least."

"It is very strange about this place," replied Mr. Cliffton. "It was built as if by magic, almost in a single night, to please the fancy of that almost omnipotent emperor. Here the court came for just twelve years; and then the marble city and the old mud village outside the gate were deserted, — absolutely deserted. No one has ever lived here since."

"How long ago was that?" Scott asked.

"A little over three hundred years."

CHAPTER XXII.

DELHI, DENNETT, AND DHONDARAM.

AS much as Scott longed to be in Delhi, it was with great regret that he left Mr. Cliffton's hospitable home, a few days later, and with Mr. Raymond took the train for Tundla, where they found the express waiting; and early the next morning they rolled over the long stone bridge, and close to the fort-wall, till they reached the station.

"There are some *dhobis* tearing some one's clothes to pieces, and breaking somebody's buttons," said Richard as they saw several native washermen in the river doing their work. "That reminds me.—Moro, bring us a *dhobi*, the first thing you do."

"Ha sahib," replied Moro, who understood perfectly, though all but the word *dhobi* Richard had spoken in English. And, as soon as they were located in comfortable quarters, Moro appeared with the desired washerman; and he and Sayad prepared the clothes, and made a list of them, which they each handed to their respective masters to look over while they counted their clothes before them.

"This is a precaution which it is second nature for them to take," Richard explained, laughing as Scott seemed reluctant to appear to distrust the boy who had served him so well. "They know themselves that they are such thieves, that they would only think you a fool if you did not keep a sharp lookout for them."

"I don't believe this fellow would steal," said Scott, looking toward Sayad.

"See that handkerchief sticking out of his girdle," said Richard. "I warned you to be careful."

Scott looked, and to his horror saw one of his own silk handkerchiefs peeping from beneath Sayad's girdle.

THE RAILROAD BRIDGE OVER THE JUMNA AT DELHI.

"The wretch!" he muttered.

"Oh, no!" replied Richard, laughing: "he's just as good a boy as he was before. He only wants looking after, that is all."

"Every city, so far, is so very different from every other," said Scott, as they took their first walk in Delhi. "There is just a sort of family resemblance, but nothing more. How broad and beautiful this avenue is, with the line of trees through the centre, and only the low houses on each side! such pretty houses, and all so different from any thing else! And this marble aqueduct, carrying such clear cold water in an open stream down each side of the street,—who ever thought of such a thing? But how cooling and refreshing it must be to the tired, heated fellows at their work!"

"You are quite right, Scott. This water is brought in the marble aqueduct for eighty-three miles, to supply the city with water that is cool and fresh when the river becomes heated and low in the dry season. It was done at the expense of one of the queens, long years ago; and when it was finished, to prevent the rich from ever monopolizing it in any way, so that the poor could not have the benefit, she decreed that the two aqueducts should extend the whole length of this street, the Chandi Chouk, or Street of Silver light, and that they should always be uncovered for the entire distance."

"That's not a bad name for a street," said Scott. "But what is this immense square that we are coming to, with that—what is it? a mosque, isn't it? it has minarets—on the right."

"Yes, it is a mosque, Scott,—the most beautiful public mosque, and the largest one, in India. Do you see, this wall extends entirely around it? and there are gates exactly like this on every side. Over the wall you can see the front of the principal arch, and the three domes of the mosque, and the minarets."

"Do they have any Sundays, and sermons in those mosques?" asked Scott.

"Friday is the Mussulman's holy day," replied Richard. "It is as much his Sunday as any day; but they never have sermons, except in times of excitement over something. They often have short lectures by the priests, but they are chiefly the repeating of the Koran. They believe in more Bible, and less expounding of it."

"That's the talk," exclaimed Scott. "I wish they'd come over and teach that doctrine to some of our ministers. Oh, how tired I get in church, sometimes!" he concluded with a sigh.

They went into a little chapel at one corner of the wall;

DELHI OF THREE THOUSAND YEARS AGO.

where, with great reverence, the priests took out for them treasure after treasure from their store of sacred relics. Rolled up in innumerable papers, they had a hair from the beard of Mohammed, an old crumbled sandal that he once wore, and a manuscript copy of the entire Koran, written by his favorite daughter, Fatima.

They climbed one of the minarets, and obtained an extensive view of the immense plain and the ruins surrounding the city.

"How old are these ruins?" asked Scott.

"That tomb with a dome, yonder, is about eleven hundred years old," replied Richard; and, while Scott tried in vain to stretch his imagination, he continued. "But there are so many interesting places there, that we must find a first-rate guide, and take two or three days to see them all. There are ruins there of buildings that were erected over three thousand years ago, and some even older. There are relics of the first Aryan conquerors, and that was nearer five thousand years."

"Oh, wait a minute! wait a minute!" cried Scott. "I have not got over the first three thousand yet. But the Aryans, did you say? Why, I thought that we in America were descended from the Aryans."

"Quite right, Scott. Five thousand years ago the Aryans divided. Half of them followed Mr. Greeley's advice, and went west; and half of them came south-east. We are directly descended from one branch, and these Hindu heathen are as directly descended from the other."

"You don't mean to say that we come from precisely the same stock?" said Scott in surprise; adopting the vernacular of the Beverly farmers, for want of any thing more expressive.

"Just precisely," replied Richard.

"Well, that's what makes the Hindus look so much like Europeans, in spite of their dark skin, — so much more than the Africans and Chinese and the Japs; isn't it?"

"That is it precisely, Scott. You're quite a philosopher. Now point the glass a little to the right till you hit the Kutub Minar, that tower that rises against the sky. Do you find it?"

"I have it, sir," replied Scott, as he found the high tower at last.

"That is a minaret," said Richard.

"A minaret!" exclaimed Scott.

"Yes, only a minaret. It was built almost a thousand years ago; and the temple about it, that has been almost demolished now, in fanatic wars, was the largest Mohammedan mosque ever built. That minaret is only forty-eight feet in diameter at the base; but, with the little cap, that has been torn away now, it was two hundred and sixty-seven feet high. It is beautifully ornamented to the very top. By and by you will be studying architecture; and, unless times change a great deal, you will learn that the campanile in Florence, built by Giotto after this mosque had begun to crumble, is the triumph of tower-building. You may find a note at the foot of the page, admitting that a possible rival may be a Mussulman or a Hindu minaret in the plain of old Delhi. This, in spite of the fact that the Kutub was higher than the campanile, that it is round where the other is angular, that it is beautifully ornamented where the other is almost plain, and that it is in vastly better proportions, according to geometric laws, than the work of Giotto."

From the Jumma Musjid they went across the square to the old fort opposite. It was more dilapidated than the fort and palaces at Agra, though in its glory it had been more beautiful.

"These walls look as if they had had the small-pox," Scott remarked as they went through the royal apartments, where the elaborate carving remained, but the jewels and gold had all been taken out.

"That is the result of the rage with which the English soldiers appropriated every thing that was valuable, to pay the Hindus for having kept them so long outside the gates.

KUTUB MINAR.

besieging the city," replied Mr. Raymond. "But there is one little gem here that they did not demolish, simply because there was nothing but white marble about it. It is the Pearl Mosque, all walled in by a high fence of white marble, where the hundred wives of the emperor worshipped. There is only one little door by which it could be entered, and that was kept guarded by eunuchs. Inside, it is a perfect gem."

From the palace they walked to the famous Cashmere gate, in the old wall about the city.

"I want you to see the breach that was made, through which the British entered the city. They tried in vain to reduce the natives here, and at last Col. Nicholson announced that the task was to be abandoned for the time unless a breach could be made in the wall. He offered an immense reward to any soldiers who would take kegs of powder up to this old wall, and blow it up. Three Hindu traitors were among those who dared to venture for the reward, and offered to run the risk. Two of the three were shot on the way. The third sprang over yonder bridge, and ran down the moat that was only half full of water. He fired the powder, and escaped. The British entered. The poor fellow only enjoyed his notoriety for a little while, however; for the mutiny was no sooner subdued than he fell dead under the dagger of Dhondaram."

"I can't help it, Mr. Raymond," Scott said a little later, as they walked along the bastion: "I somehow admire that Dhondaram."

"He is a hero, there's no doubt of that; and perhaps you are a hero-worshipper, Scott," returned Richard.

"It's not that exactly," said Scott. "I cannot help feeling that there is something good in the man: there is something that is really noble, for all it seems so wicked, in what you have told me of him. Don't you think he believes he is doing right?"

"It is vengeance and fanaticism with him," returned Mr. Raymond. "I would hardly put it that he thinks he is

THE CASHMERE GATE OF DELHI.

doing right, but I don't imagine he stops to think that he is really doing very wrong."

"There is a little English chapel, just over the knoll," Richard continued as they approached the gate, "built to commemorate the success of the British. It is dedicated as a memorial to the English martyrs who fell here. To-morrow is Sunday. Shall we go there to church?"

Scott thought upon it seriously for a moment, and replied, —

"I believe I should rather be excused. I should be mad about the mutiny, instead of mourning for the British martyrs. If there is a mission church about, I think I should rather go there, and get you to translate the sermon as you did in Bombay. Is there a mission here?"

Mr. Raymond did not answer directly, and Scott looked toward him. He had gone a little distance to one side, and was studying a paper posted on the gate. The notice was written, and officially signed, in three languages; and there were already a dozen or more reading it, or translating it to others. They seemed much excited. It must have just been put there, for a moment before there was no one at the gate. The same frown had gathered on Mr. Raymond's face that Scott had seen there once before; and looking up anxiously he asked, —

"Is there any trouble, Mr. Raymond?"

"No trouble, my boy; oh, no! I was only reading that notice, and thinking."

"What was the notice?" asked Scott.

"It says that the traitor Dhondaram is known to be in the province, and increases the reward that is offered for his head."

"Dhondaram here!" exclaimed Scott. "I should like to see him."

"You may have a chance, Scott. I thought he must be dead, but it seems they are after him as hard as ever."

While they were standing there the crowd continually increased. Just then a European pressed through, without seeming to notice any one, but in great excitement pushed to the front, and looked up at the notice. He began to read, and shuddered. He read on.

It was very near where they were standing. The crowd was becoming so dense that Scott attempted to move away. Mr. Raymond stood still. Scott spoke to him: he did not answer. Scott looked up: his face was white; his eyes were fixed on the man who was reading the notice.

"Do you know him, Scott?" Richard muttered in a low voice.

Scott looked at the man again. He finished reading, and with a hollow laugh he turned away.

"Roderick Dennett!" escaped from Scott's parted lips.

CHAPTER XXIII.

SCOTT AT THE HINDU FEAST.

HAVING once fixed his eyes on the man he was searching for, Mr. Raymond did not easily lose sight of him. Scott had no further occasion to complain of lack of energy. He walked rapidly. He seemed to be in a hurry, and the crowd was much more dense in the streets he chose than outside the gate. Mr. Raymond did not dare to follow too closely. But at a distance they saw Roderick Dennett enter the Dak Bungalow.

"He must have just come," said Richard. "Let me go in first, and you may come in a few minutes if there is no trouble. Paul is not there, I think. Probably Dennett is here to meet him, and will be frightened away by that notice. It is very likely that Dhondaram is on his path."

Richard went in. Scott was too eager to wait, and followed after only an instant's delay. Almost together they entered the bungalow. It seemed utterly deserted. Richard pushed his way without ceremony into the side room. Dennett was bending over a valise. He was evidently hurrying his things into it to leave; and, thinking it the keeper who had entered, he said, without looking up, —

"I am going on for a few days. I have some trunks and boxes at the railway, and will have them sent over here. Take care of them for me, and I will pay you well."

Then, seeming to realize that he had made a mistake, he looked up.

"Raymond!" he gasped; and, starting to his feet, he drew his revolver.

Mr. Raymond sprang upon him; and, throwing him down, wrenched the revolver from his hand before he fairly realized what was taking place.

"Ha! You've done it now. Go ahead, and kill me!" he muttered as Richard held him fast.

Richard looked at him savagely for a moment, while Scott stood in the doorway aghast. Then, shaking his head, he replied, —

"No, Roderick. You saved my life when we were boys in Beverly, and it has saved yours more than once since then. I have no desire to kill you."

"Then, give me over, and have me hung," growled Dennett through the choking grasp that Richard had fixed upon his throat.

"You deserve that richly, but I will let some one else do it," Richard replied.

"Then, what do you want of me?" he asked, looking toward the door, evidently suspicious that there were others waiting for him.

"I want several things; and every one of them I will have before you escape me, no matter what it costs." Richard spoke in a way that yielded nothing. "I want the secret records that you stole from me, and the locket you took from my room. I want the signet and the badge of the governor-general. I want the key to the safe where your counterfeit rupee stamp is kept, and directions where I can find it. I want a written statement from you that Mr. Clayton had nothing to do with the defalcation and robbery in Boston, and just what disposal you made of the bonds. And I want you to give up Paul Clayton."

"You ask too much. I will not do it," replied Roderick sullenly.

"Very well," said Richard calmly: "then I will hand you over to the British government. You will be hung as a murderer; and I shall find out all I wish without your help, and have your belt besides."

"I have no belt," gasped Roderick, making a desperate struggle to rise.

But it was impossible; for Mr. Raymond held him in a grip of iron, with muscles that had hardened in the jungle, and toughened with the rifle and the sword.

"I'm not come to dispute with you, or to treat you as I have before," he said sternly. "It's neck or nothing with you this time, Dennett. You might as well begin, and give me what I want."

Roderick hesitated for a moment.

"You've got the best of me, Raymond," he said at last. "If I do what you ask, are we quits?"

"I'll make you no promises, Roderick. Those things I will have, for they concern me."

Roderick yielded without another word; and Richard let go his hold, and, with the pistol in one hand, he said,—

"Now go on, and tell me all."

Roderick began,

"The records and badge are with the Royal Rupee Mint, and are deposited with my friend Mobarak, in his safe in the Bhendi Bazaar. I just moved them there from their last hiding-place. The locket and the signet are in my belt. The memoranda of the disposition I made of the bonds and securities are in my valise there: it is unlocked. The written statement for Mr. Clayton I will give you when you will let me write. The boy I have not got, and don't know who has. I left him with a fellow in Benares; and he got scared, and sent him away with some pilgrims. He said they were coming up to the Feast of Pungas. I came here to look for them."

Without a word, Mr. Raymond opened Roderick Dennett's coat and vest; and, reaching the belt, unbuttoned it, and drew it off. Dennett did not move, or make any remonstrance. The locket and signet were there. He opened the valise, and found the memoranda. Then he gave the valise to Moro, who stood behind the inner door. He turned to Roderick, and asked, —

"Where are the receipts for your luggage, that you said was at the station?"

"You've nothing to do with my luggage," replied Dennett sullenly.

"Give me the receipts," said Richard sternly.

The man produced them, and Richard gave them to Moro.

"Take the valise to my room, and have the luggage sent there at once," he said briefly, giving him a rupee. The boy left without a word · it was an adventure that he enjoyed.

"Sayad," said Richard, "take a *garri*, and go to Mobarak in the Bhendi Bazaar. Tell him the chief of the Bombay service, and secretary of the viceroy, commands him to come at once to the Dak Bungalow, and bring with him Roderick Dennett's box. Bring him with you: if he refuse, call the English police. Give them my card, and have him brought."

With military precision, as though he was entirely used to the business, Sayad departed.

Richard took paper and pen from the table in the room; and, releasing Roderick's hands that he had bound, allowed him to sit up and write the statement, while he sat on the edge of the bed with the pistol in his hand, and Scott looked at his friend in astonishment.

When the paper was ready, Mr. Raymond looked at it, nodded his head approvingly, signed it himself, asked Scott to sign it, and then put it in his pocket.

"Now about the boy," said Richard. "Have you lied to me?"

"I might well have lied about the whole," replied Roderick with a sneer. "You're not dealing on the square with me, Rich. Raymond."

"No?" said Richard.

"It's none of your business to meddle with me, now that you've got the signet and the badge and the rupee press," muttered Roderick in a surly way.

"Thank fortune, it's not an absolute duty of my office to turn you over to be hanged!" replied Richard; "but it would be a favor that the government would remember, and reward well, I assure you."

Roderick made no reply; and Richard asked again, —

"How is it about the boy?"

"Just as I told you."

"But no one is going to keep him without being paid for it," said Richard sternly. And while he sat carefully watching the man, he began with one hand to take rolls of Bank-of-England notes for immense sums from the belt; then he carefully put them back again, and folding the belt up, he put it in his coat-pocket.

"The fellow gave the pilgrims a hundred pounds to take the child off his hands," said Roderick. "And he says he promised a hundred more when they delivered him to me here in Delhi. I don't know who I'm waiting for; but I'm waiting for them here, and I expect they'll find me some way; but now, if you've taken up the trail, I'll let it drop. 'Twas rough luck for me that I got you to run away to sea with me," he added with a sneer.

"You might have had friends who would have served you worse," replied Richard calmly. "But you must not leave me just now. You will be more likely to find the boy than I shall, and I'll keep this belt till you do find him. You can go ahead, and find the boy: and when you have brought him to me, I will return the belt; it will be ten times the reward that is offered for him," he added, smiling sarcastically.

Just then Sayad came in triumphantly, followed by a native of Africa, black as the blackest men of Zanzibar. He was much agitated, and dropped on the floor as he entered, touching his forehead a dozen times to the ground.

He brought with him a leather portmanteau, that was sealed over the keyhole, and evidently very heavy. He laid it at Mr. Raymond's feet; and, without a word, Roderick took a key from his pocket, and passed it to Sayad, who gave it to Mr. Raymond.

"Ha, you! Mobarak, I have seen you before," said Richard. "You used to live in Bombay. You were a bad man then; and you have been growing worse, it seems. The air of Delhi does not agree with you. Go over there in the corner, and sit down on the floor. Don't you move, or I will shoot you dead before you can shut your eyes."

He took a pistol from his pocket, and handed it to Sayad, directing him to watch the African banker, who had been engaged in passing Dennett's counterfeit rupees, and possibly in manufacturing them. Then he proceeded to open the valise, and seemed satisfied with the contents, as he closed it again, and, rising, asked Sayad if the carriage was at the door.

"Get up on the top, you drop of Afric's sunny fountains," he said to the black banker, who instantly obeyed. "I'm going to take you back to your booth, and let you go on with your business. But let me hear of your passing another of these rupees, and it's a prison for life for you. Roderick, I hope to hear from you directly," he added as they all left the Bungalow.

The banker made a profound salaam, touching the earth again in his gratitude: then he climbed to a seat beside the driver of the *garri*.

"We have taken another step," said Richard as they were being driven away; "and I hope the next will be the finding of little Paul." He spoke as calmly as though they had only seen another ruin.

Then the day of the great Feast of Pungas dawned clear and warm, but nothing had been heard from Roderick Dennett.

"There is more than two hundred thousand dollars in that belt that I deposited with the English bankers," Richard said to Scott. "Depend upon it, he will redeem it."

They went out into the city, and mingled with the excited crowd. It was a novel sight to Scott, and he almost forgot his anxiety in the constant changes.

At last the grand procession of elephants was coming down the street. It would pass the open square before the Cashmere gate.

"We will get into a good position here where we can see it," said Richard; and they stationed themselves as near the track as the already dense crowd would permit. They were in the very front before the procession passed.

The long lines of gaudily decked elephants were on their way. One end had already disappeared before the other end came in sight. Scott was beginning to grow weary, when his eyes fell upon a little boy in European clothes, all alone in the dense throng of natives. He started: he trembled in every limb. The crowd swept on, and he lost sight of the boy. He caught Mr. Raymond's hand; he tried in vain to speak; he pointed, and dragged him forward. A sharp cry broke upon his ear from the voice he so well remembered. He was so excited that he did not distinguish the words, but others less interested heard,—

"Dhondaram, Dhondaram!"

"In a moment the entire throng was transformed. It was electrified: it was demoralized. Cries of "Dhondaram!" "Dhondaram!" rose on every side. Richard forgot Scott; and, freeing himself from his grasp, he started forward, thinking only of Dhondaram.

At the instant that the voice sounded, Scott, who was a little in advance of Mr. Raymond, had seen the little figure of his brother Paul dart before a huge elephant. He sprang after him. The elephant moved his trunk to one side to avoid the little stranger, and it struck Scott a severe blow that threw him down. In an instant the excited crowd was trampling upon him. He gave a sharp cry of pain, and a moment later was dragged from his perilous position, and in the strong arms of Mr. Raymond was carried away to the hotel.

Scott was severely bruised. For three days his mind wandered, and Mr. Raymond and the best doctors that could be obtained fought with a raging fever that almost defied them. He incessantly talked of Paul and Dhondaram; and, when he came to himself again, he repeated almost the same thing, only that then he did not associate Dhondaram with Paul.

Mr. Raymond did not feel at all sure that Scott was cor-

MASSURI IN THE MOUNTAINS.

rect, and that it was not a dream of his delirium; but he allowed him to have his way, and pretended to believe that he had really seen Paul somewhere in the procession.

A week later, when Scott had nearly recovered, Richard receved a telegram, as follows:—

"Come to Massuri at once. Paul is in the mountains: I dare not follow alone. There is something wrong.

"Roderick Dennett."

"The mountain air will be the best thing for you, Scott," said Richard; "and I would rather take you with me than leave you behind. You can stop at Massuri if there is trouble, or you are not strong."

"Indeed, I will go!" exclaimed Scott eagerly.

"Very well, then: we will leave for the Himalaya Mountains on the express to-night," replied Richard.

CHAPTER XXIV.

YOU SHALL BE MY HARI-SAHIB.

WHEN he had finished his supper of milk and rice-cakes,— and little Paul was very hungry, for he had eaten nothing but sweet limes and bananas, and had taken a long walk, and suffered a deal of anxiety for a small boy in the mean time,— Dhondaram ate what was left, and sat down beside him.

"Did you bring that for your supper too, Dhondaram?" asked Paul, looking up into the face that so many feared to the very marrow of their bones. "I wasn't very good to eat so much of it;" and he stroked the bearded cheek, and put his little white hands over the black eyes that had made the blood of many a strong man turn cold.

"I was only helping the little Feringhi," replied Dhondaram gently. "And now is my little sahib sleepy? Will he lie down in this poor place, and shut his pretty blue eyes? It is not comfortable."

"Anywhere where you are, Dhondaram, is very nice. I will not stay again in a place like the *biri* wallah's, where you left me this morning. I will follow you without waiting. I am glad I came and found you."

"I am glad too," replied Dhondaram as he spread out a mat on the hard floor, and made it as soft as he could by folding another mat under it, and putting his turban under the top to act as a pillow. He did not tell little Paul that the remnant of his supper was all he had eaten since the night before on the banks of the Jumna, or that there was not another mat for him to lie on. He brought a little cup of water, and washed Paul's face and hands as tenderly as a mother could have done it, — though not so proficiently, of course, — and wiped them on his girdle. Then he laid the little fellow upon the mats, and cross-legged sat down beside him.

"Kashibai will be here in the morning," he said; "and she will make the place more comfortable."

"Who is Kashibai, Dhondaram?" asked Paul as he lay comfortably stretched on the mats.

"She is very good; she is Gunga's mother: she will love you," replied the muni.

"I love Gunga," said the boy. "When am I going to see her?"

"Soon, soon," replied Dhondaram.

"Dhondaram," said Paul looking up, "who gave you your name?"

"My mother," replied Dhondaram solemnly.

"Who is my mother, Dhondaram?"

The muni hesitated for a moment. "Gunga's mother, Kashibai, will be your mother: she will love you."

"Will she give me a name too?" asked Paul. "You have nothing to call me by but Feringhi, and that means 'something different;' and I don't want to be something different; I want to be just the same. I am sorry I am white. Couldn't you make me dark, like you, Dhondaram?"

A fire seemed flashing from Dhondaram's eyes. He was silent for a moment: then he said suddenly, "Yes; if you would like it I can make the little Feringhi almost as dark as I am."

"And call me something like you too," exclaimed the boy, sitting upright with a cry of joy.

"You shall be my brother, my Dhakta Bhai. No, no!" he added hurriedly, "I am not good enough for that. You shall be my master, — my Swami. Your name shall be Hari. It is the name of my God."

"I be your master, and you mind little me! you're terribly big for that!" said Hari-Paul; but he threw himself into the arms that had held the knotted rumal and the blood-stained dagger, and nestled there; sending a thrill through the iron heart to stop whose beating the British government offered to pay over ten thousand dollars in gold.

"I can mind you all the better for being large," said the muni at last; but the voice trembled that had rung firm and clear before death and all sorts of terrible dangers, and the eyes that had never flinched were dimmed with tears.

"I want you to be my elephant, and carry me as the elephants did the men to-day," said Paul at last, clapping his hands, and starting to his feet.

"I'm hardly big enough for that," said Dhondaram; "but I can be your horse. Come you, my Hari-Sahib, get on my back, and we will go where you will."

And the bare-headed muni, the terror of India, on his hands and knees went galloping round the bare floor of that dimly lighted, wretched room, with the pale-faced, blue-eyed, brown-haired Hari-Paul crowing and laughing and shouting on his back, his little hands clinging mercilessly to the lock of long black hair that in Hindu fashion grew from the top of his horse's head.

It mattered little that he had walked all night with the boy upon his shoulder, and that he had walked all day in the

THE DYERS.

procession: Dhondaram was as wild and happy as Paul. And yet the boy was not quite happy; for the very excitement of the game seemed to bring back to him other hours, — hours full of sunshine and laughing, — and other surroundings, when he had not been the Hindu Hari, but —

He tried in vain to catch the dream. It vanished, as it always had, just as it touched his eyes.

When the sport was ended, Hari, at a loss for something new, said, —

"Now you must make me dark, just like you, Dhondaram."

"I will get something to put on your hands, and let you see how you like it, my Hari-Sahib," replied the muni. "I will come back at once, and bring it with me."

He went out, and Paul began to be frightened again the moment he was alone. He would have followed had he not found the door locked again. But Dhondaram had only gone around one corner to a dye-house, where he was sure he was unknown, and there procured the material with which he stained the boy's hands and face a delicate brown. They were not so dark as the muni's, but they were no longer white; and Paul was happy. He lay down again, and this time he was fast asleep in a moment.

He slept soundly. He did not know that the muni, close to his little brown head, sat cross-legged on the floor, leaning against the wall, and only half sleeping, anxiously starting up at every sound; and that many a time he put his hand out in the dark to see if all were well with his little god Hari. Near morning he gently cut off one of the brown curls that clustered about the boy's head, but it did not disturb him.

When Paul awoke in the morning the room was much

changed. There were two small screens and several mats; there was a little fire in a small iron stove that could be carried about in the hand, burning in one corner, and over it a woman was cooking the breakfast. She was a Hindu woman, very delicate and pretty in figure, wearing only a little close-fitting *chouli* about her shoulders, that hardly reached her waist, and a bright cloth bound closely about her hips. Her legs and arms were bare, except for broad bands of gold and silver that circled her wrists and ankles; and there were large ear-rings in her ears, and a little gold star on one side of her nose. On her toes were silver rings, that clinked as she walked on the bare places on the floor. Beside the fire sat Dhondaram. Paul knew it was Dhondaram, for he heard his voice. But what a change! A huge red turban was twisted about his head in graceful, but brigandish folds. His beard was shaven off, leaving only a heavy mustache that looked fiercer than ever. Instead of the plain muni's frock that was all he had worn, bound at the waist with a simple girdle, he wore a loose woollen jacket, with flowing sleeves. An enormous girdle, the same color as his turban, was wound about his waist; and he wore a pair of loose woollen breeches to the knees, and a pair of heavy

DHONDARAM IN ARMOR.

sandals on his feet. Leaning against the wall behind him was a sword almost five feet long.

Dhondaram and the woman were engaged in earnest conversation in a low tone, but Paul could distinctly hear and understand most of what they said.

"Why should I defile myself?" muttered the woman. "Am I not a Bramhan woman? Are you not a Bramhan? Am I not desolate that you wander as you do? Do I not die every day, till the wind is ever in my bones? Am I not cursed by the breath that I breathe, and the food that I eat? Have I not already defiled myself a thousand times, till my penance and purification keep me the day long, and the voice of the mother speaks feebly now, and sometimes not at all? When will this wandering cease, Dhondaram? When will these wild ideas of yours have rest? The boy is well enough. I wish him no ill. I would do him no ill. I would injure no one. I hate no one except the ones you hate, and who have injured you. But why, in the blissful moment when the gods and the mother smile upon me, and place the rose in my bosom, the attar on my hair; when the star is once more in my heaven, and the breath again in my body; when I can cook the food that Dhondaram eats, and fan Dhondaram while he eats it; when I live again, O jewel of my crown of joy! — why ask me to die in this hour, and defile myself again? And yet I will do it. Yes, I will feed and bathe the Feringhi. Yes, I will care for him. Yes, by the mother, on the neck of my daughter Gunga, I swear I would nurse a pariah upon my breast if Dhondaram should ask it."

"Dhondaram does not ask it," replied the muni. "Cursed be the day, and defiled he that breathes in the hour, that Dhondaram asks any thing of any one. To the viceroy from

England, to the guru, the pundit, the rajah, Dhondaram speaks; and cursed is he who forgets to hear. Who will not tell you so? Did you not hear the city howling yesterday with the name of Dhondaram? It will howl again and again, till Dhondaram's thirst is quenched. But to you Dhondaram does not speak. He thinks; and you read his thoughts, and do as it pleases you. Who ever bound thy hand? Thou art Kashibai. I am Dhondaram. Thou art the holy mother's, and I am — well, I am Bhowani's too; but to you she is soft and gentle; she is fairest of all the blest in the paradise of Indra: to me she is blood and death and cruelty. Who am I, that I should wish you to do what I would do willingly? No: the little Feringhi shall go with me."

He turned to Paul; and, seeing that he was awake, he crossed the room, and bending over him he asked, —

"Would the little Sahib like to go into the mountains with me?"

Paul's lip trembled. He had been frightened by the conversation that he had overheard, and by the new costume that made Dhondaram look so savage. He realized that the woman did not like to have him there. In fact, though he did not know it, he was homesick; and the name by which Dhondaram called him was the last straw. He turned over on the mat, and began to cry.

"Oh, I am not a Feringhi! I am not a Feringhi! I am not 'something different'! I wish it were last night," he sobbed. "Look at my hands, Dhondaram, look! I am black. I am like you."

He held up his little hands. The muni caught them, and pressed them to his forehead.

"It is last night now, and always will be while Dhondaram

is free," he responded solemnly. "You are my Hari, my god of gods, now and always. It is not that I am rich that you love me. I have given you no gold ornaments. I have, only a little water here with which to bathe you. I will bring you some breakfast and sweet limes then, and to-night we will start for the mountains."

"I want to see Gunga," said Paul, still sobbing a little.

At four o'clock that afternoon, right through the crowded streets of Delhi, a Brinjari chieftain walked slowly, with head erect, and a little Persian boy beside him, affectionately clinging to his hand. The light brown skin of the Persian contrasted peculiarly with the darker hue of the Brinjari chief in his dashing costume; and many a one, as they passed, stopped to look at the bright blue eyes that were so peculiar and unusual, and shuddered at sight of the ugly sword hanging over the right shoulder of the chief. Many even stopped the servant who was carrying a large bundle on his head behind them, to ask him which of the great men of his people this one was. But he only stared at them, and shook his head. Scott would hardly have recognized little Paul, and no one in all Delhi repeated the name of Dhondaram when they saw the chief.

They stopped at a booth in the outskirts of the bazaar; and Dhondaram bought a sack of maize meal, and a small bunch of little red peppers, which the servant added to the bundle upon his head.

They even walked directly to the English railway-station, and in the mountain dialect the servant purchased tickets in the third-class car for Amritsar. Dhondaram and Paul stopped for a moment before such a notice as Scott saw on the Cashmere gate, then took their places in a car already crowded with natives. They fell back, and gave them more room than any one else had in the car; looking suspiciously at the long sword, but not suspiciously at Dhondaram.

They stopped when within twenty miles of the city. Dhondaram was perfectly informed about every thing, and

THE CORN-CHANDLER.

knew that a caravan he wished to join had not yet reached the station.

It was a little lonely country town, on a narrow, rushing mountain river. Dhondaram, with Paul and his servant, walked up the bank a little way, and took a native boat, to be carried to the caravan trail that passed at no great distance.

As they were about to embark, Paul caught sight of a little stone figure that looked like a tiny elephant sitting on his haunches, and having fore-feet like his own hands and arms.

"What is it? what is it?" he asked eagerly, as a native, bareheaded, came up to the little image, and began to pour water over it, and to drape it with flowers.

Dhondaram's lips curved scornfully, much as they had

BATHING AN IDOL.

when looking at the image of Kali. He was evidently not the devout Hindu that many thought him.

"An atom of God," he replied in an undertone. "That man is bathing his preserver. He is praying," he said aloud.

"Do you never pray in that way?" asked Paul: "if you do, will you teach me?"

"Why should I pray like that?" said the muni. "God is everywhere. The great essence of Bramha fills all space. If I would pray to an elephant, it should be to one that God had made, and not to one that some beggar had manufactured to earn his bread."

"But I never pray at all, Dhondaram. And now I am like you, and have a name, and all that; and I want to learn to pray. Can't I pray without pounding myself the way you do? I tried to do that when I was at the *biri* wallah's, and found you were not there; but it hurt me."

The muni stroked his little hand; and answered, —

"That was only for the boatmen: I was not praying to God. The great, real Bramha cannot be pleased to see men hurt themselves. No, no, my Hari! I know very little: I am perplexed. Religion is a myth, a folly: God alone is a reality. There is some way to worship him, but it is not as I and my people do it. You are little now, but you will know it all some day; and when you have found out what God is, and how he is best worshipped, if Dhondaram is still alive, you must come back and tell him, and he will kneel at your feet and worship God, — your God, my Hari."

"How could I come back to you when I am never, never going away from you, Dhondaram!" exclaimed Paul. "Teach me, oh, teach me to pray like you and every one else!"

They had been floating rapidly down the river, and now were landed where they had but a short walk over the hills to the caravan trail. The boat moved away; and, sending the servant on ahead, Dhondaram sat upon the ground close upon the bank of the river, and, drawing Paul to him, said, —

"I will teach you a prayer, little Hari-Sahib, — a prayer that you will never be told not to say; and I can show you how to say it. I cannot say it in the language that we are speaking, but in my own language, the Marathi. You will not understand it all; but you can remember it, and know that you are praying to God."

He bathed his face and hands that he might be clean, according to his own teaching; and very slowly he repeated, and Paul followed him, —

"He amachya Akashantil Bapa, tujhe nam pavitra manile zavo; tujhe rajya yevo; jase akaṣhant tase prithvivarahi tujhya ichchhepramane hovo; amachi rozachi bharkar az amhas de; ani jase amhi apalya rinyas sodato, tase tu amachi rine amhas sod; ani amhas parikshent neu nako, tar amhas waitapasun sodiv; kaki rajya ani parakram ani mahima hi sarvakal tujhi ahet. Amen."

Over and over again they went through the prayer, till Paul could repeat it almost without a mistake, kneeling by the muni's side, and closing his brown hands before his breast.

Then suddenly they heard the voice of the servant calling from the top of the hill, that the caravan was already in sight; and taking Paul on his shoulder, Dhondaram hurried on.

Reaching the point where the servant stood, they could see a dense cloud of dust rising in the plain beyond; and through it they could discern horses and camels, and a vast herd of cattle, with men and women and children all about them. Paul clung more closely to Dhondaram.

"The little Hari must not fear," he said. "They are all friends of mine there. I feared they would not be here so soon. We shall go a little way with them, for they have news for me; and you need not be tired any more, for while we are with them you shall ride upon a fine horse, and the servant here will ride behind you to hold you fast."

"I would rather ride here on your shoulder," said Paul.

"You will have plenty of chances for this, Hari-Sahib, when we cannot find a horse."

Several of the leaders now came rapidly riding up to Dhondaram. They had no difficulty in recognizing him, and, dismounting, made very low salaams, as though he were a ruler among them.

Hastily directing his servant to mount one of the horses that those before him had brought up, he placed Paul before him, and gave the bundle to one of the soldiers of the caravan who now reached them. Then he pressed Paul's hand to his forehead, and said,—

"You are safe, little Sahib. You have but to speak, and they will bring me; and very soon I shall ride beside you."

Then, turning to the officers, he spoke in a language that Paul could not understand; nor could he have heard much, for the servant immediately drove away with him.

"What news from the Nana?" was what Dhondaram asked; and the officer replied,—

"He is still in danger: the wound mends slowly. He much fears that he may die before the work is completed."

"Send him word from me at once," said Dhondaram, "that only one of the condemned remains alive. Tell him that this one is now in these mountains; tell him that I have a magnet that is drawing him toward me, and that he shall hear of his death in less than a month. Tell him to recover; but if he dies, tell him to die in peace: Dhondaram has fulfilled the vow."

He turned abruptly; and, mounting another of the horses, evidently caring little how the fellows who had come up on them disposed of themselves, he rode on, and a moment later was beside little Paul.

The men in the caravan were generally dressed much like Dhondaram; and the women often wore long pointed ornaments on their heads, to which their veils, or *saris*, were attached. Several of them had little naked children in their arms, and there were other children riding like Paul. Paul noticed that the cows all had curious saddles, and each one was laden with a small burden. Before the whole walked an immense bull, a stately fellow, without a burden except a garland of flowers.

THE MERCHANT.

Some of the merchants travelling with the caravan were most elaborately decorated. Their packs were on their camels' backs, — sometimes silk and costly cashmeres, sometimes precious stones or oils. They often had servants, and some of them a few private soldiers with them. They were often rolled up in limitless folds of cloth, over head and all, and always carried on their shoulders a long-barrelled and richly ornamented gun.

A half hour before twilight the stately bull seemed to be examining the sun. It was round and red. Very soon he stopped, and began to eat the grass that grew abundantly in the valley. Then all the natives along the line, in their scanty costumes and with long blunt spears, who had been keeping the cows in motion when they would have stopped to eat, drove them together, and removed the saddles, letting them wander where they would. The horses were tethered by ropes from their necks to their fore-ankle. Here and there Paul noticed a man go a little way apart from the rest. They were Mussulmans, — though Paul did not know what that had

THE DAY'S MARCH THROUGH THE MOUNTAINS.

to do with it, — and, dismounting from their camels, before they set them free they knelt beside them in prayer. They spread little mats upon the ground, and, taking off their shoes, stood erect, placing their thumbs to their ears, and opening their hands so that the palms were presented toward

Mecca: thus they began the prayer. Then they folded their hands upon their breasts, and with their heads bowed they prayed again; then placed their hands upon their knees; then knelt, with their hands still on their knees, and continued. After this they laid their hands upon the ground, and touched their foreheads several times to the earth.

"That's another kind of praying, isn't it?" asked Paul, who, with Dhondaram, sat upon a little rug eating the food that the servant had prepared for them.

"Yes," replied the muni, with a sneer: "they call it praying."

"Isn't it so good as mine?" the boy asked earnestly.

"God may hear it; but, if he does, it is through pity," replied the muni, with another sneer.

"See if I can say my prayer," said Paul; and, without waiting for an answer, he bathed his face and hands in Hindu fashion, by turning a little water for the purpose from a basin before him, and catching it in his hands; then, kneeling by Dhondaram's knee, he repeated over and over again the prayer that the muni had taught him, needing much help, but every time improving. It became dark while he was praying, and a few torches and a few large fires were lighted to keep off the wild beasts.

Suddenly a clear voice sounded from no great distance, chanting in Hindustani the old, old desert hymn of the Mussulman. Paul understood every word.

"Whoever thou art, whose need is great,
In the name of God, the compassionate
And the merciful one,
For thee I wait."

THE CLOUD MOUNTAIN BY THE MOON.

"That's pretty good," said Paul, as it sounded again and again and again from different parts of the caravan, where Mussulmans were wrapping themselves up for the night.

"It would be," replied Dhondaram, "if they meant it."

"How are we to sleep?" asked Paul, who noticed for the first time, that, instead of the sun, it was the moon that was shining brightly; and in the moonlight, the plain before them that had appeared so fresh and green with its grass and little flowers was now but a barren mass of ragged rocks outlined against the shadows, and by the moon there seemed to rise a huge mountain. Paul had not seen it before, and eagerly asked,—

"Where did that come from, Dhondaram?"

"It is only a cloud," said the muni, "driven up by currents of air through the gorges. One sees very curious things here in the mountains. But we shall have a good place to sleep. They have prepared a tent for us." And rising, he took Paul in his arms, dreading even to let him touch his little feet to the uncertain ground, and carried him to a low camel's-hair tent, of black and white stripes, under which they both crept, and where Paul slept as soundly on the strong arm of Dhondaram as though it had been upon a soft white pillow in the cottage at Beverly Farms.

The next day the caravan wound up a river-bank. Ragged mountains rose up almost directly out of the water. Upon their rocky sides deodars were growing, straight as arrows, though they were rooted only in clefts of the rocks in almost perpendicular precipices, and fed only on the dying lichens, and icy rills from the melting snows up above.

Paul looked long and earnestly at the snowy peaks.

"Where have I ever seen snow before?" he asked Dhondaram.

"In your home, Hari-Sahib," he replied.

"Have I a home?" he asked again. Dhondaram looked down at him. He was riding now before the muni. The blue eyes looked up wonderingly.

"You must go to it, my treasure. You shall go to it. Dhondaram will not keep you."

UP AMONG THE SNOWS.

"But I want you to go, too, Dhondaram. Where is it? Is it far from here?" asked Paul.

"Far?" the muni laughed. "Far? Yes: it is far from here." There was a strange tremor in his voice: it was very unnatural. Paul said suddenly,—

"But you will go, Dhondaram? You must go. Where is it?"

"You shall know before long. You shall know all about

it," remarked the muni sadly; "and you will not forget old Dhondaram. No, you will not forget him."

Paul threw one arm around the muni's neck: tears filled the clear blue eyes, and ran down over the brown cheeks. They were not so brown as at first. The dye was not lasting, and was wearing off. Dhondaram would not have renewed

THE GOLDEN TEMPLE.

it for the world. His treasure was the pale-faced boy. There were tears, too, in the muni's eyes.

When they reached Amritsar they only remained to visit the beautiful golden temple, in the centre of the clear, cold mountain lake, and to exchange a few sentences in a language that Paul could not understand, with several bands of munis and pilgrims that were there.

The city was greatly disturbed by notices posted everywhere, stating that the great Guru, or the high priest of the golden temple, had seen in a vision that his holy father, who lately died, had been transformed into a fish, and was then swimming about in the lake. On account of this he forbade any one, under penalty of death, to catch a fish in the lake. The greater part of the population of the city was composed of poor or pilgrims, who depended chiefly upon the fish in the lake for food, and something like starvation stared them in the face. But Paul cared very little for Amritsar or the mandate, as he held fast to the muni's hand, and looked only into his face.

It produced no effect on the boy when the muni said to him, "We must go to Massuri: it is a hard journey, but we will make it easy for the little Hari-Sahib," any more than it would if he had said "We will go to the other end of the world to-morrow." If Dhondaram only went with him he did not care.

With a small escort of mountaineers they started into the defiles, the soldiers taking the lead and bringing up the rear.

Sometimes the way led through beautiful valleys, with lovely flowers, and giant trees, and roaring mountain streams, with little bridges across them that were composed simply of branches of birch-trees twisted together; and they would sag and bend and tremble when they were on them. But Paul clasped the muni's hand so much the closer, and followed where he led, only keeping quiet when he was frightened, and laughing when he was not.

His face and hands became quite white again; and he asked to have them once more colored, "With a black that will go all over me, and last till I am a great man like you."

But the muni only assured him that he had no more of the material with him, and that he must wait; and, as long as Dhondaram did not call him Feringhi, it made less difference.

Sometimes they were under the shadow of towering mountains, where the eternal snows lay in the gorges; and Paul was carried in a sort of bag, hung on a bamboo pole that rested on the shoulders of sturdy mountaineers. The bag was open on one side; and as he sat in it his feet hung out, and to prevent them from striking against the rocks, or being injured, they rested in a smaller bag just below. A *dandi* the mountaineers called the carriage; and, as Paul was very light, they carried him so easily that he thought it almost as comfortable as riding on Dhondaram's shoulder.

A CURIOUS PEOPLE.

Often among the peaks and gorges there were curious stone houses, where they could rest for the night, — "caravan-sarais" Dhondaram called them; and the people that clustered about them from the little hamlets in those almost inaccessible recesses were as peculiar and interesting to Paul as was the little white-faced boy to them.

While the servant who had come with them from Delhi

was preparing the fire and supper, these people would gather round, anxious to see and speak with any one who had come from "the world," as they called anywhere out of the Himalayas.

Many of them who had never seen a white boy before would creep up timidly and touch Paul's cheek, and then look at their fingers to see if the white came off. Their clothes were ugly; but their faces were kind, and the smiles were pleasant. Many a merry time had the boy in playing with the superstitious children, who were mortally afraid of him if he really approached them, and in laughing over their struggles to speak Hindustani, in which, unwittingly, he had become a very competent little scholar.

THE WOODCUTTER.

The older and braver would take off his hat, and proudly walk about beneath it, and question him, till his brain became bewildered, about the dye he used to make his hair so brown; while they displayed with pride the reddish-yellow ends of their own black hair.

Wood-cutters at their work in the vast forests would stop with their bundles on their heads, and drop their straight-helved axes to look at the little Feringhi riding past them in a *dandi;* and shepherdesses, with rings in their noses, and leather belts full of turquoise about their waists, and large bundles of hay balanced on their heads, would pause as they leaped over the rocks after the goats, to make a salaam to the white sahib, and wish him a godspeed (the speed of a heathen god, at least) down out of the mountains.

SHEPHERDESS.

Going as he did, Paul found a trip through the Himalayas a very much easier affair than many older ones have found it. He did not realize the dangers of the precipice. He had not been told that he should be dizzy, and that his head should swim, as he looked down those perpendicular cliffs, sometimes three thousand feet and more into the black gorges, where he could not even distinguish the great towering deodars: so, holding fast to Dhondaram's hand, he looked down and laughed, and pretended he was about to jump, to see the muni spring and catch him.

He would sometimes even laugh on the trembling birch-branch bridges crossing the deep gorges. What did he care for the roaring mountain rivers, though they were five hundred feet below? He would have stood under an avalanche, tearing down the mountain-side, and jumped for joy to see

THE BLACK GORGES.

the great masses come bounding on; he would have waited to watch the progress of some of the fearful land-slides, so much more dreaded than the avalanches; he would have shouted in concert with the numberless echoes of the crash, crash, crash, of some great bowlder tearing down the mountain-side, though it came directly toward him, so long as he held that sinewy brown hand in his, and felt the hard muscles of the fingers as they gently clasped his little palm.

What did he know about the blood-stained daggers and knotted rumals, and vows of terrible vengeance against a long list that Dhondaram and Nana Sahib called the "condemned," and all the rest? What did it matter?

It grew colder as they went higher; but Dhondaram had known what was before them, and provided warm blankets of goatskin, in which Paul was so perfectly enveloped that the air proved but bracing, and the roses came back again to the cheeks that had been very pale ever since the terrible drugs to which Roderick Dennett had subjected him. He grew stronger every day. A European, to cross those passes, would have made out an endless list of necessities. He would have had a small army of servants. He would have suffered all the way. Dhondaram had crossed the mountains many times before. He knew just what little was a necessity, and where and how to provide every thing else by the way.

At last they reached a little village far up among the snow peaks, in a little gorge between the eternal ice, where three or four hundred people live, no one knows how or why. They do nothing, they export nothing, they import nothing (nothing but tobacco, which they obtain in exchange for goatskins). The houses were all front doors and one large hole dug out of the mountain behind them. It was in the midst of ice, yet it was not cold there; and very near at hand the goats — the village was supplied with several hundred — found abundant pasturage, often being obliged to stand almost erect, the cliffs upon which they feed are so nearly perpendicular.

The people lived upon the goats' milk and the goats' flesh, and made their clothes from the goats' skins. They made very bad liquor, upon which they succeeded in getting drunk, out of the cedars growing just below; and while the warm winds blew they raised just enough grain to keep them from starving till they could raise more. They sat in those front doors and smoked their *hookahs* all day long, for want of any thing in the world to do. For the rest that was absolutely necessary, they trusted to what little money they might receive from passing travellers.

"This is the last but one, I think," said Dhondaram, as they pitched their tents for the servants and soldiers, and they themselves took refuge in one of the huts. "To-morrow we shall begin to go down the mountains, and we shall be among the flowers again."

"But where are we going, Dhondaram? I want to go and see Gunga and Prita," said Paul.

The muni had grown more sad as days went by, and it made the boy sober. He only stroked the soft cheek, and replied, "The day after to-morrow, if I am told truly, you shall be with the ones you wish to see."

"I wish I might see a great many things," said Paul a moment later.

"You will soon know a great many things, and see more," replied the muni.

With returning strength and rapid regaining of health, Paul philosophized more than he had; and, as the muni dropped hint after hint, as though anxious to lead him on, he remembered more and more, though nothing perfectly.

Early the next morning they began to go down the mountain. Dhondaram had sat all night by the side of his charge, communicating something of his own feeling, perhaps; for Paul had waked up several times in the night, but always to find the muni bending over him.

Perhaps it was weariness after such a night, or perhaps it was the grandeur of the scenery through which they passed, that made both Paul and his friend silent and sad through the long morning as they wandered on, more rapidly now, for the day's march before them was a long one.

The tremendous peaks rose against the sky, white as marble at the summit; and a soft and most delicate pink tint covered the broad snow-fields below. They seemed to Paul to be very near, though they were a hundred and fifty miles away. The air of the mountains is so clear and pure that even the dark outlines of the gorges seemed perfectly defined. There was wall after wall of these mountains, not like the sharp peaks of ranges anywhere else in the world, but hurled together. Great domes and circling crowns, rising in such masses as to dispel the impression of their real height, though most of them were over twenty thousand feet above the sea. Little Paul in his *dandi* had been higher up than the summit of Mont Blanc, the highest peak in Europe.

As soon as the sun rose, the distant rumbling and low grumbling of glaciers, and the occasional thundering of avalanches and land-slides, filled the air with an incessant din, that grew louder and louder as the day wore on.

The servant who accompanied them from Delhi had left earlier than they in the morning; but he had started earlier every morning for several days, only to appear again at night. To-day, however, it was long before sundown that he returned. He hurried to Dhondaram, and anxiously said, "Their coolies are setting up the tents on the heights just below. They remain there to-night, and go on by way of the clay caravansarai in the morning."

THE CAMP ON THE HEIGHTS.

"'Tis well," replied Dhondaram; and a strange low fire seemed lurking in his eyes. "We must reach the caravansarai, and sleep there to-night. How many are there? and who is the party?"

"There are two white men. He is one; and the other is from Bombay, with a young man who does not speak the languages. Their escort is five Rajpoots; their company, twenty servants."

"'Tis well," said Dhondaram again. "Were the escort five hundred Rajpoots, or five regiments of British soldiers, what would it avail? Why should I continue flying like a cursed sore over a man's body? Move on! Move on rapidly! It will be long after dark, and the way is dangerous."

The train began again to move: and just as the sun was setting, they passed the heights that the servant had spoken of, where a large European tent was pitched; and at a little distance, on the ground, sat a dozen or more native servants. The train moved a little below the heights; but Dhondaram left it, and, walking up to the servants, began to talk with them: within full view two Europeans were standing by the tent.

A little later the muni was again beside his charge; and little Paul clasped his hand, and pleaded till he took him out of the *dandi*, and for another hour bore him through the darkling jungle upon his shoulder.

"This is like the time when the boat was smashed," said Paul, patting the dark cheek that he could no longer see.

The sinewy arm clasped close about the child. A shudder shook the strong man. He walked unsteadily. He almost fell on the uneven path.

"If you should fall, I should fall too, shouldn't I?" asked the boy, laughing.

"I will not fall while my Hari-Sahib is on my shoulder," replied Dhondaram, strengthening himself to the task, and walking more rapidly and firmly.

"I don't care if you fall," said Paul carelessly: "'twould be fun. It wouldn't hurt me."

"How does the little Hari know that?" asked the muni, patting the shoulder upon which his uplifted hand rested.

"Oh! you wouldn't let it hurt me," replied Paul confidently. "I like to be where I'm afraid, and be with you."

It was dark. He could not see the tears roll down the furrowed face of the black-hearted murderer.

For a moment the muni strode on through the darkness in silence. Even the touch of his feet in the track made no noise. At last, however, he lifted Paul from his shoulder, and took him across his breast. It rose and fell in deep and painful respirations.

"Never mind," he said at last: "they will take better care of you than Dhondaram can; for he is rough and rude, and only a Hindu. They are like you. They will love you." His arms drew so close about the boy as almost to crush him, but Paul did not feel the pain. The muni added, "But they cannot love you more. No, no. It would be impossible."

"Who will?" asked Paul indignantly.

"You will know to-morrow. To-night you are Dhondaram's. Yes, to-night you are Dhondaram's."

"I'm always yours," said Paul, as they reached the clay caravansarai.

In the morning Dhondaram bathed Paul tenderly, and took from his bundle the prettiest suit of European clothes. At first Paul objected to taking off the bright Persian costume, bordered with fur, and the soft goat-skin robe that had protected him so perfectly from the cold: but there was something of his dreams in the other clothes; and they looked so pretty, after all, that he began to dance about the absolutely bare room of the caravansarai, and called to the rough mountain soldiers that had been their escort, to come in, and look at him.

The stockings and shoes were almost more than Dhondaram could master. But he who had grimly grasped the throat of many a fellow-man, and calmly stood over him to see him die of suffocation; he who had smiled in the ghastly eyes that stared at him while his dagger lay buried in the victim's heart; he who had laughed when infuriated crowds shouted, "Down with the outlaw Dhondaram! Curses on the terror of India!" he who had calmly led surging throngs of fanatics in even more terrible struggles than those reported of the mutiny; he who knew neither shiver from the frozen mountain peaks, nor terror from the torrid heat of the plains, whose name was banned, whose heart was fearless, — knelt upon the clay floor, and patiently struggled to button the little shoes with his rough fingers, while he chatted to keep the child from being weary, and jumped about like an acrobat at a circus, to make him laugh, when his awkwardness had pinched the flesh, and started the tears into the blue eyes.

The work was done at last, however: and, combing the brown hair with its persistent curls as nearly in European fashion as his unaccustomed hands could do it, he took a jaunty little American hat from the bundle; and, putting it on Paul's head, he stepped back to look at him. And he smiled approvingly; though the iron heart was throbbing hard beneath the dark brown breast, and the perspiration standing on the broad, stern forehead.

One of the soldiers entered, and spoke to him.

"I am none too soon," he replied. "Hold them at bay; fire high: there is no need to kill even a Rajpoot. And look to your lives that no European is struck by a ball! All will go well: there is no chance for mistake. When they turn and retreat, let them go." And taking Paul on his shoulder, he

HE HEARD A SHARP REPORT.

gathered up the bundle of clothes, and into it thrust the Persian suit and the warm goatskins. "The little Hari will need them perhaps," he said with a sigh; and from the other side of the caravansarai he sprang into the jungle.

As they left, Paul looked back. He had not understood what was said, but realized that there was danger. What did he care for it? He saw the soldiers, rough fellows, to whom blood and fighting were second nature, gathering eagerly about the door of the caravansarai; he saw the servant look sadly toward Dhondaram, and bow to the ground; he saw one of the soldiers kneel, and rest his gun upon the clay wall by the caravansarai-door; and just as Dhondaram leaped forward, and the jungle covered them, he heard a sharp report.

"What are they doing?" he asked as he clung to the muni's neck; while with leap after leap he sprang through the dense growth, and, guided by the shouts of the party that had been surprised in approaching the caravansarai, he rapidly circumvented them, and paused in a cleft between high rocks, where a little brook leaped down into the shadows,—a point that they must have lately passed. Here he placed Paul gently upon the ground. A flock of wild pigeons started from the brook, and circling about his head flew up the ravine.

"That is a good omen, little Hari-Sahib," he said, and bending over him, whispered hurriedly, "Once more the little prayer. Touch the water, kneel by the brook, and say it. There"—

He waited. Paul had well learned it by this time, and repeated it without hesitation.

"Now stay upon the knees for a little while," he added, turning his face away as the little blue eyes met his. "I must go and see what is the matter, and why they are shooting.

Nothing will hurt you here. Say the prayer over and over again, and do not move till some one calls you: you will be very happy then. Say it once more while I listen. And remember! do not get up from your knees, or something bad might happen."

Paul said the prayer again. He had heard no sound, but when he looked up the muni was gone. He started to his feet, and would have called; but he remembered the charge, and, kneeling again, repeated the prayer once more, — the little Marathi prayer, — without understanding a word of it.

The rippling brook went dancing by. Paul was only a child, and soon had forgotten the surrounding circumstances in watching the water, and playing with the pebbles, sure that in a little while he should look up and see Dhondaram coming back for him.

CHAPTER XXV.

SCOTT'S FIRST TIGER, AND FINAL PRIZE.

ON reaching Massuri, Mr. Raymond and Scott discovered a very curious state of things. Roderick Dennett was there, and working as eagerly as ever he worked in his life to regain that valuable belt. But he worked with fear and trembling, for there was something so mysterious in it all that he began to fear foul play from some of his enemies.

A messenger had come to his friend Mobarak in Delhi, leaving with him, to be given to Dennett, a package containing a lock of Paul's hair, a little shirt that he himself had bought for him, and a charm that he had worn about his neck. These were accompanied with a message that the boy was in the defiles of the Himalaya Mountains, between Amritsar and Massuri, and that if he would see him alive he must go there for him within a month. He had started at once, but when he reached Massuri fear so overcame him that he sent for Mr. Raymond.

"We must begin the search at once," said Mr. Raymond. "Never mind the foul play: I think there is none. It is probably only a native dodge to see how anxious you are."

They studied the routes together; they sent out spies; they made every effort, but in vain.

"We must go ourselves," said Richard a week later. "Scott is hardly well enough to risk the first passes; but, while you go over the mountains, we will take the longer route on elephants through the lower hills, and meet you on the tenth day. From there we will go on together."

There was no avoiding this, and Dennett accepted the terms.

RAJPOOT GUARD.

Five of the famously brave Rajpoot soldiers were sent for from Delhi to accompany them as escort.

"I do not like these mountaineers for guards," said Richard, "especially when we are attempting to discover any thing in which other mountaineers may be interested. We shall have to employ them in districts where the rajahs oblige us to, but we will have our own men beside."

Mountaineers were hired to carry the baggage, provisions, and tents.

"What a frightful looking set of fellows!" exclaimed Scott as they came together for the start. "I'd rather trust my life with Thugs."

"They're not so bad as they look," replied Richard.

"But what in the world do we need such a crowd for?" Scott asked.

"Because the legal burden of these men is the weight of twelve quart bottles of water, and not a drop more. It is quite enough, too, in some of the climbing."

"Does every one always pet the same bundle?" asked Scott.

"Not by any means. They will fight for an hour every morning for the first choice, if they think one of the bundles weighs a little less than the rest."

"They look like regular buck-knots for toughness," Scott remarked, with a shadow of admiration after all for the ungainly fellows.

"So they are," replied his friend; "and yet the chances are, that at the foot of every bad hill they come to they will lie down and begin to cry."

"What for?" asked Scott.

"Oh! they will say that you are killing them with over-work; that you have brought them up there expressly to murder them; and that they are dying, while you look on and do not care a straw."

"What can one do with them?" questioned Scott again.

"Why, the best way is to tell them they are quite correct about it, and let them get over it as soon as they like: unless one is in a hurry, and then he must give them some back-sheesh; that is what they really want."

"I'd give them a thrashing instead," said Scott.

THE MOUNTAIN COOLIES.

"It is sometimes quite refreshing to pound them a little, but they take it so meekly that one gets tired of it."

"But can't they learn in time what is wanted of them, and that they must behave?" Scott asked impatiently.

"That's quite impossible," replied Richard; "for we shall have to change them at every important town we come to. The same set of fellows never go but a little way. They spend their lives in going back and forth between two places."

The Himalaya Mountains are formed like a gigantic staircase, extending from the plains about Delhi and Agra to the inaccessible heights of which Kailas and many others are the upper tier, with Everest over twenty-nine thousand feet above the sea. The lower step of this great staircase is the elevated jungle rising out of the Terai, that swarms with ferocious beasts and venomous reptiles. During the season of rains, when the spongy Terai becomes nothing more or less than the most poisonous malarial swamp in existence, even the beasts are driven out, and take shelter in these jungles.

For three days Scott rode upon a small elephant, while Mr. Raymond followed upon a larger one, with a few servants behind, carrying the necessary baggage. They did not need the tents and clothing, as they depended upon caravansarais and villages. Richard had suggested taking their rifles, as there was a good chance for game at this season. This was a fortunate thing; for about noon on the second day, while Scott was almost asleep under the easy motion of the elephant, he was suddenly roused by a shrill cry from the beast, and a decided spring for that clumsy animal.

Scott opened his eyes instantly. The head and trunk of the animal were stretched out as far as possible. Richard called from behind. Scott turned in time to see a large tiger in mid-air, as if flying directly toward him. It was a peculiar sensation, to meet something that belonged on terra-firma gliding through the air like a bird, with no apparent exertion; but Scott had not long to enjoy the novelty.

Thanks to the elephant, whose little eyes had discovered the tiger as he sprang, and who had strained every nerve to

SCOTT'S FIRST TIGER.

get out of his way, the creature missed the high aim of the *howdah*, and struck on the haunches of the beast that bore it. There he stuck tight, fastening his great yellow claws in the elephant's flesh.

"He'll stop there for a minute. Shoot steady and sure for his breast, Scott," called Mr. Raymond, as he urged the mahout to drive his own elephant faster, and overtake the other.

The tone and timely warning had a strong tendency to quiet Scott's excitement; and, quickly placing his rifle to his shoulder, he aimed for the tiger's breast, and fired. The moment the rifle sounded, the mahout turned the elephant. This was in rule, but Scott did not know of it; and, as the beast fell with a fierce howl to the ground, Scott was thrown on his back, but fortunately not out of the *howdah*. This sudden turning has the effect to throw the tiger if he is only wounded, — as proved to be the case, — instead of allowing him to still cling, and possibly climb higher. In this case it also allowed Richard a chance to catch up.

"Up again, Scott, be lively," cried Richard as they came abreast each other. "He will spring again in an instant. Take my rifle. Look out! There he comes. Kill him this time."

The tiger lunged, tore the earth for an instant, and, seeing the elephant, made another dive; but in his haste he missed his aim again, and only caught his fore-shoulder. There he clung, looking up at Scott with his red tongue and purple gullet and glistening teeth but a few feet from the *howdah*, while hoarse and harsh his breath came wheezing and grating. Scott's hand trembled. He drew back from the fearful jaws.

"Give it to him! Give it to him, Scott!" exclaimed Mr. Raymond, seeing him under the spell of peculiar terror that so often benumbs one when first he faces one of the kings of those Indian forests; utterly unable to move, while he stood with his eyes fixed on the tiger, that now began creeping up toward the *howdah*. Then he had his mahout push the elephants together; and, even before they met, he sprang from his *howdah*, catching on the back of Scott's elephant. Clambering up with the rapidity of thought almost, he stood beside the boy as the tiger's paw rested on the opposite side of the *howdah*.

This caused Scott to recover the presence of mind that had entirely forsaken him, and that has forsaken many an older man than he under the same circumstances. He stepped bravely forward, and, hardly waiting to aim, placed the muzzle of the gun to the animal's mouth, and fired. The tiger sprang for the rifle; but, before his jaws closed, he fell back, and in a moment more lay dead upon the ground.

"Killed your first tiger!" exclaimed Richard, slapping the trembling boy upon the shoulder.

"Why didn't you shoot him, instead of giving me the rifle?" asked Scott as he climbed from the *howdah* of the elephant that now lay on the ground, and approached his first tiger.

"What was the use? He was yours, and you were perfectly able to attend to him. 'Twould have been against etiquette."

"No, I wasn't able to attend to him," replied Scott. "If you had not come, I should have stood there, and let him have me."

"That's because he was your first," said Richard. "The natives say that no man is a safe hunter till he's felt a tiger's breath. Now you've felt it, and the next time you'll have no fear of that sort."

Moro and Sayad soon came up with the light baggage. They were not skilled in the trade, but they succeeded in skinning the tiger; and with the fur, the proudest trophy of his wanderings in India, Scott mounted the elephant again, and they moved on more rapidly to make up for lost time.

The next day they left the elephants, and went on by

dandi. Scott found it a most uncomfortable mode; for he did not make the selection that Dhondaram had for Paul, and had no native to walk beside, and keep the bearers in time and temper. They succeeded in swinging the *dandi* back and forth like a pendulum, and letting him strike against every rock and sharp corner by the way, that they could possibly reach. When the way was particularly narrow, as it always is in the Himalayas, through inanimate perversity, when it leads along the brink of a precipice that is particularly high, the bearers always carried the pole on the outside shoulder; and as Scott peered over the edge of the bag in which he rode, and saw the forests hundreds of feet below, it made his blood run cold, where Paul had only laughed.

"I wonder what would happen if one of these fellows should shrug that outside shoulder?" he said to Richard with a shudder as they rode side by side in an open place after crossing one of those precipices.

"Heaven only knows," replied Mr. Raymond. "And I hope that neither you nor I will ever find out."

"Well, I am frightened to death in front, and bruised to jelly behind," said Scott. "If there's any other kind of engines here, I'm in for trying them. Haven't they any horses?"

"Plenty of them, and terrors they are too, I tell you. Over rough places like this the fellows will jump from rock to rock like chamois in the Alps, lighting all fours together every time, on little rocks that you could hardly stand on. And the little brutes will shie like the mischief too; and you know a horse will always back when he is frightened, without caring a straw where his hind feet are going. If that happens to be on a precipice, over you go before you can say boo!"

"I'd jump off," said Scott.

"No, you wouldn't," replied Richard: "you would cling to the horse and saddle for life. Then you see how the natives that we meet with packs on their backs always take the inside, and sometimes even stop and balance the bundles against the rocks, to watch us pass."

"Well, they are enough to frighten any living horse!" exclaimed Scott. "But is there nothing else?"

"There are yaks, Scott; and at the next village, where the *dandi* wallahs leave us, we will try and get some. They are safe as the mountains themselves. I never heard of a yak falling, or losing a passenger."

"They'd be as good as a Cunard steamer, then," suggested Scott, who had found to his sorrow that the fact that a line has never lost a passenger is not the only requisite to a comfortable passage.

"But they are ugly enough to frighten all the peasants in the mountains; and when you are off their backs, take care! They regard white men as the bane of all their misery, and go for them at every chance."

"Never mind that, if they are all right when I'm once on board," replied Scott; "for indeed I'm completely mashed to pieces here."

While they were talking, a small caravan passed them; and the leader, bowing very politely, saluted them,—

"Bonesore, Sahib."

"My bones are rather sore, thank you," replied Scott, as politely as possible; but as soon as they had passed he said to Richard, "Wasn't that rather cheeky, to ask me if my bones were sore?"

Mr. Raymond laughed till the bearers almost lost their balance, but at last succeeded in gasping, "He has only learned a little French, Scott, and was trying to say '*bon soir*' to you."

"Bother his French," growled Scott: "I wish I was on the back of a yak."

They had one more steep ledge to climb; and, while crossing, an incident occurred that caused Scott to declare more decidedly than ever in favor of the yak. When they were nearly half-way over one of the narrowest ledges, where a steep incline rose above them, and fell away again from their feet, a sudden roar aroused them, — a crashing and thundering from above.

Scott was then some distance behind Mr. Raymond, and was unceremoniously dropped in the path, *dandi* and all, while the bearers ran for their lives in opposite directions.

Before he could extricate himself, a mass of rock and dirt rushed down the steep declivity at a tremendous velocity, like the most formidable avalanche. By good fortune the bearers had missed in their calculations; and it passed a little behind, only covering him with dust.

At the foot of the ravine, there was a rushing river of no very dignified proportions; but it had succeeded in tearing away the frail bridge that crossed it.

"What in creation!" groaned Scott as they approached. "What are those fellows carrying on their backs? Young oxen?"

"Ferry-boats," roared Richard.

"Ferry-boats? For mercy's sake!"

When they reached the stream, the natives turned a half somerset, landing the mussok-skins stuffed with straw upon their sides in the water.

"How much does this show cost?" asked Scott, as they landed safe and dry at last.

"Just a half of one cent apiece," replied Richard solemnly.

"Great Cæsar's ghost!" muttered Scott, as he again seated himself in the *dandi*, and was borne up the opposite hill: "I suppose the benighted fellows think they are doing a good business."

One of the first things Scott saw upon approaching the village was a great, grim, ugly, ungainly yak. He knew at first sight that it was a yak, for in all his circus-going he had never seen any thing so horrible. There was an old man holding the creature by a ring in his nose.

"What a haul Barnum would make if he could have that thing on his bill, man and all!" Scott observed admiringly, estimating his chances on the creature's back, from a safe distance. The old man was muttering, —

"Om, Om, Om, Om, Om, Om!" as rapidly as possible, and took no notice of them.

"What's the matter with him? Is he sick?" asked Scott as they passed.

"He is going somewhere with the yak; and before he starts he is saying a part of the great Llama prayer," replied Richard. "'Om mani padme hum,' is the sum and substance of their longest prayer; and the more they say that word 'Om,' which is the name of God, so much the holier they are."

They entered the house that usually served as an inn for those who did not wish to provide for themselves at the caravansarai.

Here was an old woman cooking over a hole in the floor, and a young woman sitting by the fire, with two boys about three years old on her knees. She was swinging something like an old-fashioned watchman's rattle over the children's heads, and saying "Om, Om, Om, Om, Om!" just like the old fellow with the yak.

"She's got it too, and got it bad," said Scott with a sigh; "but what has she in her hand?"

"A praying-stick," replied Richard. "That same prayer is written all over that stick, and every time it turns round it is as good as repeating the prayer as many times as it is written on the stick. Didn't you see the men that came up with us stop at those little wheels by the way, and set them spinning?"

"Of course I did, but I thought they did it for fun. So they were praying-sticks too. And I suppose the young woman there is going it double, turning the stick and saying the prayer at the same time, because she has twins."

Richard spoke for a moment with four or five men sitting about the hut, who had moved a little, without more ado than a simple salutation, to make room for them as they came in. Then turning to Scott, he replied,—

"That boy on her right knee is her son, and the other one is her husband."

"Husband!" exclaimed Scott, "why, I thought one of those grown fellows was her husband."

"So they are, every one of them; and she has two more out in the mountains, with two husbands of the old woman there, who is their mother."

"Great Cæsar! that's worse than harems," said Scott. "I'll have to tell mother about this. Is that the way they all do business here?"

"That is the way they all do business here; for you know we have got well up into the mountains now, and down on the Thibitan side is one great centre of polyandry."

"Poor things," groaned Scott: "there are women in America who can't stand one: wouldn't they open their eyes if we should tell them about this?"

Two days of climbing upon yak-back proved much more comfortable than the days in the *dandi*, and brought them to the meeting-place, where Roderick Dennett was already encamped; and two days more brought them to the heights where they pitched their tents, where Paul and Dhondaram passed them just as the sun was setting.

Little Paul had not even seen the camp. The *dandi* in which he was carried was purposely turned, that it might open on the other side. Dhondaram had calmly walked up to the servants, and conversed with them: he had asked them where they were going, and many questions about the members of the party.

In the morning there was snow half a foot deep over the ground; but with the first rays of sunlight the snow disappeared like a morning mist, while from under it there suddenly appeared a thick carpet of beautiful mountain flowers, just as fresh and fragrant as if they had only come from a bath in the morning dew. Even the glacier that they crossed an hour later was a broad river of mountain flowers.

As Scott's eyes became weary of watching the changes with the rising of the flashing, glaring sun, he went toward the cook, who sat by his fire. A pot of tea was boiling furiously; yet he saw the fellow pour out a cup for himself, and drink it down without waiting a moment for it to cool.

"He must have a throat of cast iron," said Scott to Mr. Raymond, who had joined him; but he opened his eyes in astonishment when Richard went up to the fire, and did precisely the same thing.

"Try it," said Richard, giving him the steaming cup. He daintily touched it to his lips, and looked up in surprise.

"Why, it is hardly warmer than new milk!" he exclaimed: "it must cool rapidly."

"It is not that exactly," Richard replied; "but when you have graduated from college you will know, that, on general principles, at this elevation water will boil away before it is really hot. You couldn't boil a leg of mutton here if you should try all day. But breakfast is ready, and we must be under way. We have a few more places to search before we climb the highest pass and go down on the other side."

"What a place for Englishmen this would be!" Scott remarked, still thinking of the boiled mutton, as he sat down on the ground and began his breakfast.

At the end of a two hours' march they were brought to a stand by a shot from a mountain soldier's gun, fired from above the parapet of a caravansarai, at an incline of forty-five degrees above them.

"Stop, stop!" cried Dennett: "there is trouble there! There are robbers, or no one knows what not. Wait till I go back and hurry on the rest of the escort."

They drew back a little out of range, and held a consultation; but nothing but his first proposition would satisfy Roderick Dennett. He had no intention of advancing into unknown danger, and started back, resolved that the others should try the danger before he threw himself into it.

"Coward!" said Richard scornfully, when the man had disappeared. "There is no danger. The fellow fired into the air. We will go on."

So they started forward again, without Dennett, after having waited less than half an hour; when an old, tottering, ragged, dirt-grimed pilgrim came slowly up the way behind them, climbing with difficulty, and bending wearily upon a knotted cane.

He had almost reached them, when, seeing that they were moving on, he hailed them in a weak voice. They waited.

"You are white. You are Englishmen," he said, catching his breath like one who had very little to spare for speak-

"PAUL! PAUL!"

ing. "I climbed up a little brook to reach yonder haven by a short cut. You will cross it down the track, and going down the stream you will go as I came. I passed a little child down there. He was kneeling by the water, weeping. He was white: I could not touch him; but you might," he added with a scornful sneer.

Electrified by the intelligence, Mr. Raymond and Scott turned back down the narrow way, without waiting to hear more. They had hardly gone a quarter of a mile when before them, in the path, upon his back, stark dead and staring at the sky, lay Roderick Dennett. His face was horribly discolored, and his throat swollen from strangling, while blood-stains on his vest betrayed a dagger-thrust.

They stood for a moment aghast, when Richard discovered something printed in blood upon the bosom of the dead man's shirt.

He bent forward, and in Marathi read, —

"The last of the 'condemned.' The eighty-third traitor who has fallen beneath the hand of Dhondaram for his treason to India. The muni has fulfilled his vows. The outlaw has avenged his country. Dhondaram is no more."

"Scott," said Richard, rising, "you said once that you would like to see Dhondaram."

"So I did," replied Scott, standing, very pale, before the corpse.

"That old pilgrim was the man. This is his last victim."

Scott started. "And Paul!" he gasped.

"I do not know," said Richard. "It may be only an accident that he took this way of bringing us here. Let us go on."

Strained to the utmost in every nerve, Scott hurried on faster than Richard could follow him. He found the brook: he leaped from rock to rock to follow it. He sprang through a narrow cleft. Before him knelt a little child playing with the water.

"Paul! Paul!" burst from his lips.

The boy looked up. He started back. The veil that had shrouded the past was suddenly swept away.

"O Scott! my Scott!" he cried, and sprang into his arms.

CHAPTER XXVI.

IT WAS MY OWN DHONDARAM!

ONLY the narrow space between the time that Paul left his father's house with Roderick Dennett till he took the hand of the muni always remained a period of the utmost uncertainty to him. The happy hours at home, he remembered all of them. The time that he spent with the muni, he never forgot one minute of it. It was a long time before he perfectly discriminated between Hindustani and English, in speaking; and it was one of the most curious sensations that Scott had ever experienced, to hear his petted little baby brother chatting briskly with the Hindus and Mussulmans, ordering them about, understanding their ways, and explaining to him their peculiar customs.

When Richard came upon the brothers, still locked in each other's embrace, he could not refrain from wonder at the rosy cheeks, the tastefully curling hair, the bright blue eyes, the fashionable little suit of clothes, the shining boots, and the dignified bearing, which latter had been instinctively copied from Dhondaram.

When at last they turned to leave the place, Paul pointed to the bundle that had followed him so long, and in Hindustani said, —

"There are my clothes. But I am not going away till Dhondaram comes back."

"Dhondaram!" Richard started, and looked at Scott. Scott caught the name, and looked at Richard.

"Who is Dhondaram, Paul?" Mr. Raymond asked.

"I am Hari-Paul: not Paul all alone," replied the boy promptly. "Dhondaram called me his Hari-Sahib; and Dhondaram,—don't you know him? He is one of the best men in the world. Dhondaram! Oh, he is the very best! He is my servant, my horse, my every thing. No indeed! I'll not go till Dhondaram comes."

It was two hours before they could persuade the boy, with tears in his eyes, to go away from the spot where Dhondaram had left him.

From that moment they made the most rapid progress possible toward the south. And many and many a word that Paul spoke of his friend, the muni, as they went, brought fresh astonishment to Mr. Raymond, as it told of the heart in Dhondaram's breast. Morning and night, and whenever they halted by a stream, Richard noted with horror that little Paul carefully bathed his face and hands, and repeated something very gravely, with his hands clasped before him, while he knelt with his head bowed. He supposed it was some Hindu devotion that Dhondaram had taught him. But at last he succeeded in being near enough to overhear the little Marathi prayer. Scott was beside him, and, noticing his emotion, asked,—

"What is it, Mr. Raymond?"

Richard did not answer directly; but, as Paul rose from his knees, he asked,—

"Where did you learn that, Paul?"

"Call me Hari-Paul," said the boy sternly. "If I have lost my dear, dear Dhondaram, I will not lose the name he gave me. He taught me that prayer, and taught me how to say it; and I will always say it,—yes, I will always say it."

"That is right, Hari-Paul, say it always,—always say it," replied Richard fervently; and Paul loved him better from that moment. Then turning to Scott, with tears in his eyes, Richard replied, "It is,—

"'Our Father which art in heaven, hallowed be thy name.'"

"Dhondaram told me that no one would ever say I should not repeat that prayer," said Paul triumphantly.

They were bound for Calcutta, but on the way were obliged to stop for a day at Benares, as Mr. Raymond wanted to see the half-caste foreman concerning some of Roderick Dennett's papers that he could not fully understand; and to occupy the time pleasantly for Paul, who still was often very sad over the loss of his friend, they drove all the afternoon about the outskirts of the city. It was a Hindu festival. All the temples were crowded with pilgrims. In their brightest holiday attire were the priests and dancing-girls in the Temple of Bhowani, in the extreme suburbs of the city. The sight was so tempting that Richard proposed that they stop and watch the ceremony.

It was early for the special service before the Mother; and while some of the *murli* girls clustered about the altar, some were yet at the tank, where they had been bathing as a form of purification. Beyond this tank stretched the plain, dotted with ruins, and the road leading toward Sarnath, where Scott had driven with Mr. Raymond.

It was a picturesque spot, bordered by clusters of flowering shrubs, made more attractive by the bright costumes of the dancers in several little groups about the tank. The three wandered through the throng down toward it, instead of entering the temple. Beside the marble steps, leaning against the parapet and one of the slender shrubs, stood one of the principal and most beautiful dancers. She had thrown her *sari* behind her, and laid some of her ornaments upon the ledge, preparatory to stepping into the bath; but she had evidently forgotten the temple, its accessories, the dance, and the throng that was gathering, and in her thoughts was far away,—perhaps on the snowy slopes of the mountains, perhaps in the humid heat of the plains, surely not where she was standing.

Scott pointed to the girl, and said to Mr. Raymond, "How sad she looks! I wonder what troubles her."

Paul followed the direction; and what was the astonishment of the two when he broke from them, and, rushing toward her, sprang into her arms, crying "Gunga! O Gunga!"

What was their *amazement* when the beautiful *murli* bent forward, and, clasping the little fellow to her heart, burst into a passionate flood of tears.

As they drew near, they heard Paul ask eagerly, "O Gunga! where is Dhondaram? I am crying! I am dying for my Dhondaram!"

"Dhondaram is in prison, bound with chains, in Calcutta," Gunga answered sadly.

Richard frowned, and said anxiously to Scott, "I read in the papers this morning that Dhondaram had given himself up to the English, and was taken to Calcutta. I did not dare to speak of it, for I feared that Paul might hear."

"O Gunga, it must not be so! I will break the chains! No one shall hurt my Dhondaram!" said Paul.

"But he did it himself," answered Gunga. "He sent me word that I must not try to help him, for he would have it as it was."

"But O Gunga, I love him so!" sobbed Paul.

"And so do I," said Gunga sadly. "He is my father."

GUNGA.

It was not until Gunga was obliged to prepare for the temple that Paul would leave her; and then only on the positive promise that as soon as was possible he should be allowed to see her again, but that first he must go to his home in America. He little dreamed how far away it was.

They went on to Calcutta. Paul remembered the name, and demanded that he be taken to see Dhondaram. It was a strangely affecting sight, the meeting of the two, — the hardened criminal, as the law considered the muni, weeping over and caressing the blue-eyed boy; and the little white hands fondling the roughly furrowed face.

Paul would not leave him; and through Mr. Raymond's intervention Dhondaram was moved to a better room, that was carefully guarded; and Paul remained with him over night, sleeping, as he had not slept since the night in the clay caravansarai, on the arm of the cold-blooded murderer.

Mr. Raymond stopped at the Great Eastern Hotel, in the English quarter of the immense city, where he was well known and as influential as Scott had found him all over India. He exerted himself to the utmost to do something for Dhondaram in the few days that remained before the steamer sailed from that port, by which they should return to America by way of the beautiful island of Ceylon. He secured a promise that the utmost mercy of the law should be extended, and finally, to the astonishment of all, that the sentence of death should not be passed in case the muni would take the most solemn of his oaths, and swear on the neck of the little Paul that he was entirely penitent, would never attempt to escape and resume his former life, and would give the government information that should result in the capture of Nana Sahib.

The court-room was crowded with prominent officials, all anxious to see the famous Dhondaram. He was led in in chains; and many a low hiss sounded from different parts of the room, to which he paid no attention, as proudly he walked between the soldiers to his position. Paul was sitting on the opposite side of the bar; and, in spite of every endeavor to restrain him, he walked across the room directly in front of the highest dignitaries of the law, paying no heed to them, and fondly clasped the hard hand of Dhondaram in both of his. An audible murmur ran over the room, but neither Paul nor the muni noticed it.

The officer rose; and, when order was gained, the long list of charges was read, and the deserved condemnation of death alluded to.

"If you kill my Dhondaram, I will kill you!" cried the clear, ringing voice of a child; and many started, and looked in astonishment at the flushed face of little Paul. But, without heeding the interruption, the officer read the terms upon which the death-sentence might be relieved.

The room was still. All waited breathlessly the reply of the outlaw.

"Dhondaram gave himself up to the English because he was ready to receive what they might have for him," he replied slowly, with true Hindu dignity. "It was not to re-purchase his freedom. Had he wished to be free, he would be free this day. No one captured him: no one was able to. And do you think that Dhondaram came here to be a traitor to his own? Did any one ever hear of Dhondaram's betraying a friend of India?" He waited a moment: then added solemnly, "No worm upon the ground, no bird in the air, shall be able to say over the ashes of Dhondaram, that he was a traitor. No! not though the English burn me alive, as they have one of my countrymen; not though they blow me to pieces from the cannon's mouth, as they have many of my people; not though they torture me, defile me, hang me, starve me to death, as they have thousands of Hindus already. And do the English think that I would take an oath, even to do what I wished to do, upon this little neck, more sacred to me than all my gods?" He laid his hand tenderly over the clustering brown hair. "No! not for life and liberty! No! not for the surety of an eternity of bliss in the paradise of Indra would I defile this little one with an oath of the blood-stained Dhondaram!"

A murmur of applause replaced the hisses that had greeted the entrance of the muni. He was remanded to prison. But Mr. Raymond assured Paul that there was no danger of the sentence of death being passed, and that he must return to India by and by, and see his friend again.

The child's heart was partially comforted by this; and, as they had one day left before the steamer sailed, they spent it in riding about the city to try and occupy his mind. But he was much more interested in stopping on their way home upon one of the little branches of the Hoogly, where native boats were moored all along the banks, and native farmers who had come down with their products were wandering on the sand waiting for purchasers.

In a peculiar way Paul had eaten the lotos that draws many an older Occidental heart back again to Oriental India; and he laughed and chatted with the peasants, and dug in the sand with the native children, just as he had often played upon the coast at Beverly.

Mr. Raymond was too well pleased to see him enjoying

himself to disturb the pleasure, and he and Scott sat together on the bank.

"There are thousands of more beautiful things in India that you have not seen than all we have looked at, Scott," said he; "and I hope some other time to be able to show

BLACK MARBLE CHAMBER.

them to you; but the first steamer will be none too soon to take Paul back to anxious hearts that are waiting for him. There is a magnificent palace not far from here, with an enormous hall of three galleries, divided by long rows of black-marble pillars, wonderfully carved, that I wish you might see when the sun is setting, as it is now, and its red light floods the long galleries, making a dark garnet and purple out of the black: you would think it one of the grandest corridors in the world. Then there is all of Southern India. Oh, there is a wonderful world that you have not seen yet! You must surely come again."

"I certainly shall," replied Scott earnestly.

"You will stop for a few hours at Madras, on the southern coast, as you go down to Ceylon in the steamer, and a few hours at the beautiful and almost landlocked harbor of Point de Galle, on the Island of Ceylon, where an unbroken line of cocoanut-palms grows upon the very water's edge. You must make the most of the time you have at each of those places."

"*I* must?" Scott asked, looking up in surprise. "Are you not going too?"

"I am very sorry, but I cannot go," Richard replied sadly. "I have had my vacation; and I have work that I must attend to at once in Bombay, in connection with Roderick Dennett's misdeeds. But a very dear friend of mine, a missionary from the interior, leaves with his family on the steamer for America, and will be delighted to do every thing for you and Paul. You will have a very pleasant trip. You will carry very good news too. I will give you a sealed package containing Dennett's confession of the bank-robbery, entirely freeing your father from the suspicion that he must have been complicated in some way; and by good fortune I shall be able to send security, too, for nearly the entire amount of which Dennett robbed the bank, for I have learned of several large deposits that he made here."

"But there is the reward for finding Paul," said Scott, "and all of my expenses."

"I have had a very pleasant visit from you, Scott," replied

Richard, smiling. "I shall be very glad to pay your expenses over here again, any time that you will come to see me. I do not want the money. The only living relative I have is my sister in Beverly, who is well married, and needs nothing. I am abundantly wealthy, and have no family. There is no use in my hoarding up money. Besides, *you* found Paul. I did not find him. I suppose there would be perhaps a legal claim for me, so I have enclosed an order for the money to be paid to you."

"You are a very strange man," Scott stammered.

"I told you long ago," Richard answered, smiling, "that you must never take it for granted that what any one does is through purely disinterested motives. It will not do. I wanted to find Roderick Dennett. I should have taken any amount of pains to find him. He escaped from me on the express to London, when I followed him there. I told you how while we were in England. Do you remember?"

"Was that the man that the old woman stopped the car for?" asked Scott in surprise.

"That was the very man. I did not know then that he had gone to America. No one knew it; for no one knew his real name, till I chanced to read the old name in a Boston paper, as cashier of your father's bank. I went to America expressly to find him. I have accomplished the business much better than I could if he had remained there. And all I ask of you, Scott, is, that you let me know, by and by, how you dispose of the money."

"That I can tell you now," replied Scott earnestly. "Half of it I shall give to the American Board for India as soon as I receive it, and the other half I shall save to distribute here myself. I made up my mind to one thing a long time ago—a month at least," he hesitated.

"What was that?" asked Mr. Raymond.

"Why, Paul and I broke wishbones with Bess and Kittie at the party the night he was stolen. We each had the long end. Paul wished that he might see India, and I wished that I might have an opportunity to be a hero. Paul has had his wish, and I have had mine. I saw what good people the Hindus might be, and what kind of a hero it was that I ought to be; and I promised myself that if we found Paul all safe, and took him back to America again, I would be a missionary: and so I will."

"God bless you, Scott!" exclaimed Mr. Raymond fervently. "You have your wish,—an opportunity to be a hero. Go it with all your soul. Be a *good* missionary, and you will be one of the greatest heroes on earth. Paul has set you an example already as to the right way to work, in his power over that strange man Dhondaram. Go it, Scott. You're on the right track."

The steamer was a large one, and was lying in the river instead of at the wharf. They were obliged to take a boat to reach her. Paul rebelled against going away without seeing Dhondaram; but Mr. Raymond at last succeeded in persuading him, as he feared a last interview.

When they reached the wharves, a long ride from the city proper, one of the ugly, hooded boatmen caught Paul in his arms, and ran for a dingi.

"Confound their impertinence!" muttered Richard. "These boatmen will do any thing to secure passengers. I've a mind to refuse him."

"It doesn't matter," replied Scott. "One dingi is as good as another. It is only for a moment."

They reached the steamer; and, as the same fellow again took Paul in his arms to carry him up the swinging steps, Mr. Raymond and Scott went on ahead.

As Paul was being borne up the ladder, the boatman put his lips close to the child's ear, and whispered eagerly, —

"Hari-Sahib, don't speak! don't speak, or they will kill me. No dungeon-bars could keep me from asking a blessing

THE LAST OF INDIA.

from my Hari before he left. Remember the little prayer I taught you, and pray for me, that I may be your servant, your horse, your dog, in the Christian heaven where you will go. Pray for my Gunga and Prita and Kashibai too. Let us all follow you, Hari! my Hari!"

Paul threw his arms around the rough boatman's neck, and kissed his dark lips, just as they reached the top of the ladder. The boatman hastily freed himself, and, seeing that Mr. Raymond and Scott were looking at him, he bent very low, and, kissing the little white hands, pressed them upon his forehead. Then, without rising again so that they could see his face, he ran down the ladder, and into the boat.

The missionary was standing beside Mr. Raymond, and remarked carelessly, "These superstitious fellows are very eager to receive a blessing from any one going on a long journey." Then taking Paul's hand, he said, "Well, Master Paul, I trust we shall be the best of friends before we reach America."

Paul snatched his hand away. "No, sir!" he exclaimed in Hindustani (for in his excitement he had forgotten which language he should speak): "not if you call me Paul. Hari is my name, and always shall be." (A resolve that he still firmly adheres to.)

"Very well, then," replied the missionary: "I will always call you Harry. It is a very pretty name."

But Mr. Raymond had seen more than the blessing that the missionary spoke of; and, taking Paul in his arms, he whispered, "Hari-Paul, did you know the boatman who brought you up?"

Paul looked at him suspiciously for a moment; but, reading only friendship in his eyes, he answered with a sob,—

"It was my own Dhondaram."